GREEN DEATH

High above center stage one of the hologram projector's lasers suddenly blazed to life. It pulsed—full power—directly down into the heart of the meteorite. Green light flooded the stage, blazing all around Jacobi and the boy.

Stuart Harrison began to convulse. He shook so violently that Jacobi was thrown back. A few yards up the aisle, Stuart's mother began to scream. Stuart collapsed onto the stage, dropping the meteorite.

Clark was out of his seat in an instant, but as he reached the stage where Stuart lay, his knees began to buckle. He could see the veins of his hands writhing and pulsing, turning a sickly greenish-black.

Jacobi leaned over them, holding the meteorite, its green glow casting over Stuart . . . and Clark.

SMALLVILLE

STRANGE VISITORS

ROGER STERN

**Superman created by
Jerry Siegel and Joe Shuster**

ASPECT®

WARNER BOOKS

An AOL Time Warner Company

WARNER BOOKS EDITION

Copyright © 2002 by DC Comics
All rights reserved under international copyright conventions. No part of this book may be reproduced in any form or by any electronic or mechanical means, including information storage and retrieval systems, without permission in writing from DC Comics, except by a reviewer who may quote brief passages in a review. Inquiries should be addressed to DC Comics, 1700 Broadway, New York, New York 10019.

Cover design by Don Puckey
Book design by L&G McRee

Warner Books, Inc.
1271 Avenue of the Americas
New York, NY 10020

Visit our Web site at
www.twbookmark.com.

Visit DC Comics on-line at keyword DCComics on America Online or at http://www.dccomics.com.

Ⓦ An AOL Time Warner Company

Printed in the United States of America

First Printing: October 2002

10 9 8 7 6 5 4 3 2 1

For Carmela and Joanne

ACKNOWLEDGMENTS

The book you're about to read—assuming that you haven't skipped over this part—is an original story based on the characters appearing in the WB television series *Smallville*.

This story—and for that matter, the television series itself—could never have existed without the work of Jerry Siegel and Joe Shuster. Nearly seventy years ago, they created Clark Kent, and so changed the world.

Since then, many talented people have contributed to Clark's story. His story has been told in radio dramas, motion pictures, animated cartoons, television series, a Broadway musical, two newspaper comic strips, and thousands of comic books. Clark has appeared in every medium known to mankind—from the printed word to on-line animation—and as new media are invented, he appears in them, too.

But it all started with Jerry's and Joe's amazing creation, in the pages of a comic book.

Many of you may think you already have a pretty good idea of who Clark Kent is. Mild-mannered reporter for a great metropolitan newspaper. Secretly Superman, strange being from another planet who came to Earth with powers and abilities far beyond those of mortal men. Fights a never-ending battle for truth, justice, and the American way. Faster than a speeding bullet and all that, right?

Well, sure. But did you ever wonder how he got to be that amazing hero?

That is the story of *Smallville* . . . the story of Clark Kent as a young man. It's a story that is never-ending and forever young. (Not at all surprising, when you stop to consider that he was created by a couple of guys in their teens.)

* * *

Just as Clark wouldn't have existed without Jerry and Joe, *Smallville* wouldn't have existed without Alfred Gough and Miles Millar, who wrote the pilot episode and continue to oversee the ongoing series.

I especially want to thank Al for taking time from his busy broadcast day to fill me in on the background of the citizens of Smallville . . . and a lot of the secret stuff being planned for the future. (My lips are sealed.)

Thanks, too, to all the other writers on the show—Greg Walker, Mark Verheiden, Michael Green, Doris Egan, Cherie Bennett, Jeff Gottesfeld, Tim Schlattmann, and Philip Levens—who through their scripts established the stories of all the good people of Smallville (not to mention the bad ones!).

And I'd be remiss if I didn't mention Tom Welling, Kristin Kreuk, Michael Rosenbaum, John Schneider, Annette O'Toole, Sam Jones III, Allison Mack, Eric Johnson, John Glover, Joe Morton, and Tom O'Brien. These actors, the cast of *Smallville,* were an inspiration, helping me capture the form, the movement, and the voices of the people of Lowell County.

[Oh, and for those faithful viewers who like to keep track of such things, this story takes place chronologically between the "Zero" and the "Nicodemus" episodes of the television series.]

In writing this novel, I also received invaluable advice and support from a number of fine folks.

I'd like to thank paramedics Joel Cadbury and Mark Spadolini, who took time to advise me on medical procedures.

Thanks to Jack and Rose Marie Bley, for details of a vehicular nature.

Thanks to Rich Thomas, Trent Duffy, John Aherne, Sara Schwager, and all the good folks at DC Comics and Warner Books who worked anonymously behind the scenes in the production of this book.

Thanks to my editor, Steve Korté, who called me up and kept after me with phone calls and e-mail until I agreed to write the story that became *Strange Visitors*. Easygoing and a genuinely funny guy, Steve provided guidance and suggestions that were invaluable. Not only that, but he answered his e-mail promptly. (Hey, is that a great editor, or what?)

And a most very special thanks to my lovely wife, Carmela Merlo. As always, Carmela kept me centered and reminded me of all the important things. She made notes, double-checked my science, kept track of outlines and time lines, ran down research, and proofread all my many drafts. When problems arose, she helped brainstorm solutions. I really couldn't have written this story without Carmela's love and help. She remains my strength and inspiration. And now, after twenty years of marriage, she still laughs at my jokes.

—Roger Stern
4-14-2002

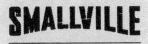

STRANGE
VISITORS

CHAPTER 1

Halfway to the Moon, Clark Kent stopped and looked back over his shoulder. The whole of the Earth seemed to float in space behind him, and he turned to admire it. *What is it that they used to call it,* he thought, *the big blue marble? It's big and blue, all right, but more like a soccer ball at this distance. Beautiful . . .*

Clark held one hand out at arm's length, as if balancing the Earth on his palm. *Looks like I could reach right out and touch it!* It was hard to believe that little ball was where he had grown up, where he had spent the last twelve years of his life. *Yeah, the last twelve. The first few are still a total mystery. Earth is home now, but it's not where I originally came from. I'm really from somewhere else . . .*

He made a lazy circle back toward the Moon. *Somewhere out here . . . but where? Not the Moon. It's nothing but a big, gray rock.* The lunar surface seemed to beckon to him. *Men walked on that moon . . . left their footprints on its surface. That was twenty years before I even came to Earth. No one goes there anymore. But I can . . . !*

On he flew, effortlessly, through the void . . . only vaguely aware that he didn't seem to need a space suit, or even an external air supply. He was like a pearl diver, plunging into the shallows of space on a single breath.

The Moon loomed large before Clark, as the meteor swarm came into view. On a whim he flew toward the swarm, spiraling around it like a porpoise. *Another cluster of space rocks . . . like the meteors that followed me down to Earth.*

Playfully, Clark plucked a baseball-sized meteor from

that swarm. *Now pitching for Smallville . . . Clark Kent!* He went into his windup and hurled the meteor back into the swarm, where it slammed into another, larger rock, breaking both open. Clark's grin faded. From within the rubble of the larger meteor came an eerie green glow. A phosphorescent crystal, big as a goose egg, came tumbling right toward him. Desperately, Clark turned to get out of its way, but his speed was fading fast. So were his strength and toughness. He started to feel the chill of space, clutching at his bones.

The green rock slammed into him.

Clark reflexively opened his mouth to scream, but there was no sound. Instead, the precious air rushed from his lungs. *No!*

Tumbling out of control, Clark fell toward the surface of the Moon. *No one'll ever know what happened to me . . . they'll never even find my body . . . !*

Craters rose up all around Clark. All he could see was gray. Clark hit and bounced, hit and bounced again. Dust rose up all around him, choking him.

"NO!"

Clark awoke with a start, gasping for breath. "Huu-whah!" His hands pressed down, sinking deep into a soft, spongy substance, and more dust rose up around him. "Wha—? Where?" Chest heaving, Clark rolled over and tumbled another foot and a half, landing hard on his back. He turned over, getting to his hands and knees, and felt the grain of rough wood beneath his fingers. *Wood? There's no wood on the Moon!* Clark pushed up from a wooden floor, looking about wildly—and found himself in the old familiar surroundings of the barn loft.

The light of the full moon streamed down on him through the open loft door. A gentle breeze wafted through the open gable door, carrying with it the scent of straw and fresh cow manure. Clark reached out and touched the cushion of a dusty old swaybacked couch that sat in the shadow of the rafters, the couch he had just fallen from. *A dream . . . ? It was just a dream?*

Clark scrambled to his feet and paced around the loft. He knew this place. He'd claimed it for himself years ago, when he was just a boy, after his family had built the newer live-stock barn. The main level of the old barn became home to the tractor and other large machinery, and the loft became his private fortress. In the half-light, he could see his old bookcase and an old steamer trunk, both filled with boyhood treasures.

And in the middle, sitting on its tripod next to the open loft door, was the telescope his father had given him. Clark stepped into the shaft of moonlight and ran his hand down the length of the telescope. He stared uneasily up at the sky. *I was checking out the Moon earlier this evening, before I went to bed. To bed . . .* Clark looked down at his T-shirt and boxers. That was what he had worn to bed, all right. *So what am I doing in the barn?*

Clark leaned out of the open loft door to look at the farm-house. There was his room on the second floor. The window was open . . . *just the way I left it. No, wait!* The screen was now open as well. *I don't remember opening that.* He could feel his pulse start racing again. *Did I walk out here in my sleep? Or . . . did I float?*

Once before, Clark had awoken from a flying dream to find himself floating above his bed. That had been disorient-ing enough, but at least then he was still in his room. This time—! *Could I have floated out of bed . . . unlatched the screen . . . and drifted all the way out to the barn and up into the loft?* He backed away from the open door and sat down on top of the trunk.

I really didn't need this. Going through the "normal" changes of puberty was strange enough. But being able to defy gravity, to see through walls, even being able to bend steel in his bare hands—! *The floating . . . that's the weirdest.*

Clark's extraordinary strength had developed slowly, almost slowly enough that he could adjust to it as he'd grown. He hadn't accidentally broken any furniture in a long time—not beyond repair anyway—and he could juggle eggs without cracking a single shell. Besides, some people simply were stronger than others. His folks, for example. They'd both stayed in great shape, running the farm. His mom was stronger than some kids' fathers, and his dad was much stronger than most guys his age. Variations in strength were normal.

Even his "X-ray vision"—the most recent development—had some analogs in nature. Clark had done some research on the Web, and learned that there were numerous creatures that could see beyond the spectrum of so-called visible light. None of those creatures was *human*, but still, they existed. That had given him a little perspective to go along with his parents' reassurances.

The first time Clark discovered that he could see through solid matter, he'd lost his grip. Literally. He'd been in gym class, halfway up a climbing rope, when he suddenly started seeing *through* Pete Ross's face, right through his buddy's dark skin to the muscles underneath. Startled, Clark let go of the rope and crashed to the gym floor. (That he wasn't hurt by the fall didn't make the experience any less strange.)

Lately, he'd gained reasonably good control of his X-ray vision. It hadn't kicked in without warning for some time, and he could usually prompt it to function if he focused properly. He was coming around to accept that being able to "tune in" to X-rays and other penetrating radiation—radiation far beyond the visible spectrum—was, in a way, just an extreme extension of natural vision.

But being able to fly without wings, without a plane around him—that was just plain freaky. Even his father had been taken aback when Clark told him about the first flying dream.

"Clark, I honestly don't know," Jonathan had said. "Soon as you start breaking the law of gravity, we're definitely in uncharted territory."

Clark smiled wryly at the memory. *We hate it when our parents think they have all the answers, but we're not crazy about the times when they don't, either.*

Clark got up and again looked out at the farmyard. *No one in sight . . . no one will see me.* And then, he jumped from the open loft door. He landed effortlessly, his knees slightly flexed, easily absorbing the impact of the story-and-a-half fall. Clark dashed to the side of the farmhouse and, glancing about again, leaped up to his second-floor window in a single bound. Grabbing hold of the window frame, he swung both legs through the opening. Clark sat there on the windowsill for a second, staring back at the loft. Then he slipped inside his room as quietly as he could manage. *Don't want Mom and Dad waking up, thinking someone's breaking in.* Clark immediately turned and slid the screen back down, feeling the satisfying click as it locked into place. He gazed back out at the moon. *Even if I did float out to the barn, so what? I couldn't possibly float all the way to the Moon . . . could I?* Clark shuddered, remembering all too vividly how his dream had ended. He closed his window tight and locked it. *Yeah, like a locked window would stop me.*

Clark sat down on the edge of his bed. *A wall wouldn't stop me! But smashing through a window or a wall would wake me up, wouldn't it? Yeah, I couldn't sleep through that!* He lay down, his head sinking into the pillow, and shot a glimpse at his alarm clock. Dawn was just a few hours away.

Could I really survive in space? Hard to believe I could

go that far on a single breath. How long can I hold my breath anyway? Clark thought back. *There was the time I swam to the bottom of Jennings Pond . . . must've been down ten or fifteen minutes. Mom looked pretty frantic by the time I finally came up. But I'm a lot stronger now. And that was—what?—a couple of years ago?* He frowned. *Yeah, before I found out that I came from outer space.*

Clark had known for years that he was adopted. His parents had explained that much to him before he first went off to kindergarten. But it had been just a few months ago that Jonathan Kent had finally taken Clark down into the storm cellar and shown him the tiny spacecraft that had brought him to Earth. *And we still don't know where I'm from. Or who sent me. Or even what I am . . . really.* The questions never ended. *It's like thinking about breathing . . . once you start, it's hard to get it out of your mind.*

Clark tried to think of something else, and his mind wandered back to the flying dreams. The first one, when he'd woken up in midair, had happened within a day or so after Jonathan had told him that his biological parents "weren't exactly from around here." Did learning about his past somehow help to *trigger* whatever it was that made him able to defy gravity?

And if it had . . . what additional changes might occur if he ever learned the answers to his other questions?

Clark tossed restlessly on his bed. His alarm clock showed that ten minutes had passed, and he was still wide-awake. *Great, just great! If this keeps up, I'll be a zombie by morning. I've got chores . . . school . . . I would have to have that stupid dream on a Monday!* Clark gave a heavy sigh, then rolled over on his side and tried to fall back to sleep.

◆◆◆

In a dark motel room one time zone away, Donald Jacobi stared intently at the screen of his laptop computer. His smile grew wider as he clicked from one page to another.

"Shape-changing teenagers ... bug boys ... pyrokinetics!" Jacobi leaned back in his chair and massaged the ache out of his neck. "Marvelous! Absolutely marvelous!" He glanced down at a small metal case on the floor beside his bed.

Jacobi knelt down and snapped open the latches that secured the lid of the case. As he lifted the lid, a gentle green glow began to illuminate the room. Jacobi reached in and pulled out a small irregular hemisphere of rock. Most of the rock was a dull charcoal gray, but embedded in its middle was a small green crystal, the source of the glow.

"And to think, old friend, they're crediting the creation of all those freaks to the likes of you." Jacobi patted the rock as if it were a faithful dog. "No doubt they're afraid of you. It's the same old story. They fear what they don't understand. Well, we'll just have to show them the light, won't we?"

Jacobi rose to his feet and threw open the door that connected his room to the next. "Jimmy! Jimmy, wake up!"

The heavy-set figure in the bed groaned and turned away, pulling the covers up over his head, as if to block out the green glow that was invading his space. Jacobi grabbed the side of the mattress and shook it hard. "Come on, Brother Wolfe. Up and at 'em!"

"A'right, a'right! Stop a'ready!" James Wolfe began to unwind himself from the sheets. "What is it? What's wrong?"

"Not a single thing, Jimmy. Things are righter than they've ever been. I have seen the future!"

"Terrific." Wolfe let out a weary yawn and pulled himself

upright. "Couldn't this wait until the near future? Daybreak, at least?"

"This is too good to wait for morning. I know where we must go next."

"Y'mean, after Atlanta?"

"Forget Atlanta. Forget the whole Southern tour! We're going to Kansas."

"*Kansas?*" Wolfe fumbled for the lamp, almost knocking it over. After a few fitful stabs, he finally managed to find the switch and turn it on. "What the devil is in Kansas?"

Jacobi smiled in the glow of the geode. "A little town called Smallville."

CHAPTER 2

James Wolfe frowned into his second cup of coffee. "Let's go over this one more time. You want to drop everything, cancel all of next month's bookings, and go visit some little cow town out in the middle of nowhere. Is that what you're telling me, Don?"

"Smallville isn't a 'cow town,' Jimmy." Jacobi looked up from his laptop. "According to the town website, it was once considered the 'Creamed Corn Capital of the World.'"

"Wonderful." Wolfe drained the dregs of his cup. "And how many fine citizens reside in this Mecca of Maize?"

"Currently, around forty-five thousand."

"Don, we stand to draw more than that in the Southern tour. Who do you expect will come hear us in Smalltown?"

"Small*ville*. And in addition to the locals, I expect that we'll pull in a good crowd from Metropolis, Kansas City, and Wichita. Not to mention Denver, Dallas, Chicago—"

"Wait a minute!" Wolfe pulled a road atlas from one of their bags and plopped it down on top of the room's mini-fridge. It took him a few minutes just to locate Smallville on the map of Kansas. "You expect people to travel hundreds of miles to some little burg out in the sticks?"

"Oh, they'll come, Jimmy. In case you haven't noticed, we're starting to develop quite a faithful following in some circles. Our new website gets more and more hits every week. We already have over three thousand subscribers, and many of them are starting to follow us from city to city."

"We're not a rock band, Don, and this isn't a city we're talking about. Why would they want to follow us to Smallville?"

"Because, Jimmy, that's where my meteorite came from."

Wolfe straightened up. "I thought you found that thing in Arizona."

"I *bought* it in Arizona—from a disgruntled former employee of STAR Labs. But, no, my miracle meteorite fell to Earth in a storm that pounded Smallville and portions of rural Lowell County in October of 1989. Did quite a bit of damage. Some loss of life, too. Very sad." Jacobi paused to consider that. "Very, very sad. The largest, most impressive fragments were carted off for study by the National Science Foundation, Metropolis University, NASA, STAR, all the usual suspects. But the land around Smallville is still littered with chunks of nickel-iron space rocks. And many of those rocks have glowing green crystals at their center . . . just like mine."

"Okay, I can see why that might interest you, but we could get more fragments anytime."

"No, Jimmy. Now! As soon as possible!" Jacobi's mellow tones took on a hint of iron. "Things are starting to happen in Smallville. Things we must take advantage of. I've found the most amazing website here, see?"

Wolfe looked over Jacobi's shoulder. "Football coach bursts into flame . . . girl changes shape . . . is this some kind of joke?"

"No, it is quite sincere. From what I've gathered, the meteor storm apparently had a mutagenic effect on those close to the point of impact, especially the younger ones. And now, over twelve years later, those effects are becoming more obvious, more pronounced. Jimmy, I feel certain that the meteorites caused a genetic change."

"Which fits right in with your lectures."

"Precisely! This is an opportunity we dare not pass up!"

"Okay, I can see that. But can't this wait until after Atlanta?"

"No. There's far too much chance of someone else beating us to this." There was a hint of concern in Jacobi's gray eyes. "To be honest with you, I'm surprised that someone hasn't already. No, this absolutely can't wait!"

"But where would we set up? There can't be a hall big enough in all of Smallville for the kind of crowds you're talking about drawing."

"I doubt it. We'll have to arrange for tents."

"*Tents?*" Wolfe spat the word out. "That's crazy! I haven't put together a tent show in nearly a decade. You don't know what kind of logistical nightmare that can be!"

"I have every confidence in your abilities, Jimmy. Remember when that hurricane scuttled the South Florida tour? You had us back on the road with new bookings in Louisiana within twenty-four hours. On a Sunday!"

Wolfe stifled a yawn. "That was different."

"Nonsense! You've done it before, you can do it again." Jacobi shoved a fresh cup of coffee into his partner's hand. "Now, go boot up your laptop and start working your magic! We'll need all the usual equipment, plus the tent, and a good-sized site to pitch it. Oh, and transportation for all of that, as well as for us. You know what's needed."

"Don, a lot of the places I'd need to contact aren't even open yet."

"Then start with the ones that are."

"Look, you're asking the impossible! And how do you know that this website you've found isn't the product of some delusional idiot?"

"I've been over it most thoroughly, Jimmy. And I've already found partial confirmation of these stories on the website of the local newspaper. If it makes you feel any better, I'm going to continue chasing this down, while you make the preliminary arrangements."

"But—"

"If I find anything that completely discredits this website, then I'll call this off, all right? And all we'll have lost is a few hours on the Internet. You waste more time than that web-surfing every week."

Wolfe looked at his watch and scowled. "Not at this hour of the morning."

"Trust me, Jimmy, it'll be worth it."

"Oh, really? Do you have any idea how much this could cost? No, Don, I don't want to do this!"

Jacobi's eyes narrowed. His voice turned brittle. "Jimmy, we must all do what is necessary."

"It's out of the question! We can't afford—!"

"We can't afford not to. You, especially, can't afford not to. Do I have to remind you about what happened in Cleveland?"

"No." Wolfe turned ashen. "No, you don't."

"I didn't think so. Okay, it's settled then. Start making the arrangements. I want to leave for Smallville as soon as possible."

◆◆◆

The skies over Kansas were still dark when Jonathan Kent padded downstairs. The lights were already on in the kitchen, and Martha Kent sat at the kitchen table, nursing a cup of coffee as she pored over a textbook.

"Good morning, hon!" Jon bent down and kissed his wife. "How is it that you can get up even earlier than I do and still manage to look so gorgeous?"

"Gorgeous? Oh, please! I just ran a comb through my hair and threw on yesterday's clothes. I'm lucky I don't look like the Wicked Witch of the West."

"Well, you still look beautiful to me." Jonathan poured himself a tumbler of orange juice. "You're up awfully early, though."

"So are you." Martha picked up a marker and highlighted a line in the text. "You're just itching to get started on that new fence, aren't you?"

"No. First, the new drainage ditch, then the fence." He finished his juice and started pouring himself a cup of coffee. "Is this a glamorous life or what? But why are *you* up so early? Couldn't sleep?"

Martha shook her head. "I slept just fine until about an hour ago, then I woke up and started thinking about this advanced accounting class." She tapped the textbook. "The exam is this evening, remember? So, I decided to get up and work a few extra cases." She checked the clock on the wall. "But the time slipped away from me. I should make you some breakfast—!"

"No, that's okay. I want to get a quick start. You finish your cases, and I'll make myself a peanut butter and jelly sandwich to tide me over." Jonathan was already pulling jars from the refrigerator. "But, when you come to a good stopping point, maybe you could nuke some of those homemade waffles you stashed away in the deep freeze?"

"All right, but don't you work too long. Not on just a sandwich!"

"Hey, this is one of *my* sandwiches!"

"Even one of yours, 'Dagwood.'"

The eastern sky was just starting to lighten along the horizon as Jonathan headed out the back door, a half-eaten sandwich in hand. He rounded the tool shed and stopped short, so startled that he nearly dropped his sandwich.

The drainage ditch had already been rerouted.

There were, in fact, no signs of the ditch's original path. The sides had been smoothly rebanked. The ground on both sides had been gently tamped down and mulched. Jonathan lifted the corner of the mulch with the toe of one boot. *Seeded with new ground cover, too. Pretty good job!*

Jonathan slowly paced along the new ditch, wondering if he was completely awake. Maybe he was still in bed, and this was all part of some pleasant dream. Then his boot heel caught on something half-hidden in the mulch, and he almost lost his footing. Jonathan reached down with his free hand and picked up a wooden stake. *Okay, now I know I'm awake.* He recognized the stake as one of several that he had set in the ground the evening before, to mark out the path of the new ditch. Someone had tossed this stake aside, presumably, the same person who had rerouted the ditch. *And unless a group of vigilante ditch-diggers came through here in the middle of the night, I suspect that someone was Clark.*

Jonathan weighed the stake thoughtfully in his hand as he finished his sandwich. In some ways, life with Clark was like life with a poltergeist . . . a *friendly* poltergeist. Things just . . . happened . . . at odd hours and often without warning. Especially since Clark had reached his teens. Jonathan flipped the stake up and caught it on the downspin. *Looks like we all got up before the chickens today. I wonder what's on Clark's mind?*

Whatever it was, Jon knew it had to be fairly distracting. Scattered near the tool shed, he found the rest of the stakes and a wide board that showed signs of having been used to tamp down earth. *Oh, well. When I was his age, I didn't always put stuff away properly, either. Even when I wasn't preoccupied with something.* He smiled. *Used to drive my dad nuts.*

Jonathan brushed the dirt from the tamping board. *No sense in letting it stay out here on the ground and warp.* He piled the stakes on top of it and carried the whole pile into the tool shed. He started to cross the shed toward the lumber rack, but then thought better of it and set the big board across a five-gallon bucket. *It'll dry faster there.*

On a hunch, Jonathan strode toward the field where he'd planned to fence off a section of pasture. Sure enough, all the new post holes had been dug. The fence posts, true and level, were centered in concrete. And this time, there were no stray tools or materials. No piles of dirt or half-empty bags of cement. This job site had been left as tidy as Jonathan (at least, the adult Jonathan) would have left it, as tidy as *Martha* would have left it.

I'd almost swear he does it deliberately, just to keep me off-balance. Jonathan shook his head, but had to smile all the same. *Lord knows, I never wanted my dad to think that he had* me *all figured out.*

The smile faded a bit as he added up the work involved. The post-hole digger's engine was noisy—considerably so. It would have woken him up, if Clark had used it. *He must have done all this digging with a pick and shovel . . . or possibly with his bare hands.* Jonathan understood using sheer physical labor as a stress reliever; it was by far his own preferred form of therapy. But he had to wonder just what could have stressed out his son so much that he would need to do all of this. Was he brooding over some fresh calamity at school? Or was this connected to the family's deep, dark secret?

Jonathan reflected on how ridiculous that sounded, like something out of a Gothic thriller. *Then again, I have a spaceship hidden away in the storm cellar. My son's from another planet.* He shook his head. *A Gothic* science fiction *thriller!*

Well, if something serious has come up, Clark'll tell me in good time, I guess. Shouldn't be too hard to steer the conversation in that direction. "Good job on the fence posts, Son . . ." Lost in thought, Jonathan was halfway back to the house before he noticed that the work lights were on in the barn. "Clark? Are you in there?"

"Yeah, Dad! Good morning. I was just checking out the tractor. Come take a look."

Jonathan strolled into the barn. *Okay, first we'll talk about the tractor. Gotta start somewhere.* "Good morning yourself, Son. Guess we're all up a little early today. So, the tractor, huh? Did you figure out what's wrong with it?"

"You know, I think I did." Clark came around from the side of the tractor, wiping his hands on an old rag. He was grubby but cheerful. In fact, he looked quite pleased with himself. "Better yet, I'm pretty sure I have it fixed!"

"No kidding? That is *very* good news." The tractor had been running poorly for a few weeks, sometimes—but not always—refusing to start. "What did you find?"

"A loose electrical connection." Clark tapped the cap of the distributor. "Solenoid wasn't making contact. In fact, when I looked in there, the connecting wire was flopping around free. We've had those intermittent problems for what, a couple—three weeks now? I bet the screw shook loose last month."

"Makes sense. I bounced this poor old tractor over a lot of hard ground last month. Looking back, I guess it isn't surprising that something jarred loose."

Clark closed the engine cover. "I got it tightened back down pretty good. Give her a try and see if she'll turn over."

Jonathan hopped up on the seat and turned the key. The tractor immediately roared to life. "Good work, Clark." He shut the engine down, looking mildly chagrined. "Probably should have thought of that myself."

Clark grinned at his father. "Probably! Anyway, after I found that, I started wondering if maybe the old girl had taken any other hits, so I checked the undercarriage and what do you know? I found a hairline crack along the bottom of the crankcase, up near the front wheels. Here, let me give you a better look."

Jonathan fully expected to see Clark hoist the front end of the tractor up off the floor. Instead, his son walked around to the other side of the vehicle and crouched down out of sight.

"Clark . . . ?"

"Just a sec, Dad." Clark hummed a random tune and ran his palms along the tractor's undercarriage. He felt around for balance points and made certain that he'd picked a couple of sturdy spots. Then, Clark began to straighten up and lift, as easily as he might lift a fifty-pound bag of feed.

And the tractor began to rise, straight up into the air.

Jonathan took a step back. He couldn't help himself.

Since childhood, Clark had grown strong enough to lift the end of a truck. In private moments, he and Jonathan had shared a laugh or two over what they called his "human jack" routine. But this was something else.

Clark stood stock-still in the middle of the barn floor, holding the tractor over his head. Jonathan gaped at the sight.

Clark smiled. "Not bad, huh?" He raised his arms to their fullest extension, and then lowered them a few inches, shoulder-pressing the tractor up and down.

That broke the spell. Jonathan stepped forward, arms crossed, pretending to look stern. "Okay, now you're just showing off."

"You think?" Clark tilted his head way back so that he could look straight up at the tractor. Then he looked back at his father and grinned. "Well, maybe a little. I just thought you could get a better look, if I got the whole thing up off the ground."

"I see. So this is for my benefit."

"Exactly. Step right up!" Clark held the tractor aloft with such total confidence that Jonathan found himself doing just that. Clark pointed up at the crankcase with his chin. "Over there, see?"

Jonathan pulled a penlight flash from his pocket and pointed it where his son had indicated. Sure enough, the light caught a jagged line of leaking lubricant. "Oh, yeah, I see it now. Good catch, Son."

"Think we can patch it with some of that miracle epoxy you always swear by?"

"Sure. A little epoxy now will prevent a world of trouble later. I'll go get it."

Jonathan backed out from under the tractor, and stared up at it again. *Amazing. Clark's not even breaking a sweat. He just keeps getting stronger.* He walked over to a metal cabinet along one wall. "It'll take me a minute to mix the compound," he called over his shoulder. "Don't feel that you have to hold the tractor up the whole time."

"No problem." Clark lowered the tractor a few inches, then raised it again. And again. "I actually kind of like this. I found a couple of good balance points, so I know I won't lose my grip. And it's a big, rugged piece of machinery, so I know it isn't going to break. It's a good workout."

"There's a thought. Maybe we should make an exercise video. Call it *Farm Fitness*."

"Yeah, right." Clark rolled his eyes. "I can see the warning label now: 'Caution. Not recommended for persons with high blood pressure or for anyone else from the planet Earth.'"

"Yeah, I suppose the customer base would be limited." Jonathan returned with a small tray of epoxy and a putty knife. "Ohh-kay, let's see about getting this sucker patched! Little bit of the epoxy here . . . smooth it into the crack . . . yeah, that should do the trick, once it sets." He stepped back to survey the patch. "Look good to you, Son?"

"Looks good from here. You clear?"

"Free and clear!"

"Okay." Slowly, Clark lowered the tractor back down to the floor of the barn. "Mission accomplished."

Jonathan looked at his son, at the tractor, then looked back at Clark. *At this rate, he might be strong enough to lift a tank someday. Or maybe even a plane. Who knows?* He slowly shook his head. "Son, I know that sometimes your unusual abilities seem like a mixed blessing. I know that being different has caused you some grief, and I know you've wished you could be more 'normal.' But . . . damn, I wish *I* could do that!"

Jonathan was absolutely sincere, more proud than envious of his son's strength. Clark's eyes lit up, and he smiled the wide smile that meant, for the moment, everything was perfect. "Actually, Dad, I have to say, it's fun being really strong. *Hiding* it is tough. And the other abilities—being able to see through walls—that can all get a little weird." Clark hesitated, started to say something else, then shrugged and smiled again. "But being strong, and being able to run faster than an Indy car, is just plain fun. A lot of fun."

"Yeah, I bet it is." Jonathan suddenly remembered a bumper sticker that he'd seen on a day trip to Metropolis, a particularly obnoxious piece of work that announced, "My D student can beat up your honor student." *Well*, my *honor student can lift a* tractor! *Top* that!

As they strolled back toward the house, Jonathan clapped his son on the back. "By the way, Clark, excellent job on the fence posts. And on the drainage ditch. You saved me at least a day's work, maybe two. Thanks."

"Oh, that. You're welcome. I was just restless. I woke up, couldn't get back to sleep. I just kept . . . thinking. You know?"

"Sure do," Jonathan nodded. "I've had many a night like that. Usually around tax time, but other times as well."

Clark chuckled. "Yeah. Well, finally, it occurred to me that digging that ditch might put my brain in neutral. And it worked. So then I dug the holes and set the fence posts. And then I thought, hey, why not check over the tractor? It just felt good to *do* something."

"I know the feeling. That's what usually works for me."

"Yeah. For me, too. I just wish I'd thought of it sooner." Clark's half smile twisted into a deep scowl. "I must've tossed and turned for an *hour*. If I'd gone and started digging as soon as I woke up, I'd have gotten all the work done and still had time to catch a few good Z's before school."

"Clark! Don't be so hard on yourself." Jonathan put a hand on Clark's shoulder. *Lord, were my moods that volatile when I was sixteen?* He tried to remember. *Oh, yeah . . . guess they were.* "Listen, there are any number of suit-and-tie types who never—and I mean not once in their entire lives—figure out that they'd be a lot happier if they left their offices once in a while and built something. Something tangible!"

"I guess." Clark didn't look convinced.

"You guess? Hey, you can take that as *gospel*!" Jonathan looked Clark in the eye. "C'mon, Son, what's bothering you?"

"Oh . . . stuff." Clark looked away. "You need anything else dug up?"

"On a farm? You're kidding, right? Look, why don't you knock off for the morning and get cleaned up?" Jonathan checked his watch. "There's still a little over an hour before you have to catch the bus. We could all have a nice, civilized breakfast together. Haven't enjoyed one of those on a school day since . . . oh, since you were in grade school."

"Well . . . sure. Okay."

"Good! After all, with the morning you just put in, you've got to be getting pretty hungry by now."

Right on cue, Clark's stomach growled audibly, and he had to laugh. "Good call, Dad."

Jonathan waved one hand dismissively. "It's a gift. Comes with being a parent."

Clark was out of the shower and half-dressed when he stopped and sniffed. There was more than just the scent of bacon in the air. He could swear that he smelled waffles. In seconds, he finished dressing, dashed downstairs, and inventoried the breakfast table.

There was a big platter of scrambled eggs and salsa. Crispy bacon and whole-wheat toast. Milk, juice, and coffee; the milk and juice in nice pitchers. Bowls of fruit salad, Martha's homemade applesauce, and blueberries. Lightly steaming Belgian waffles. Maple syrup and sorghum.

Clark blinked and looked at his parents. "Did a week go by while I was in the shower? Is it Sunday again already?"

"Wise guy!" Martha reached up to ruffle her son's hair. "You did the work of an entire crew this morning. The least we can do is feed you like one."

Jonathan divided a waffle, placing half on Martha's plate and half on his own, and sat down. He set a waffle on Clark's plate. "Have a seat. Then have a waffle." Straight-faced, he handed over the maple syrup. "This goes on the waffle."

"You think?" Clark grinned and popped open the syrup bottle. With one hand he began pouring syrup into the pockets of his waffle. With the other hand, he grabbed a spoon and began building a small mound of scrambled eggs alongside.

Martha began to wonder if she'd made enough.

CHAPTER 3

"'Scuse me! Coming through!" Chloe Sullivan sidled along the narrow aisle of the school bus, navigating between an ill-parked trombone case and a cardboard-padded art project that threatened to snag her backpack. She glanced out the window at her house and blew a kiss to her father's old Volvo parked in the drive.

"Someday you will be mine, and all of this will be behind me."

Suddenly, the bus started up with a lurch, and Chloe grabbed hold of a seatback just in time to save herself from tumbling to the floorboard. Setting her feet, she swung around and plopped into the seat next to Peter Ross.

Quickly reaching into his windbreaker, Pete produced two prenumbered index cards and held them aloft. "A nine-point-eight! A near-perfect score for our plucky blond newcomer."

"Thank you, thank you!" Chloe returned Pete's grin. "Haven't toppled me yet, though Lord knows they've tried." She shifted the backpack onto her lap. "But . . . 'plucky'? That makes me sound like Rocky the Flying Squirrel! Am I really 'plucky'?"

"You kidding me? You are the epitome of plucky. Go ahead, look up plucky in the illustrated dictionary. Know what you'll find? Picture of yourself—complete with that plastic flower in your hair."

"The flower . . ." Chloe's hand went to it. "It's too . . . country, isn't it?"

"No, no. It looks nice. The blue matches your eyes."

Chloe briefly studied Pete's eyes—deep, deep brown, almost black—and decided that although he was teasing her (as usual), he wasn't really kidding. "Well. Thank you!"

Pete inclined his head graciously. "You're most welcome. So, what's the big news of the morning?"

"You mean, the news of the moment! Let's have a look, shall we?" Chloe pulled a sleek new laptop computer from her backpack and switched it on.

"Hey, that's not your old laptop. Is that a PowerBook?"

"An *Ultra*-PowerBook." Chloe lovingly ran her hand along the edge of the screen. "It's a loaner from the computing lab. I needed something with wireless Internet capability."

"Oh, really?"

"Don't give me that look, Pete. As editor of the *Torch*, I need to keep on top of things twenty-four/seven, at home or on the road."

"Ah, the mighty *Torch*, lighting the way for dear old Smallville High."

Chloe gave him a sharp elbow to the ribs.

"Ow! Hey, don't pick on the black guy!"

"Well, don't make light of the media." Chloe's fingers danced across the keys and started running through her e-mail. "Oh, no . . . !"

"Bad news?"

"Possibly very bad. Stuart Harrison's back in the hospital. Apparently, he had a seizure over the weekend."

"Oh, man, he was in and out of hospitals the whole first half of last year. He had surgery and chemo and all that cutting-edge *Star Trek* medicine. They gave him the *works*! That was supposed to finally *cure* him."

"Well . . . let's hope it did." Chloe gently tapped the side of the keyboard. "Having a seizure doesn't necessarily mean the cancer came back. My mom knows someone who had to have a brain tumor removed, and he had a seizure afterwards. But it wasn't related to the tumor, it was just his brain sort of rewiring itself and getting a connection wrong, I guess. He's fine now."

"He's fine, huh? Did he have that seizure a whole year after his surgery?"

"Well, no. It was more like a couple weeks."

"And did he have any previous cancer surgeries, like Stu did?"

"No, he didn't. But hey, ease up a little. Anyone would think that *you* were the muckraking journalist here." *Must be his mom's influence. Wasn't she a prosecutor before she became a judge?* "I'm just suggesting that we not jump to conclusions."

"I know, I know. Sorry." Pete shook his head ruefully. "I just wish the universe would cut Stu a break for a change. He's one of the good guys. If all seniors were like him, high school would be a whole lot easier. I've never seen him lord it over anybody."

"Me neither. I don't know Stuart as well as you guys do, but as far as I can tell, no one—from the lowliest freshman to Principal Kwan—has ever had a bad word to say about him."

"Exactly. It isn't fair he's back in the hospital after all he's been through. Man, this is gonna be a lousy Monday."

The two of them sat, still and solemn, as the bus rumbled down the highway. Chloe finally broke the silence. "Look, we can't just sit around in a funk all day. That's not going to help."

"I s'pose."

"We need something to clear our heads, raise our spirits." Chloe gave Pete a sideways glance. "Who can we always depend upon?"

"Clark . . . !" Pete brightened a bit. "And by the way, Ms.

Media, shouldn't that be 'upon whom can we always depend'?"

"Whatever. When did you join the Grammar Police?" Chloe checked her watch. "Let's see . . . Hickory Lane is just five minutes away. Skies are fair. Temperature fifty-five. I say that today Clark makes the bus!"

"Are you kidding? On a Monday?" Pete grinned and held up a folded five-dollar bill. "I've got five that says you're wrong!"

"Why, Peter!" Chloe gasped in mock dismay. "Wagering on the foibles of your best friend?"

"Don't we always?"

◆◆◆

Clark sopped up the last bit of syrup from his plate with a corner of toast, as Jonathan surveyed the vast wasteland of empty bowls and platters that littered the kitchen table. *Ah, to have that kind of metabolism again.* He could still remember what it was like to be able to put away that much food—at every meal, no less—and not show it.

Clark pushed back from his plate, stretched his arms wide, and gave a prodigious yawn. Martha flicked an eyebrow at Jonathan, and gently shook Clark's shoulder. "Hey, there! Maybe I shouldn't have let you have that third waffle. You're not going to sleep all through school today, are you?"

"Don't worry, Mom. I'll be wide awake by the time the bus gets to school." Clark gave her his most earnest look. "In fact, that's *why* I took the third waffle. I was carboloading. Like for a marathon?"

"I see. Very shrewd." Martha tilted her head sympathetically. "So . . . lots of bad dreams last night?"

"Uh . . . no. Not really."

"Mm. Just one really strange one, huh?"

Clark, about to reach for the milk, pulled back and stared at his mother with wide-eyed astonishment. "How did you know—? And don't say, 'It's a gift. It comes with being a parent'!"

Martha turned both hands palms up. "Well, it *is*. It *does*."

"Now Martha, you know that in your case, that isn't entirely true." Jonathan poured himself another cup of coffee. "You've always been very observant and extremely intuitive. You could usually guess what *I* was thinking—even before Clark came along." He turned to Clark. "*Long* before you came along."

"Jonathan—!"

"Honey, it's true." Jonathan shot his son a grin. "Clark, don't ever think that you are the only one in this family with strange powers and abilities."

Clark took a slow deep breath, as if preparing an especially dramatic sigh. But halfway through the release of air, his exasperation broke apart into a laugh. "You guys are too much. Yeah, I had a crazy dream last night. A seriously weird one. At least, it felt weird at the time. Right now . . . ?" He shrugged. "It's almost starting to seem kind of funny."

Clark glanced at the clock and got to his feet. "Maybe I'll tell you about it later. Right now, I'd better go grab my stuff. I'd feel like a real rocket scientist"—he squelched a stray laugh—"if I missed the bus now. Especially after being up and awake all morning."

Clark dashed upstairs, threw his books together, and was back in the kitchen before Martha could even draw a breath to quiz him further.

"'Bye, Mom! Great breakfast!" He gave her a quick kiss on the cheek. "Dad—!" Jonathan received a gentle clap on the back. "See ya tonight!"

Clark was a blur as he crossed to the door. And then, with

a final wave, he strolled outside and up the drive, just like a normal person.

Jon looked at his wife. "He's a teenager, Martha. It's his *job* to keep us guessing."

Martha raised an eyebrow. "You say that with considerable conviction. As though it explains everything."

"Doesn't it?"

"Well . . ." Martha chuckled. "I suppose so. The important thing is, Clark does talk with us. Eventually. Whatever's on his mind, we'll find out by and by."

"I'd say you're right on all counts." Jonathan set down his coffee cup and moved closer, putting his arm around his wife. "The other important thing is, thanks to Clark, I actually have some free time this morning." He kissed the tip of Martha's nose. "So . . . can you guess what I'm thinking right now?"

"Ah! Now let me think . . ." She smiled. "You know, I believe I can."

◆◆◆

When the school bus braked to a stop at the end of the Kents' drive, Clark was standing there, waiting nonchalantly. He bounded onto the bus, and threaded his way up the aisle toward Pete and Chloe.

"Morning, musketeers!" Clark settled into the seat in front of them and stretched out. He stifled a yawn as the bus pulled away.

Behind him, Chloe silently mouthed, "Pay up!" and Pete forked over his rumpled five.

Clark sighed, staring straight ahead as the currency changed hands behind his back. "Ya know, you two must have passed that five back and forth at least a dozen times this month alone! Isn't it about time to retire that routine?"

Chloe blinked. "You *knew*?" She shot Pete a dirty look. "You told him!"

"Uh-uh, not me!"

"Pete didn't have to say anything." Clark half turned in his seat to face them. "I'm not completely oblivious."

"See, Chloe? I told you. Pay up!"

As Chloe surrendered the five, Clark shook his head. "I don't get it. I thought she won."

"She won the 'Will he miss the bus?' bet. I won the 'Not completely oblivious' bet." Pete smoothed out the bill and kissed it. "Welcome back, Abe!"

"Oblivious, huh?" Clark raised an eyebrow. "Thanks for the vote of confidence, Chloe."

"I never said you were *completely* oblivious, just . . . detached. Sometimes." Chloe attempted a weak smile, saw that it was getting her nowhere, and tried a different tactic. "How did you know about the bet, anyway? What, do you have eyes in the back of your head? Can you read my mind or something?"

Clark just smiled.

"Give it up, Chloe!" Pete returned the bill to his wallet. "I have known Clark since first grade. It's just not easy keeping secrets around him."

"Oh, pooh! Secrecy is—!"

Clark made a choking sound. "Pete, did she just say, 'pooh'?"

Pete looked sorrowful. "I'm afraid so. And her from such a good family. What will the neighbors say?"

"They'll say you're both full of it!" Chloe sent another elbow in Pete's direction, but he managed to deflect this one.

"She should know, Clark, her dad *is* the manager of Luthor's fertilizer plant!"

"And I hear quite enough of the scatological humor from him. I don't need it from you two! Now, as I was going to say—before I was interrupted—secrecy is a way of life around here. Everyone in this high school—everyone in this *town*—is just brimming over with secrets that no one ever suspects . . . probably even *you*, Clark Kent!"

Clark started to turn away, rolling his eyes, but suddenly stopped. He stared blankly into space for a moment, then slowly turned back to face Chloe and Pete. "You're right, Chloe. I do have a secret. A big secret."

He turned a bit more in his seat and lowered his voice. "It's a terrible secret. And keeping it bottled up inside of me . . . sometimes I feel as if I'm going to explode. You know?"

"Uh-huh." Pete sounded skeptical, but there was also a hint of unease in his voice. *Where's Clark going with this?*

Chloe looked even more skeptical than Pete sounded, but she leaned forward slightly, studying Clark's face. "A big secret? And you've kept it from . . ." Her voice trailed off. *His hair is so dark. Almost jet-black. He has the most incredible eyes. I've never seen anyone with blue-green eyes before. They're gorgeous. He's—!* She shook her head slightly. *Get a grip, girl!* ". . . uh, from both of us?"

Clark nodded solemnly. "I'm really sorry. I mean, you guys are my best friends. I should have told you a long time ago."

'You guys'? A tiny frown zipped across Chloe's face in about a microsecond. She lowered her own voice. "Told us what?"

Clark took a quick, darting look around, as if making sure that no one else was paying attention. "My folks will probably kill me for telling you this, but I have to get it off my chest. Chloe, Pete . . ." They both leaned forward now, and Clark lowered his voice to a soft whisper. ". . . I'm secretly an alien from another planet."

For a second, they both looked at him in shocked silence.

And then Pete collapsed back into the corner of his seat. "Pwaaah-ha-ha!" He raised himself up, trying to speak, took one look at Chloe's outraged expression, and fell back into a stream of helpless, gurgling laughter.

"Comedians!" Chloe smacked Clark over the head with a notepad. "I'm surrounded by comedians!" She sat back, arms folded, glaring at Clark.

"Oh, man, that was so fine!" Pete reached out a hand to high-five Clark. "Remind me never to play poker with you. I can't believe you kept a straight face through all that!"

Clark smiled. "It's a gift." *And nothing works as well as telling the truth.*

◆◆◆

By the time James Wolfe shuffled back into Jacobi's motel room, the clock radio on the nightstand read 10:53 A.M. Wolfe was bleary-eyed and unshaven. He looked like he hadn't slept well in over a week. Jacobi, on the other hand, was fresh and alert.

Wolfe was suspicious. "You've been napping, haven't you?"

Jacobi just smiled. "What do you have for me, Jimmy?"

"Managed to contact a few people, an' make some tentative arrangements. It's all on this." He handed Jacobi a floppy disk. "Those're just preliminaries, mind you! Equipment rentals . . . shipping . . . lease of a recreational vehicle—"

"I take it the RV is meant to transport the two of us to Kansas?"

"That's right." Wolfe frowned. "Assuming we find a place to set up."

"Don't tell me there's no space for a tent show. It's the

Great Plains! Someone must have land that they rent out for fairs or carnivals."

"No one who would commit to me." Wolfe choked down a swallow of cold coffee, wishing it were something stronger. "I did get a line on one possibility. Problem is, it's a property currently under the control of a local savings and loan. I made an inquiry . . . details are on the disk. But I get the impression they're not that accustomed to making this kind of deal via e-mail. I think they're gonna need a little soft-soaping, a little human contact, even if it's just over the phone."

"I can handle that, Jimmy. It's my specialty, after all."

"Yeah. Good. 'Cause the way I feel right now, I couldn't sell air to a drowning man." Wolfe let out a weary yawn that seemed to originate from somewhere around his toes. "I've done all I can. Now I gotta get some sleep before my eyeballs roll outta my skull."

"You do that, Jimmy." Jacobi took his partner by the arm and steered him back toward the adjoining room. "I'm sure you've done your usual exemplary job. I'll take it from here."

Wolfe flopped into bed, and was sound asleep before the door closed.

◆◆◆

As the final bell of the day sounded for Monday classes, Clark and Pete dragged themselves down to the rooms that housed the school paper. They found the door open and Chloe typing furiously on one of the desktop computers in the *Torch* office. Behind her, most of one wall was covered with newspaper and magazine clippings of the stranger events of post-meteor-storm Lowell County. A montage of articles and photographs chronicled everything from freakish weather to the birth of two-headed calves. Chloe called it her Wall of the Weird. It formed the foundation of all her theories about the weirdness that infested Smallville.

Clark glanced over the Wall as he and Pete entered. He always checked to see if there were any new postings, especially ones that might mention him. So far, his face had yet to appear on the wall. *Nice to see that I'm not officially considered weird.*

"Hey, Chloe." Pete drummed his fingers across a file cabinet. "Tight deadline?"

"Hey, you two. No, I'm just checking out the rest of the local media, such as it is." Chloe tapped a fingernail against the glass of the monitor. "Look! Here's just another example of what's wrong with this crazy town." There on the screen was an archived image of a brightly colored billboard welcoming one and all to "Smallville, Meteor Capital of the World."

"Gaah!" She threw up her hands. "In the first place, that should read 'Meteor*ite* Capital.' Meteors are what travel through space. Once they smack into the Earth, they become meteorites."

Clark nodded. "Technically, Chloe, they're meteor*oids* when they're out in space. But, to be honest, I'm not sure even NASA calls them that anymore."

"Well, thank you, Mister Science! Anyway, terminology aside, it would be a lot more appropriate if our billboards read, 'Secrets Capital of the World.'"

"Oh, man!" Pete fell back into a chair and stared up at the ceiling. "I can't believe you're still beating that drum."

"It's true, Pete, and you know it. Ever since those flying space rocks hit the county, Smallville has harbored more dark secrets *per capita* than any town this side of Metropolis."

Pete gave a derisive snort. "Dark secrets . . . you make it sound like a soap opera."

"Exactly!" Chloe got a gleam in her eyes. "Smallville's just like *Peyton Place* . . . except that here, it's all about weirdness, instead of sex."

"Peyton Place? Where's Peyton Place?"

"Peter, Peter." Chloe sighed and shook her head. "*Peyton Place* was a best-seller written by Grace Metalious. It spawned a sequel, a movie, and at least two television series. Am I the only one here with any literary awareness?"

Clark frowned. "That's not really fair, Chloe. *Peyton Place* really wasn't intended as a classic literary novel. Besides, it was published back in the fifties, before our fathers were born."

"Then how do you know about it? What, was Lana reading *Peyton Place*?"

"Uhh . . ."

"I thought so." Chloe's smile was bittersweet. *Clark has been smitten with Lana Lang since at least middle school. And that's why I'll never be more than a bud. Not much chance of me competing with a pom-pom princess. Correction, ex-pom-pom princess.* Lana had quit the cheerleading squad when several Smallville football players were caught cheating on a major exam. That still surprised—and impressed—Chloe when she thought about it.

"Anyway, *I* was talking about secrets." Chloe started clicking through pages on the computer. "Do you realize that, so far this year, over half a dozen people have been carted away to hospitals in Metropolis? And there've been almost as many deaths . . . and all of them since Homecoming Weekend!"

"Don't remind me." Pete plucked a sheet of paper from a recycling bin and began folding it over. "High school's been a lot weirder than I ever thought it would be."

"Exactly! *We* know about the weirdness because we witnessed a lot of it. And yet, you still have to sift through the archives of the *Smallville Ledger* with a fine-toothed comb to get even *half* a clue to what's really going on. There's an almost total lack of investigative reporting from our so-called local media. And why is that?"

Clark shrugged. "I don't know. Why?"

Chloe looked up from her screen. "I'm not sure, but I have my suspicions. Here, get a load of the *Ledger* website's homepage." She turned the monitor around, and pointed to the upper corner of the screen. "See that? A direct link to LuthorCorp's public relations site."

"So?"

"LuthorCorp is the *Ledger*'s biggest advertiser. I'll bet they don't print anything that Lionel Luthor doesn't want to see in print."

"Chloe, that's just not so. Remember the banner headline they ran when people thought his son had robbed the Smallville Savings & Loan?"

"The exception that proves the rule, Clark. That robbery took place in broad daylight in front of a dozen witnesses. The *Ledger* couldn't ignore it. But they were the first paper to print a retraction when it turned out that Lex Luthor had been in Metropolis at the time. Even so, they 'somehow' neglected to mention that Lex's impersonator was a *shapechanger*!"

"Well, you have to admit it sounds . . ." Clark floundered, searching for the right word.

"Weird? It *is* weird! But it *happened*. Clark, you yourself saw Tina Greer morph into Lana, and into Whitney Fordman!"

"Yeah, but—"

"The police have to know the truth. Somebody, on some level, at the *Ledger* has to know. But the whole story is not getting into print." Chloe leaned back in her chair, arms folded, as if defying him to disagree. "My guess is that Lionel Luthor is the reason why. No one else around here has enough influence."

Pete looked up from his paper folding. "'Cept maybe for Lex."

"Oh, come on, Pete!"

"No, think about it, Clark. Lex engineered that giant fireworks display for your party . . ." Pete sent a perfect paper airplane sailing across the room. ". . . and he kept the cops away."

"Okay, he has some influence. But Lex is all right. He stood up to his father and saved a lot of jobs at the local plant, didn't he? Chloe, your dad might be out of work, if not for Lex. Who funded the school's new computer lab? Lex! And who bankrolled the renovations to the Talon downtown—?"

"Hold it, Clark!" Pete stooped to retrieve his airplane. "I know he's been your bud ever since you saved his sorry butt from drowning, but how much do we really know about him?"

"How much did we know about Chloe before we got to know her? How much do you know about me? Pete, I'm adopted. Even *I* don't know who my natural parents are!"

"Uh, guys?" Chloe waved a hand to get their attention. "Forgive me if I'm interfering with some kind of male bonding ritual, but I was trying to make a point."

"Which is—?" Pete set the airplane down on top of her computer.

"The local media, for whatever reason, is failing to adequately cover Weirdness Central. And that's where I come in."

Clark looked at Pete. "I'm almost afraid to find out."

"Me too, but I'll ask." Pete turned back to Chloe. "Tell us,

Intrepid Girl Reporter, just what do you have planned? I thought the principal put the brakes on your weirdness exposés in the school paper."

"In the paper, yes." Chloe smiled as she typed in a new Web address. "As a matter of fact, his exact words were 'don't print what you can't prove.' But he neglected to mention any restrictions in connection with the *Torch*'s website. So . . ." she stretched the word out like taffy. "I've set up a little cyberarchive of all the recent meteorite-inspired weirdness I've been able to track down. Take a look!"

Clark scrolled down the page. "You've put your Wall of the Weird on-line. Very thorough. Are you going to add the part about me being an alien?"

"Very funny!" Chloe turned the monitor away from Clark and motioned Pete over to take a look. "I just wish I still had my jpeg files of the late Coach Arnold's pyro display. But those were all lost when the *Torch* offices were . . . torched. That's why I'm saving everything to this website now."

"I don't know, Chloe." Pete looked up from the screen. "I mean, sure, we know all of this stuff happened." He grimaced. "I was there when a couple of the bodies were found. But, when you put it all together like this in one place, it reads like a year's worth of the *Weekly World News*. Who's gonna believe it? Who's even going to see it?"

◆◆◆

After a bracing afternoon swim in the motel pool, Donald Jacobi returned to his room to find his partner seated before his laptop.

"Jimmy . . . ? Looking for something?"

"I was just checking to see if you'd had any luck making contacts in Smallville, and came across your newest bookmarks." James Wolfe was freshly showered and shaved. He looked considerably better after an extra six hours of sleep, but his face bore an expression of growing disbelief. "I didn't expect to find this . . . this lunacy!"

The laptop's monitor screen showed a banner headline, declaring Smallville, Kansas, "The Land of the Weird and Home of the Strange." Below the headline was a by-line for one Chloe Sullivan.

"I wouldn't call it lunacy, Jimmy." Jacobi loomed over his shoulder. "It's actually quite inspired."

"Do you mean to stand there and tell me that this"—Wolfe angrily pointed to the screen—"this crap is what 'inspired' you to blow off our Southern tour? *This?*"

"I showed you that website earlier."

"I was still half-asleep! Don, this was created by some high-school kid!" Wolfe fought to keep his temper in check, but he was rapidly losing the battle. "You woke me out of a sound sleep and made me spend hours on-line, lining up every goddamn thing we need for a goddamn tent show, for *THIS?*"

"Calm down, Jimmy. You'll work yourself up into a stroke." Jacobi's voice flowed cool and even, like a gentle autumn breeze. "I wouldn't make a decision based on a single website. But young Ms. Sullivan's work pointed me in all the right directions. As I told you before, I was able to confirm many of these case studies on the more established local news sites. I've since cross-checked these incidents with stories which appeared in the *Metropolis Daily Planet* and their chief competitor, the *Inquisitor*."

"The *Inquisitor?*" Wolfe threw up his hands. "Oh, *that's* a reputable news source! They're just one step up from the supermarket tabloids. The stuff they've printed is probably wilder than this kid's!"

"There is a certain flamboyance to their reporting style, but it often contains a kernel of information. Sometimes, even more useful than what can be found in the *Planet*. At any rate, I've been able to verify the existence of these odd 'mutant cases.' The survivors are scattered among various hospitals and research institutes, mainly in the vicinity of Metropolis. And those centers are being extremely close-mouthed about the conditions of their patients."

"Which proves nothing."

"Perhaps, Jimmy. There could be nothing to this at all, but—reading between the lines—I don't believe that's the case. No, I think something has been happening out there in the hinterlands, something that people in authority don't wish to acknowledge. It may not be quite as freakish or extreme as Ms. Sullivan believes . . . but she does believe in it, Jimmy. And others will believe in it, too. Just as they believe what I've been teaching these past few years."

"I don't know, Don." Wolfe leaned back in the chair. "This is a far cry from lecturing about cosmic mind alignment or running aura-cleansing seminars. There are so many risk factors."

"Aren't there always? But we have to go after this, Jimmy! The meteorite connection is right there. It's too good to pass up." Jacobi smiled. "Besides, I've already been in touch with that savings and loan. The land we need for the tent show is ours. All we have to do now is sign the final papers."

"What papers? Where?"

"Here is the basic boilerplate agreement," Jacobi tapped a code into the laptop. "Now that I've cleared the way, you can iron out the final details on-line. We have until this Friday."

"Friday." Wolfe rubbed his forehead. "I'm getting too old for this crap."

"Don't be ridiculous, Jimmy. You're not that much older than I am. We're still both in the prime of life." Jacobi's voice was as smooth as honey, but underneath was the firmness of steel. "And never forget, Jimmy, we're in this together. Partners to the end."

"Right . . . partners . . ." *But you still hold all the high cards, Don.*

"That's what I want to hear! Now let's get to work. We've a lot to accomplish in the next four days."

CHAPTER 4

Friday afternoon found Clark Kent peering at the big old clock on the wall from the back of the study hall. He had finished his homework assignments in the first half of the period, and there were still several minutes left before the bell. *Wish I'd brought along an extra book to read . . . a magazine . . . anything!* Bored, Clark stared at the clockface and looked through it, into the inner workings of its electric motor. With each passing day, he was finding it easier and easier to see through solid objects. *Who needs X-ray specs? All I need is a little more practice.*

Leaning back in his seat, Clark gazed through the sidewall, and out into the corridor. There he saw Mr. Weedmore carrying a box of trumpet mutes down the hall to the band room. Concentrating a little harder, he peered through to the music instructor's skeleton. As the skeleton limped along, Clark could see the series of metal pins that army doctors had used to save Weedmore's leg after he'd taken a near hit from a mortar shell in Vietnam. Weedmore passed by a second skeleton, who appeared to be standing several feet in the air. Clark softened his focus and immediately recognized Will Grady, one of the school janitors, up on an old wooden ladder. *What's Grady working on? Hard to tell from this angle. Oh, must be the emergency lighting system.* As Clark watched, the janitor climbed down the steps and slid the ladder five feet farther down the hall. Before Grady could take another step, he reacted as if he'd heard a voice call out to him. The janitor turned and headed up the hall in response, leaving the ladder behind. With a start, Clark realized that the ladder had been left dangerously close to the door of the biology lab.

And then, the bell rang.

As the classmates around him began to collect their gear, Clark jumped up from his seat. He reached the corridor just as the door to the bio lab slammed against one leg of the ladder. The ladder swayed slightly, dislodging a big bucket of tools from one of the upper steps. The bucket fell straight toward the head of a girl who was leaving an adjacent classroom. She was completely oblivious to her danger.

As Clark raced down the corridor, everything else seemed to move in slow motion. With the tool bucket just inches from striking the girl's head, Clark reached out and yanked it away. Momentum carried him another ten feet down the corridor before he came to a stop. Setting the bucket down, Clark straightened up and looked around. Students were again surging through the corridor at normal speed. The girl looked up, a puzzled look on her face, and brushed her hand across her hair. No one paid Clark any special notice; it had all happened too fast. He casually turned and started to saunter back to the study hall.

One voice stopped him in his tracks. "Clark?"

"Lana . . . hi! What's up?"

"I wanted you to be the first to know—I aced my algebra test!"

"That's great! But I'm not surprised. I knew you could do it!"

"Well, I wasn't so sure of that, until you helped me with that last study session. I really understand how to handle the equations now. I can't thank you enough."

"I'm glad I could help." Clark returned Lana's smile. It was the most beautiful smile he'd ever seen. He had thought so for years, and couldn't imagine ever thinking otherwise.

Clark still remembered the first time he'd noticed Lana
Lang, across a crowded middle-school cafeteria. She had
beautiful long hair, glossy and straight and dark auburn
brown, an amazing color. Until that moment, Clark had
thought that his mother had the prettiest hair he'd ever seen.
Sorry, Mom. You lose. Lana half turned, talking with a
friend, and he fell completely, totally in love. Even then,
Lana was gorgeous.

A week later, after steeling his nerve, Clark walked up to
her. He hadn't heard her say anything nasty or mean to
anyone—he had been covertly watching Lana the past few
days—and had decided it was safe to say hello and intro-
duce himself. Clark had gotten close enough to notice that
Lana had the most amazing green eyes. Then he'd tripped
over his own feet and wound up stumbling to the floor.

Lana had been very kind, shushing the kids who laughed
at him and helping him retrieve his scattered textbooks.
That, of course, just made the situation even worse. Clark
retreated more awkwardly than in his worst nightmare, half-
paralyzed and having trouble breathing. If the Earth could
have swallowed him up, it would've been all right by him.

It was nearly a month before he had the nerve to approach
her again. In the weeks that followed, he tried again and
again to talk with Lana. But every time, he broke out in a
sweat and felt weak in the knees.

Jonathan had tried to reassure him. "You have to understand, Clark, you're at that age when boys start becoming
men and girls start becoming women. It's like with the birds
and the bees—"

"We live on a *farm*, Dad. You and I already had that talk.
Besides, I learned all about that sex-ed stuff in grade
school."

"Oh . . . yeah." Jonathan had looked completely flummoxed. "I keep forgetting they start teaching that at a younger age these days."

"Uh, Dad? About my problem? Is this like a hormonal imbalance or something?"

"Not exactly. You see, Clark, you're going through a lot of changes, and it just takes time to adjust to them. There'll be times when you feel awkward around a pretty girl. But it's nothing to worry about. It's perfectly natural."

It was good advice, but Jonathan had been wrong on one count. Clark's weakness around Lana had not been born entirely of adolescent anxiety. It had mostly been caused by her necklace.

For years, Lana had worn a small green crystal on a chain around her neck, a tiny piece of one of the meteors that had struck Smallville when she was a little girl. It wasn't until recent months that Lana had put the necklace away. Once she'd stopped wearing it, Clark found he could finally approach her and have a normal conversation with no more than the expected nervousness. She had even confided in him a few times, telling him about her parents, and the necklace, and—

◆◆◆

"Lana!" Whitney Fordman's booming voice completely destroyed the moment. "I've been looking all over for you. Oh, hiya, Kent."

"Whitney." Clark tried to hang on to his smile as the upperclassman approached, but without a whole lot of success. Fordman was tall, almost as tall as Clark. He was also a senior, very popular, and—worst of all—Lana's first serious boyfriend.

"Whitney?" Lana read something troubling in his eyes. "Is something wrong?"

"You knew Stu Harrison's been back in the hospital all week?"

"Yes . . . ? Oh—!" Lana stepped closer to Whitney and put a hand on his arm. "It's bad, isn't it?"

"It's really bad. It's about as bad as it gets." Whitney's jaws clenched, and he looked down at the floor. "They found new tumors in his brain, a bunch of 'em this time. The doctors say there's not much they can do. So he's decided to come home for . . . for as long as he's got." Tears started to well up at the corners of his eyes, and he wiped one hand across his face. "This . . . this just sucks!"

Lana hugged Whitney tight. "I know."

"I've known Stu since kindergarten! There's never been a nicer guy. Stu's the best! He doesn't deserve this!"

Clark put a hand on Whitney's shoulder. "No, he doesn't. Nobody does."

Whitney looked up and blinked. He'd almost forgotten Clark was there. "Yeah. You're right, Kent. What Stu's gone through, I wouldn't wish on my worst enemy."

"I feel like we should be doing something." Lana bit her lip in frustration.

"Not much we can do, babe. The doctors will be supplying meds to keep Stu comfortable. Some of the guys on the team have talked about going over to see him, maybe take along some comedy videos—y'know, like Laurel & Hardy and the Stooges—to keep his spirits up."

"That's a good idea." Clark thought for a moment. "What about his parents? How are they holding up?"

"'Bout as well as they can, but they're hurting. My mom was saying that their insurance has run out. They may have to take out a second mortgage to pay the doctor bills."

"Then maybe we could hold a fund-raiser for them. They shouldn't have to lose their house, too. It's bad enough . . ." Clark let the words trail off.

"That's a wonderful idea, Clark!" Lana pulled out a notepad. "We could hold a benefit dance . . . bring in a few bands . . . I know we could get the Student Council to sponsor it!"

"Yeah." Whitney began to brighten a little. "Yeah, that would be good for Stu, too, knowing that his folks had fewer money worries."

"We should check with the principal to see if we can use the auditorium." Lana started scribbling down ideas. "We'll need to hold a planning meeting . . . maybe after school at the Talon. Whitney—?"

"Wish I could, babe. I can give you a lift downtown, but I have to work at the store tonight."

"That's all right. I know it's short notice." She looked up from her pad. "What about you, Clark? Can you be there?"

"Uh, sure. No, wait—! I promised Mr. Ambrose that I'd help set up the Earth Science labs for next week's experiments." He tried mightily to conceal his disappointment. *If Whitney knew how bummed I am, he'd move heaven and Earth to find a sub for his shift at the store.* "But that shouldn't take too long. If you need a hand, I'll get there somehow. I just might be a little late."

"That would be great, Clark. There'll be a lot to organize, and we don't even have much time before the next bell. See you later!"

"Yeah, see ya, Kent."

"Right. Later." Clark quickly ducked back into the study hall to grab his notebooks. *For once, I'm not going to just stand there and feel sorry for myself while Lana and Whitney walk off together.*

As the last bell signaled the end of classes, Clark made his way toward the science wing. He crossed the main corridor just in time to see Lana and Whitney leaving, arm in arm.

Despite his earlier resolve, Clark stood and watched wistfully as the two of them crossed the parking lot to Whitney's pickup truck.

Lana had started dating Whitney before the end of her first week in high school. *Easy to see why,* thought Clark. *He's Smallville's golden boy. Starting quarterback on the football team, family owns a department store . . . hard for a farm boy to compete with all that.* Whitney and Lana had broken up once or twice, but they kept getting back together. Even after the time when Lana learned of the "Smallville Scarecrow."

The Scarecrow was an old football tradition at Smallville High School. No one knew exactly how old, because few students openly talked about it. Before the annual Homecoming Game, a few football players would select a freshman, drag him out to Riley Field, strip him to his underwear, paint an "S" on his chest, and then string him up on a pole like a scarecrow. This little exercise in ritual humiliation was thought to bring the team good luck.

The week before the past season's Homecoming, Whitney had caught Clark talking with Lana outside her house. In a fit of jealous rage, the quarterback chose Clark to be the new Scarecrow.

Normally, that couldn't have happened. Clark was strong enough to take on the entire football team. But at the time, Whitney was carrying Lana's necklace for luck in the big game. Under the influence of the crystal's radiation, Clark had fallen like a sack of bricks. Whitney and two of his teammates had tied him up in the field near the LuthorCorp fertilizer plant, and left Lana's necklace around his neck as a taunting final touch.

"Enjoy it," Whitney had sneered. "Because that's as close to her as you're ever going to get."

The scary thing is, he was almost right. That green rock left me feeling half-dead. Usually, if the Scarecrow didn't manage to work his way loose, he would be released after the game. But sometimes, the team would get caught up in their victory and forget all about him until the next day. *If Lex hadn't come along when he did, I don't know what would have happened.* It had been well after dark when Lex Luthor found him in the field. Lex scrambled to free his friend, and in the process the necklace had come loose and tumbled several feet away, far enough for Clark's strength to return.

When Lana found out about the Scarecrow thing, she broke up with Whitney. Clark stood at a window by the main entrance, watching Fordman's shiny new pickup carry Lana away. *All right, so they got back together later. But Whitney's wrecked a couple of trucks . . . his father developed a heart condition . . . and he was passed over for a scholarship to Kansas State. Sometimes, it seems as though he's been paying for that night ever since.*

The old clock in the main hall cycled over to the next minute with an audible click, and Clark remembered his promise to Mr. Ambrose. He turned away from the windows and headed up the wing to the Earth Science lab. *Yeah, maybe Whitney's had some bad breaks, but his problems are nothing compared to Stuart's. Whitney still has his whole life ahead of him . . . we all do.*

◆◆◆

Midway between Metropolis and Smallville, a golden Lamborghini Diablo 6.0 exited I-35 and headed west along the Argonia Pike. The old Kansas roadway was flat and straight, and the Lamborghini was soon shooting by cornfields in excess of ninety miles per hour. Behind the wheel, Lex Luthor slipped a compact disk into the custom stereo system, and in seconds the two-seater's speakers roared with the sound of "The Ride of the Valkyries."

Lex smiled. *Life is good. I managed to get into and out of the city without once having to deal with my father. Nothing could spoil this day.*

Then he spotted the semis.

There were at least two semitrailers, lumbering along at roughly half his speed, just a couple of miles ahead, exactly at the spot where the road began a gentle curve to the right. Had he still been on the interstate, Lex would have just blown past them. But he knew from experience that there could be unpleasant surprises along these two-lane back roads. Lex hit the brakes and quickly downshifted, managing to slow to fifty just two car lengths behind the rear truck. No sooner had the Lamborghini fallen in line behind the semi than a rusty old pickup, loaded down with bags of fertilizer, rumbled past in the eastbound lane. As the pickup dwindled in his rearview mirror, Lex noted the familiar LuthorCorp logo on the bags.

That would have been an embarrassing way to die, done in by a truckload of the company's product. Especially that particular product.

Lex took a couple of long, deep breaths, dropping back an additional three car lengths and taking time to consider the freshly painted markings on the back of the semitrailer ahead of him. Bold letters across the top of the double doors read: **FULFILL YOUR DESTINY!** In the middle was a strange graphic that looked like an oddly twisted rope ladder. And, indeed, beneath the graphic was stenciled **www.cosmic-ladder.com**. After a moment, Lex realized that the graphic was an abstract representation of the DNA helix. *What the devil is* that *supposed to be selling? And how far are they going?*

Lex punched a button on his sound system, and the Wagnerian crescendos were instantly muted, replaced by the staticky crackle of citizens' band chatter.

"Li'l Duck, this is Mother Duck . . . do you see what's followin' us? C'mon?"

"Hoo-wee, I do for true! That's one fine-lookin' set o' wheels! Whaddya think it is?"

Lex pulled a wireless headset from a compartment beneath his seat and switched on the mike. "Breaker one-nine, you copy, Ducks? It's a Lamborghini Diablo 6.0."

"This is Mother Duck . . . howdy, stranger. Where are you? What's your handle?"

"I'm driving the Diablo. You can call me"—Lex grinned sardonically as he ran a hand over his hairless scalp—"Mr. Clean. Where are you boys headed?"

"Wide spot in the road called Smallville, Mr. Clean. You heard of it?"

Lex held back a disappointed sigh. "That I have, Ducks. Headed that way, myself. You mind if I play through?"

"Not at all, Clean. There's just us two big rigs, and an RV leadin' this li'l caravan. I'm showin' straight, empty road ahead an' not a Smokey in sight. You put the pedal to it, and there should be smooth sailin'! Me, I'd like to see whatcha got! C'mon."

"Much obliged, Ducks!" Lex swung the Lamborghini into the left lane and pushed his foot to the floor. He shot past the semis and the lead RV as though they were standing still. In seconds they were just a big spot in his mirror. "Enjoy your stay in Smallville."

Far behind, the truckers were still flashing their lights and sounding their horns in salute.

"Eh?" Don Jacobi awoke in the front passenger seat of the RV just in time to see the glint of the Lamborghini as it disappeared over the horizon. "What was that?"

Behind the wheel, James Wolfe sat slack-jawed. "I'm not sure. But it was gold, and it had wheels."

CHAPTER 5

Clark checked his watch as he dashed down the main steps of the school, mentally calculating the distance to the Talon cafe and the quickest way to get there. Clark knew that he could be downtown in under a minute, but running full speed through the middle of Smallville was out of the question. Fortunately, there were still some undeveloped areas between the school grounds and the middle of town. Once he reached those, he could sprint halfway to the Talon virtually unseen.

Clark was about to cross the parking lot when a trumpeting car horn caught his attention. He turned to see an exotic golden wedge glide to a stop just a few feet away. *This can only be Lex.* As Clark drew near, the passenger-side door swiveled up and open.

"Hello in there!"

"Hello out there! I thought that was you, Clark. Need a lift?"

"Need? No. Will I take one? You bet!" Clark slid in and sank back into the soft leather seat. "Oh, this is too much."

"There's no such thing as too much, Clark." With the flip of a switch, Lex closed and sealed the car. The Lamborghini began a gentle glide across the parking lot, to the appreciative and envious stares of a few teachers who stood near a line of humbler vehicles. "Where to?"

"The Talon."

"Good choice. I could use a latte."

"Do I dare ask how fast this thing can go?"

"Let's just say it can easily exceed the posted limits."

Clark shook his head. "And I'm sure you've already put that to the test."

Lex laughed. "You should have been with me earlier. I was the soul of courteous driving."

Clark looked skeptical.

"It's true. I even maintained a safe distance while following a truck." Lex braked to a gentle stop, checking for oncoming traffic before pulling out onto the main road. "Seriously. I know I have a lead foot, but I'm working on it."

"Good. You do that." *Because the next time you barrel off a bridge—!*

"There are no guarantees in life, Clark. If I take another header off a bridge, you might not be there to pull me out."

Clark blinked in surprise. "That's just what I was thinking."

"What can I say?" Lex grinned. "Great minds think alike."

"I guess so." *But not exactly alike.* Clark glanced at his friend, recalling the day they first met. *You got a glimpse of your own mortality that day. I got my first hard look at how different I really am . . .*

◆◆◆

The accident had been just a few months ago, the day Lex Luthor moved to town to take over as president and general manager of LuthorCorp's fertilizer plant. Clark had been walking across the Old Mill Bridge, staring off into the water, lost in thought. He scarcely noticed the passing truck that hit a pothole at the edge of the bridge. The truck lost a bale of barbed wire, just before a late-model Porsche approached from the opposite direction.

Lex was behind the wheel of the Porsche, speeding around the bend, when his cell phone began to ring. Momentarily distracted, he was reaching for it when he belatedly saw the bale of wire in his path. Lex dropped the phone and hit the brakes, but it was too little too late. The car hit the bale, blew both front tires, and went airborne—flying right toward Clark. For a split second their eyes locked. Both young men froze.

Lex had no clear memory of what happened next, but Clark remembered it all too well. The Porsche slammed into him with the force of a two-and-a-half-ton fist, driving him through the bridge's guardrail. In free fall, Clark reflexively sucked in a deep breath of air, just before he and the vehicle hit the river.

Once underwater, it took him several seconds to get his bearings. The river ran cold that day, but Clark never felt it. As he turned, trying to orient himself, he saw the Porsche, its crumpled front end embedded in the riverbed. And through the shattered windshield, he saw the driver— unconscious—his head bobbing gently against the deflating air bag.

Two quick strokes propelled Clark down to the Porsche. He reached into the yawning space where the top of the windshield had once been, grabbed hold of the car's roof and, with a single yank, peeled it open. Leaning down into the wreck, he pulled the driver free and kicked off for the surface.

Lex's lips were turning blue as Clark dragged him onto the rocky shore. Remembering his CPR classes, Clark knelt over the bald young man and tilted his head back. *Airway looks clear, but he's not breathing.* He pinched Lex's nose shut and, taking another deep breath, placed his mouth over the victim's and blew a lungful of air into the unconscious form. Clark checked for a pulse, but couldn't find one. He brought his hands together over Lex's sternum and pushed down hard, again and again.

"Come on, don't die on me!"

Another compression, and Lex jerked back to life, turning his head to cough up a lungful of river water. Shaking, both from the cold and the heaves, Lex looked back up. It took a couple of seconds for his eyes to refocus, and then he stared at Clark with a mixture of wonder and disbelief.

"I could have sworn I hit you."

"Well, if you did, then I'd be . . . I'd be dead." Clark looked back at the bridge, at the mangled guardrail. And then, the realization, the enormity of what had happened began to sink in. Clark felt a biting cold, a freezing sensation he had never for a moment felt underwater. He glanced down at his hands, the hands that had gripped broken glass and shredded steel. Not a scratch. His back felt fine. He ran a hand across his chest. It was a little sore from where the car had hit him, but there was no blood, no broken bones. Clark dropped to one knee, swayed a moment, and somehow managed to sit rather than sprawl on the rocky ground.

Lex pushed himself up to a sitting position, shivering as the wind whipped over his sodden clothes. "Are you okay?"

"Yeah." Clark's voice sounded distant and strange to his own ears. "Yeah, I'm fine." He really was fine—and that was the whole problem.

Clark had never been in an accident like that before. Growing up, he had known that he was stronger, faster, tougher than the other kids. His parents had always cautioned him to keep his physical power secret, to avoid drawing attention to himself—and he had. But until that moment, he had never realized just how tough he really was.

When the deputy sheriff and the paramedics arrived, they all accepted Clark's story—that he had been on the bridge when Lex lost control of his car, that he dove in and pulled Lex out.

"It all happened pretty fast." Clark hadn't offered much

more than that. He didn't have to. They wouldn't have believed the whole truth anyway.

. . . At the time, I wasn't sure that I believed it.

"I still owe you my life, you know." Lex glanced over at Clark.

"No, you don't. You rescued me from playing Scarecrow."

Lex shook his head. "I still can't believe that you didn't press charges against those idiots. You're entirely too forgiving."

"Don't worry, Lex. It was dealt with." While Whitney and his friends were enjoying the Homecoming Dance, Clark found their pickup trucks parked side by side in the school lot—and left them neatly stacked on top of each other, just like pancakes. It was too much for the local wrecker service to handle. They had to bring in a crane to get the trucks down. *I got back at them in my own way.*

Clark looked around as Lex steered the Lamborghini into the heart of Smallville's downtown. "We're getting a lot of stares."

"Nothing new for me. Don't worry, they can't see you through the tinted glass. You can make faces at them if you like."

"Do *you* ever . . . ?"

"Not for years." Lex grinned at his passenger. "But for a while, after I lost my hair . . . all the time. The first two years were the worst. People would assume I was on chemo, but when they found out I wasn't, I started hearing the 'baldy' jokes."

"Kids can be pretty mean."

"Yes. Kids, too." Lex braked for a stop sign. "I learned to

tune it out after a while. Before that, my nicknames had been 'Red' and 'Weezer.'"

"Okay, 'Red' for your hair? But why 'Weezer'?"

"I used to have asthma."

"I never knew that."

"Inhalers were my oldest friends. But I got over it. The condition cleared up shortly after I lost my hair. Probably all tied up with the damned meteor storm."

Clark considered that. He knew that Lex had first visited Smallville years ago. He had arrived with his father, Lionel, who had come to the area to close a business deal. While Lionel was signing a deal to purchase the Ross family's corn-processing factory, Lex had wandered off into the fields. *And that's when the meteors hit.* The first strike slammed into the ground not far from the younger Luthor. The impact knocked him off his feet, and left him prematurely bald.

"So, you think the meteors cured your asthma?"

Lex shrugged. "They may have. Or maybe I just outgrew it. Though I'm sure your friend Chloe would prefer the former explanation."

"By a country mile, as my dad would say. Funny, though, I've never thought of you as one of Chloe's meteor freaks."

"Why, thank you, Clark. 'Not a freak' . . . that's one of the highest compliments I've been paid all month. With that kind of charm, it's easy to see why you get all the girls."

"No, no! I meant—!"

"Kidding, Clark. I know what you meant." Lex smiled. "It isn't always easy being my friend, is it?"

"Well, it's different. This car must cost more than most of my other friends' houses."

"'Different,' eh? Very diplomatic. Ah, here we are . . ." Lex neatly slipped the car into a parking space at the curb just twenty feet from the door of the Talon. ". . . Smallville's finest new cafe and bookstore."

"You mean, Smallville's only cafe and bookstore."

"There's that charm again."

Lex and Clark emerged from the Lamborghini, to be greeted by a blare of truck horns. Two semi drivers waved wildly, calling out to Lex as they followed an RV through town. Lex just laughed and waved back.

Clark looked confused. "Were they singing the old Mr. Clean jingle?"

"It's quite possible."

"Who are they? And what's cosmicladder.com?"

"I don't know, Clark. But I intend to find out."

◆◆◆

The RV pulled over to the curb in the center of Smallville, and James Wolfe leaned out the window. He called out to the driver of the lead truck. "This shouldn't take long. There's a diner up the street. You boys take a break, and we'll join you as soon as the papers are signed."

"Sure thing. You're the boss!"

"If I was really the boss, we wouldn't be here," Wolfe muttered under his breath. He looked up as Jacobi came out of the RV's toilet. "Ready?"

"Fresh, clean, and ready to do business, Jimmy. Let's not keep the bankers waiting."

Wolfe locked up the RV and fell in step behind Jacobi as his partner entered the Smallville Savings & Loan. Confidently, Jacobi strode over to a row of desks, picking out a likely-looking individual.

"Mr. Eaton?"

"Yes?" A balding man in his forties looked up from a computer monitor. "I'm William Eaton. May I help you?"

Jacobi reached out a hand. "I'm Dr. Donald Jacobi and

this is my associate, Mr. Wolfe. We spoke on the phone earlier in the week . . . about an available property?"

"Oh, yes. Yes!" Eaton rose and eagerly shook the offered
hand. "It's good to finally meet you, Dr. Jacobi . . . Mr.
Wolfe. Please, have a seat. May I offer you some coffee?"

"No, thank you, William. May I call you William?"

"Please, call me Will."

"Will, we're working under some serious time con-
straints, and we'd like to get the paperwork taken care of as
expeditiously as possible."

"Of course, Doctor. I have the final papers right here,
ready for your signatures."

"Excellent. James, if you would do the honors?"

Wolfe pulled a pair of half-glasses from within his suit
jacket and began to scan the sheaf of papers.

"I think you'll find everything is in order." Eaton smiled
at the two men. "It's a basic three-month lease with option
to buy. Fifty acres of prime land, complete with house and
barn . . . a very good buy."

Wolfe frowned over his glasses. "If the property's in such
good shape, why was it foreclosed upon?"

Eaton gave a low, mournful sigh, like an old tire leaking
air. "It was a small family farm, and there was a death in the
family. The survivors weren't able to make a go of it and . . .
well, we hated to foreclose, but after a while we had little
choice. Besides, I was given to understand that you're interested in the property for something other than farming."

"Yes, that's the case. Our foundation will be presenting a
series of lectures and educational symposiums. I expect that
we will be attracting quite a crowd during our stay. Many of
our attendees will be traveling a great distance and will require space for parking and perhaps even for temporary on-
site housing."

"Ah, yes! Where did I write that down?" Eaton rummaged

through his notes. "Your earlier messages indicated that part of the property might be utilized as a sort of campground?"

"That's right." Wolfe frowned again. "And we want to make sure that all the proper requirements are met. You did look into the zoning as per our request?"

"Yes, yes. I have the confirmation from the county right here. The zoning for that parcel is perfectly in line with what you've described. I've gathered all the permits you will need. Once everything is signed, I can have them notarized and filed with the courthouse for you."

Jacobi beamed at the bank manager. "I knew you were a man we could count on, Will. Well, James?"

Wolfe looked up from the papers, allowing the suggestion of a smile to flicker across his face. "Everything here is just as Mr. Eaton described. I believe we have but one final requirement to fulfill." He again reached into an inner pocket, this time producing an oversize business envelope. "Here is a cashier's check for the full lease amount. In addition, within a week, we will be arranging for several accounts at the Smallville Savings & Loan, the better to handle our expenditures while we are in the area."

"I trust that all this is satisfactory, Will?"

"Most satisfactory, gentlemen! We will be more than happy to administer your accounts."

"Good. Now, where do we sign?"

◆◆◆

At the Uptown Diner, Marc Greenwood and Mac Raeburn sat themselves down at the counter, each taking an appreciative sniff. The air was rich with the aroma of coffee and grilled onions.

"Coffee, gents?" Edna Mae Benson approached, clutching two large mugs in one hand and a fresh pot in the other.

"Today's specials are liver & onions and beef Manhattan. Both come with two sides and dessert."

Mac took one mug in hand and gave Edna Mae his most charming grin as she poured. "That sounds real temptin', Sweetness, but we drive the long hauls, and my stomach's been stuck on Pacific Time all month. 'Fraid it's still too early for me to be thinkin' of dinner."

Marc flipped through the laminated menu. "I like the sound of dessert, though."

Behind him, a voice remarked, "I hear the pie is especially good."

Edna Mae's eyes grew wide as Lex Luthor sauntered into the diner and plopped down next to the truckers. She had seen him driving through town before, in one fancy car or another, but she'd never expected him to be one for diner food.

"Hey, it's our buddy, Mr. Clean!" Mac threw a playful punch to Lex's shoulder. "Man, I gotta tell ya, that li'l buggy of yours is the sweetest thing I've seen this side of a NASCAR track. Whaddya got under the hood? V-8?"

"A V-12, actually. And you'd be . . . 'Mother Duck'?"

"Right the first time. I'm Mac, an' this is Marc. He's the Li'l Duck an' I'm the Mother!"

"He sure is!" snorted Marc. "But you were sayin' somethin' 'bout pie?"

Lex pointed out a sign high on the wall. "Baked fresh daily. What's the pie *du jour*, Edna Mae?"

"Wha—?" Edna Mae was flustered that Lex knew her name, forgetting for the moment that it was embroidered on her blouse. "Oh . . . pie. Well, today we have apple, blueberry, peach, pineapple, and sweet-potato-pecan. And I think there're a couple of slices of banana-cream left. I could check . . . !"

"Not necessary, Sweetness. I'll have a slab of that pineapple pie."

Marc folded the menu. "Sweet-potato-pecan for me."

Edna Mae looked expectantly at Lex. "And you, sir?"

"Just coffee. Light. And this is all on me."

"Hey, thanks, buddy."

"My pleasure. So, what brings you to these parts, Mac?"

"Oh, this's strictly a one-way haul. The Doc and his buddy hired us to pull their gear out here. Once we reach the site, Marc an' me unhitch and we're outta here. We're due in Albuquerque tomorrow." Mac took a big swallow of coffee. "They got people comin' later to unload an' pitch the tent."

"The tent?"

"That's what I said. Yep, they're rentin' land outside o' town for some sorta show. Pretty good-sized one, too, I'd guess."

"Really . . . ?"

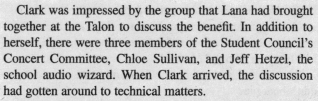

Clark was impressed by the group that Lana had brought together at the Talon to discuss the benefit. In addition to herself, there were three members of the Student Council's Concert Committee, Chloe Sullivan, and Jeff Hetzel, the school audio wizard. When Clark arrived, the discussion had gotten around to technical matters.

Lana checked something off her list. "And suppose an outside group wants to use its own audio equipment?"

"Not a problem!" Jeff added to a schematic diagram he'd sketched out. "I'd set up their equipment in front here and run a line feed off their amp into our system"—he added a few arrows—"as backup, just in case."

"That's great—I followed that completely!" Lana looked up at Jeff. "Is there any chance you could take over teaching my algebra class?"

Jeff laughed. "Trust me, you wouldn't really want that.

Math for math's sake isn't my favorite subject." He inclined his head and executed a gracious half bow. "But thanks all the same for the compliment."

Lana smiled, almost blushing, and Clark had to hide his own grin. *Too bad Whitney isn't here to see that. He'd have a cow!* Clark, who happened to know that Jeff was dating a very nice girl he'd known since grade school, felt only a minor twinge of jealousy. In fact, he resolved to practice that bow. *Nice move!*

After a heated discussion of what bands they should contact, everyone broke into subgroups, and Clark motioned Chloe to one side. "I came in late. How did you wind up as part of this little gathering?"

"Lana asked me, same as you. She figured that I'd be a good choice to handle publicity." Chloe saw the corners of his mouth start to crinkle. "Don't laugh!"

"Sorry."

"I *am* a good choice!"

"I never said you weren't, Chloe." Clark took a sip of coffee. "It's just that there's not much of a weirdness angle to this."

"I write up all sorts of news for the *Torch*. And as editor, I oversee the reporting of everything from scholarship announcements to—!"

"Sports?" He grinned, knowing her distaste for athletics.

"Yes." Chloe gritted her teeth. "Even. Sports."

"Yeah, I guess high-school newspaper work can't be glamorous and exciting all the time."

"Stop it! This is for a good cause."

"You're right. I'm sorry. You'll do a great job with publicity."

"Thanks. And I'm sure I can count on you and Pete to help."

"Of course you can."

"I can?"

"Sure." Clark set down his cup. "I figured you'd be ask-ing when you first mentioned publicity. That's why I pre-emptively busted your chops."

Chloe poked a finger to his chest. "You're a devious man, Clark Kent. Almost as devious as I am. Sometimes."

Lana breezed over, an optimistic smile on her face. "I think we've already made a lot of progress for the first meet-ing. Charlie and Sylvia know all the local bands, and Harry has contacts with a Metropolis booking agent. He thinks there's a chance that we might be able to get a name act to appear. A lot depends on scheduling. We're already promised the auditorium for the first Saturday of next month."

"There's another factor which you may want to take into consideration." Lex stalked across the cafe, a sleek leather satchel in hand. Before anyone could question him further, he flagged down a passing waitress. "A double mocha latte, please, and an almond croissant. As quickly as you can hu-manly manage. And a glass of water, no ice. I need some-thing to clear my palate."

Lex slipped into a seat at a corner table as Lana, Clark, and Chloe gathered around.

Lana looked concerned. "What are you talking about, Lex?"

"Does this have anything to do with those semis?" asked Clark.

"Stop, stop!" Chloe held up both hands. "What factor? What semis?"

"A moment . . . !" Lex accepted a tumbler of water from the returning waitress and drained about a third of it. "That's better. A word of caution: If you ever enter the Uptown Diner, avoid the coffee."

"Wait a minute!" Chloe gaped in disbelief. "You—Lex

Luthor—went into the Uptown? What were you doing there? That place couldn't get four stars from the Board of Health!"

"Not my usual milieu, but a charming establishment in its own retro way. Their coffee, however, is a crime against nature. I believe they still brew it in urns. Ah!" Lex gratefully received his mocha latte and cradled the cup in his hands, breathing in the aroma, as he waited for it to cool. "Now, to answer your questions . . . I went to the Uptown looking for information." He lifted his cup in a little salute to Chloe. "As a journalist, I hope you'll appreciate my sacrifice, Ms. Sullivan."

Chloe put her hand over her heart. "I'll remember it forever. Now, what did you learn?"

Lex took a sip of the mocha latte and smiled blissfully. "That Smallville is about to host some new visitors. A pair of semis that Clark and I saw earlier were hauling equipment for some sort of attraction that's coming to the area. Precisely what, I've yet to discover. But it does involve a tent, a good deal of audio gear, and a laser light show."

"You mean . . . like for a concert?"

"The men I spoke with weren't certain, Lana. All they could really tell me was that they were hired by two men named Jacobi and Wolfe." Lex took a bite of the croissant and chewed thoughtfully. "Jacobi is apparently a doctor, though of what the men didn't know. Jacobi and Wolfe were conducting business at the savings and loan this afternoon, but by the time I found that out, it had closed for the day."

"Jacobi and Wolfe . . . Jacobi and Wolfe." Chloe looked pensive. "Sounds like a law firm. Could they be promoters?"

"Just please don't let them be *concert* promoters." Lana fidgeted nervously. "That could ruin everything."

Clark gently touched Lana's shoulder. "Hey, no sense in worrying about this until we learn more. Right, Lex?"

"Absolutely." Lex paused over another sip. "For what it's worth, Lana, I get the impression that this is something other than a concert. Believe me, I want to get to the bottom of this as much as you do. I'll make a few calls. But in the meantime, let's see what we can find in the horse's mouth, so to speak."

Lex unzipped the leather satchel and opened up a silver-gray laptop. He pressed a recessed switch and the system was up in a second. Two more clicks and he was on-line. "I love the twenty-first century."

Chloe's eyes goggled. "What do you have in that thing?"

"My travel laptop? Not all that much." He typed in www.cosmicladder.com and a homepage appeared instantly. "Probably be needing to upgrade soon.

"Looks like they put some effort into this. Good website design. Nice, smooth homepage download." Lex read the banner out loud. "'Welcome to the Ascendance Foundation!'"

Clark looked over his shoulder. "'Fulfill your destiny!' That was the slogan from the back of the semis, all right."

Lex accessed the site's main menu and clicked on "History." The others drifted over as a much more elaborate webpage began to appear. They all read the page silently. Finally, Lex asked, of no one in particular, "Anyone here have any experience with concepts like these?"

"Sure, some of them." They all turned to Jeff. He waited a beat, then added, "Whenever I play a cleric in Dungeons & Dragons!"

CHAPTER 6

Saturday morning, Jonathan Kent was among the first to see the tent going up. He had just left the house on an errand to pick up cattle feed, when he spotted two pickup trucks pulled off by the side of Old Carter Road. Recognizing the trucks, Jonathan pulled off as well, and called out to their owners.

"Bob . . . Forrest?"

"'Morning, Jon! Come get a load of this!"

Jonathan followed the voices, joining his neighbors where they stood alongside a new fence. From their vantage point, they could see a dozen men, spread out over nearly an acre of land, working hard to convert the farmland into something else. Dump trucks poured loads of gravel into a curving roadway. Big metal stanchions rose from the prairie. Thick nylon rope began to pull a brilliant white canvas up over a framework of poles and cables.

"They started arriving last night." Bob Gundersen gestured toward the work area. "There'd been talk that someone from outta town was gonna rent the old Davis place, but I never expected anything like this."

"I can't rightly figure out what they're setting up." Forrest Morrison pulled off his cap to scratch at the back of his head. "When I saw them spreading sawdust and hauling that canvas, my first thought was that a circus had come to town. But unless they're hiding more canvas somewhere, that tent won't nearly be big enough. And it's wide-open at one end."

"That's not for any circus." Bob shielded his eyes with his hand. "Look, down at that far end . . . that's a stage they're puttin' up there, Forrest. And check out all of them speakers!" He shaded his eyes and looked off toward the east. "Appears to me like they're markin' off that old pasture for campgrounds. I'll bet someone's getting ready to hold one of them music festivals, like Woodstock or somethin'. What do you think, Jon?"

"A festival? More like a carnival." Jonathan considered the layout of the site. "Or a sideshow. My boy Clark heard about this show yesterday . . . said one of his friends checked out its website."

Forrest's eyebrows shot up. "It has a website?"

"These days, what doesn't? Yeah, this whole shebang is being run by some out-of-state foundation. They're supposed to stage some kind of lectures about alternate healing, 'cosmic fulfillment,' and I don't know what all. Sounds like a bunch of New Age bull to me." Jonathan watched as a truck pulled up and workers started off-loading Porta Johns. "I don't know who these foundation people are, or what they're selling, but they surely seem prepared to host a good-sized crowd."

◆◆◆

Saturday afternoon, posters began to appear around Smallville. Emblazoned with a "FULFILL YOUR DESTINY!" banner, the posters spoke of great new discoveries that promised new opportunities for a better, more fulfilling life. They invited the general public to a free lecture the following Wednesday by Dr. Jacobi of the Ascendance Foundation. After a brief listing of time and place, the posters directed those with computer access to the Foundation's website.

Those who accessed the website found a brief history of the Ascendance Foundation, a new listing of the times of upcoming lectures and seminars, and an offer to become a Foundation member and thus gain access to more privileged information for just $14.95 a month. Most locals declined the offer.

But the Foundation already boasted many members, scattered across the country. E-mail announcements of the new lecture series had gone out to them just minutes after Jacobi and Wolfe had finalized their lease. And the most devoted members were already on their way to Smallville.

The first of them began to arrive late Saturday afternoon. Some found lodging in the motels around Smallville. Others parked their RVs or pitched tents on space made available— for a modest fee—on the old Davis farm. They all came eager to hear more from the great Dr. Jacobi, and to do all that they could to help the Foundation.

Wolfe gratefully put the early arrivals to work. After volunteers had thoroughly cleaned the old Davis farmhouse, Jacobi and Wolfe took up residence on the second floor and set up an operations center on the first floor. On-site members were organized into teams to handle security, maintenance, and logistics for what they were already starting to call the Foundation Compound.

By Sunday morning, Wolfe was able to replace all of his hired workers with member volunteers. As night fell Sunday, the Compound's campground was nearly a quarter full. Jacobi stood out on the front steps of their farmhouse headquarters, greeting the newest arrivals, as Wolfe led them inside to collate flyers and stuff envelopes for the Foundation's mass mailings.

Eight-thirty, Monday morning, Wolfe walked out onto the back porch, nursing a cup of coffee. It had been many long years since he'd staged a tent show. The last time had been when he was touring the Southwest with the Reverend Mike. *Mike could "cure" everything from malaria to a goi-*

ter, thought Wolfe, *and every*one *except himself. But he taught me a lot, God rest his conniving soul.*

This show would be a little different. Jacobi wasn't posing as a faith healer . . . *Thank God!* If he were, they'd need a full-time staffer or two just to help handle the crowds, people fully in on the game, people who could gently turn away the obviously hopeless cases before they ever got near the stage. No, he and Jacobi ran a slicker operation; they had always managed with volunteer ushers.

Wolfe blew across the cup to cool his coffee. He knew from experience that audiences often became less inhibited under the canvas than they would in an indoor auditorium. A little extra briefing would be in order for this latest crop of ushers.

And therein was the challenge—if Wolfe was too diplomatic, the ushers wouldn't get the point that part of their job was to protect Jacobi from embarrassment. If he was too blunt, the eager young volunteers might get a glimpse of the real truth about the Foundation.

Wolfe leaned on the rail of the back porch and looked out over the Compound. Fifty feet away, a security volunteer, wearing an orange vest and a Foundation ball cap, directed a Volkswagen minivan toward the campgrounds. A small team of volunteers policed the grounds, picking up litter and trimming the grass and shrubbery. Another team was setting up ladders in preparation to paint the barn.

By God, we just might make this work after all!

◆◆◆

From the Monday edition of the *Smallville Ledger* . . .

National Foundation Announces Local Lecture Series

SMALLVILLE—The Ascendance Foundation of Smyrna, Delaware, will host a series of lectures and seminars this month at their new compound at 1027 Old Carter Road, Smallville. Dr. Donald Jacobi will speak of great new potential for the treatment of disease and improving the quality of life.

Jacobi, an internationally renowned geneticist, is a director of the Ascendance Foundation. He has devoted much of his career to unraveling the secrets of the human genome.

"The more we understand about the building blocks of life, and what affects them, the better we shall be able to treat our ailments, both common and life-threatening," Jacobi said.

Jacobi's first, introductory lecture will be held this Wednesday night at the Foundation Compound, and is free to the public. An admission of $7.50 will be charged for lectures to follow on Friday, Saturday, and Sunday. All lectures are scheduled to begin at 7:30 P.M.

Additional information about the lecture and seminar series and Dr. Jacobi's work is available on the Foundation's website at www.cosmicladder.com, and through the *Ledger*'s on-line calendar.

◆◆◆

Monday night, after dinner, Stuart Harrison shuffled into his family's living room and all but fell back into the big recliner that faced the television. When his mother joined him a few minutes later, she found him zapping with the remote from channel to channel, never lingering on any one for more than a few seconds.

"I don't know how you can get enjoyment from that."

"Not much on right now, Mom. *The Daily Show*'s a repeat that I've seen twice already. There's a great movie on TCM later, but it won't start for an hour."

"Well, while you're waiting, why don't we watch something on tape?" Mary Harrison picked through a small stack of videocassettes. "You know, it was very nice of your friends to bring these over."

"Yeah, good ol' Fordman. He knows my tastes better than just about anybody." Stuart smiled softly. "Remind me—what are the choices there?"

"Let's see . . . *Best of NFL Bloopers* . . . *Zombies of the Stratosphere*, that looks like an old serial . . . several Three Stooges tapes . . ."

"The Stooges? Do we have the one where they're plumbers?"

"Which version? *A Plumbing We Will Go* or *Vagabond Loafers*?"

Stuart sat up in the recliner. "I didn't know there were two."

"Oh, yes. Curly was in the original, where the boys were pretending to be plumbers. In the remake, with Shemp, they actually were plumbers. That's the one involving the theft of the valuable painting." Mary pulled out two cassettes. "Oh, good, they're both here. They're both very funny."

Stu stared at his mother. "How did you come to know so much about the Three Stooges?"

"Oh, I used to watch them on TV with my brother Fred when I was a little girl. It was Fred's idea of baby-sitting."

"*Uncle Fred* likes the Stooges?" Mary's older brother was an elementary-school principal in Connecticut. Stuart couldn't think of any less-likely Stooge fans than his mother and uncle.

"He certainly did when we were kids. I imagine he still

does. We'll have to ask him when he and Aunt Ev call next weekend."

"Sure! I wanna hear about *his* favorite Stooges shorts." He looked at his mother, still not quite believing. "You know, most guys' mothers hate the Stooges. You really liked them, huh?"

"Well, not at first. They scared me. I was just a little girl then." *And I didn't know about the really frightening things, like metastatic cancer.* Mary sat down on the floor next to the VCR. "But Fred just kept telling me it was all make-believe, that they weren't really hurting anyone. Where we grew up, there used to be a kids' show host who introduced each episode. He said the same nice, reassuring things." She smiled at the memory. "Sometimes he'd even show pictures of the Stooges with their families. That's when I realized that they were really nice, normal people who just happened to have unusual jobs. That's when they became funny to me."

"Huh! I guess I never gave it that much thought before. To me, the Stooges were like cartoons that were acted out by people."

"Works for me. So, what'll it be?" Mary waved the two cassettes at her son. "Curly or Shemp?"

"Let's watch 'em both. Curly first. I want to see how different they are." Stuart settled back into the recliner. "And then, maybe you can tell me more about Uncle Fred and your adventures in baby-sitting."

In the kitchen, Ray Harrison looked up from a stack of papers and grinned as he heard the opening notes of an old familiar theme song. "Hey, you knuckleheads! You watchin' the Stooges in there?"

"Why, sointenly!" croaked Stuart. "Come join us, Dad."

"Be there in a minute." Ray turned his attention back to

the papers. There were brochures from alternative healing
clinics, literature from the local hospice organization, and
bills . . . always bills. He set those aside and thumbed
through the brochures. The clinics all seemed to be in Mexico or California. *No big surprise there*, thought Ray. A trip
to any of those clinics would be expensive, and even if they
could scrape together the money, he wasn't sure his son
could survive the trip.

Ray flipped through the material that had been left by the
hospice volunteer. *"The five stages of grief—denial, anger,
bargaining, despair, acceptance."* He knew them all too
well. He'd been through this before, when he was a boy, and
his grandfather was dying. People didn't talk much about
grief in those days and even less about cancer. Ray had been
kept in the dark the whole time, told only that his grandfather was "very sick." *Don't know if Gramps accepted what
was happening to him or not. Momma was denying it up till
the day he died.*

Ray knew more about cancer than his entire family had
known back then, more than he wanted to know. He had
watched his son and his wife progress through to the acceptance stage. Ray himself was stuck at anger, and had been
ever since Stu's first diagnosis. Mary had tried to tell him
that it wasn't healthy to stay angry, but he'd dismissed that.
Anger was natural. It was *cancer* that wasn't healthy. Besides, it wasn't like Ray ever turned his anger on anyone.
(Okay, he'd yelled at a couple of doctors, but that was different.) He didn't smash things or get drunk. Ray looked
over at the empty beer bottles on the counter. *Two an
evening, same as always. Pretty damned moderate for a
fella whose old man used to put away a case of the stuff
every day.*

Ray's anger had fueled a ferocious drive to learn everything he could about the disease that was claiming his son. Unfortunately, what he'd learned was depressing as hell.

The first cancer had been a malignant melanoma—on Stuart's scalp, for God's sake. Their barber had spotted it. None of the Harrisons was particularly dark-complected, but they weren't exactly albinos, either. Ray didn't need a medical degree to know it was a god-awful bad sign when his son was diagnosed with the most serious kind of skin cancer. Most people would never get a melanoma even if they spent their whole lives out in the sun.

Still, the surgery and follow-up treatments had gone well, and the doctors were "cautiously optimistic" that the cancer hadn't already spread. Stuart had three pretty good years, then he started to stumble and run into things. For a boy who'd played baseball and soccer since he was six, it was a bad sign. And it was the one time that Ray—briefly—moved past anger long enough to pray: "Please, God, if it has to be a disease, let it be something like multiple sclerosis. Something he can live with."

But it was cancer again. In his brain this time. Like it wasn't satisfied, taking part of his scalp. Oh, no, it had to go deeper. This time there was neurosurgery, monoclonal antibodies, radioactive iodine . . . a whole raft of biomedical jargon that Ray would remember for the rest of his life. They did "complementary medicine" as well. All three Harrisons joined support groups and learned guided imagery. Stuart started to keep a journal. And those things did help some. From the doctors, there was more cautious optimism: Malignant brain tumors used to be an automatic death sentence, but the new combined therapies had shown considerable success for many patients.

Which just meant that they didn't work for everybody.

The doctors gave it their best shot, and they had a helluva lot more ammunition than they did when Ray's grandfather took sick, but even the best shots can miss. Now it was time to try something else, something drastic. There would be time enough later for despair and acceptance, but now it was time to stay angry.

Ray picked up another clinic brochure. He would accept the situation after his son died. Not a minute before.

By the time Ray finally wandered into the living room, Stuart was asleep in the recliner, the television still on. Ray picked up the remote and hit the mute switch. For several minutes he stood there in the silence of the room, watching Stuart in the light of the picture tube.

"Ray?" Mary stirred from the couch, her voice a hushed whisper. "Let him sleep there. It's all right."

"It's not all right, Mary. It'll never be right." Ray clenched his big hands into fists.

Mary got up and crossed the room to her husband. Ray Harrison was a big, physically strong man. She knew how bitterly frustrating this was for him, knew how much he wanted to strike back at the disease that was killing their son. *If only there were a way Ray could grab hold of cancer and wrestle it into submission, Stuart would have been completely cured years ago.*

Ray stared down at the boy. "Stu sleeps more an' more every day. How long'll it be—how many weeks—before he falls asleep an' never wakes up?"

Mary shook her head. It was an awful question, and she didn't want to consider the answer. "The dishes are all done and put away. If you don't mind, I'll just stay in here a while . . . in case Stuart wakes up and needs something."

"Sure. You do that." Ray took a couple of deep breaths, gave a weary sigh, and unclenched his fists. "Call me if there's anything I can do." He kissed his wife gently on the forehead and left the room.

In stocking feet, Ray padded off down the hall to his den. There, he sank down into his desk chair and wheeled closer to his desk. A stack of medical journals sat piled on a table to Ray's right, pages folded back and information highlighted. He had read through them all dozens of times, searching for something—anything—that might lead to a cure for his son.

There had been nothing.

Maybe there'll be something new on the Internet. Ray punched the power switch on his old Packard Bell desktop and started leafing through the day's paper while he waited for the computer to boot up. He was halfway to the sports page, when a line of type seemed to jump out at him:

". . . new potential for the treatment of disease and improving the quality of life."

Ray read back through the *Ledger* article. "The Ascendance Foundation . . . Dr. Donald Jacobi . . . internationally renowned geneticist . . ." Why did that sound familiar? Then he remembered the poster he had seen in the window of the Corner Drugstore, the one that said, "Fulfill your destiny!" Ray thought about that. *Worth a try, I guess.* He went on-line and typed in www.cosmicladder.com.

Fifteen minutes later, Ray had read and reread most of the material easily accessible on the Ascendance Foundation's website. A year ago, he would've passed right over a site like that. But now, the more he read, the more he saw reason for hope. *Says here that Dr. Jacobi's spent years studying alternative medical treatments. Maybe I can't get Stu into one of those clinics out West. But this fella's come* here . . . *to us!* Ray thought about that. *Maybe it's a sign . . .*

But the next page looked like a dead end. More information about Dr. Jacobi's research was available only for member-subscribers. Ray impatiently clicked on a box labeled "How to Join," and read over the solicitation. He didn't have to think twice. *What the hell, it's only fifteen bucks.*

Ray clicked on "Subscribe Now" and began to enter his credit card number.

◆◆◆

By Wednesday evening, the big tent on the Foundation Compound was abuzz with the voices of the gathering audience. Ushers scurried about, seating people and taking orders from an unseen director via the tiny wireless earphones they all wore.

"All right, people, snap to it!" From a command center set up just behind the stage, James Wolfe adjusted his headset. "Remember what I told you—stay alert to your surroundings and the people around you. If you see anyone who appears to have a problem, try to reassure them—but don't let them interrupt the proceedings without the Doctor's or my approval. If they have a serious problem, tell them that they can talk privately with Dr. Jacobi after the lecture, when we can offer them more personal attention." He took a long drink from a large plastic cup.

"Okay, let's get ready. Five minutes to showtime!" Wolfe checked a row of video monitors which showed various views of the big tent's interior. *Looking good out there, but it's about time we gave the crowd a little something to put them in the mood.* He punched a series of buttons. Soft music began to build over speakers situated throughout the tent, and the large screen that backed the stage started showing a moving starscape.

Jacobi came up behind him. "Don't tell me you're swilling another of those noxious sports drinks!"

"Hey, manning the board is thirsty work." Wolfe held his cup up and swirled the bluish liquid around. "Besides, this is good for me. Helps replenish needed electrolytes and helps me stay on the wagon."

"I think it would *drive* me to drink, but to each his own. How do I look, Jimmy?"

Wolfe cast an eye over Jacobi. His partner wore a tan turtleneck, dark brown pants, and a light brown sport coat with patches on the elbows. Academic, but not stuffy. Just the right note for the Doctor's face and manner. Jacobi had gray eyes, a warm gray, set in a face that managed to look both friendly and distinguished. People seemed to instinctively trust him, especially when he smiled. Wolfe's own eyes were a pale, icy shade of blue; he sometimes made people uneasy without even meaning to. It was interesting, that so much could turn on such little things . . .

"Jimmy? Something wrong?"

"No. No, you look very trustworthy. Like a young Carl Sagan—with better hair."

"Perfect. Where's my earplug?"

"Right here." Wolfe handed his partner the tiny plastic device. "You're on channel one, as usual. M.C.'s on channel two, the ushers on three." As the plug disappeared into Jacobi's right ear, Wolfe half turned away and cupped his hand around his headset's microphone. "You hear me okay?"

Jacobi smiled. "Loud and clear, Jimmy. How's our turnout?"

"A few hundred. We've filled a little less than half the seats, and there are maybe thirty to forty curious locals scattered amongst the devoted faithful. Frankly, that is a lot better than I'd expected, especially for the middle of the week. Must be too many reruns on TV." Wolfe scratched his chin. "I wish we hadn't set up so many chairs, it makes us look bad."

"Not to worry. By the time we start charging admission, we'll have standing room only."

"I hope so. We can't afford to go on this way for long."

"Just stay on top of the board and leave the rest to me. Is our volunteer M.C. ready?"

Wolfe looked over at the screens. Monitor three showed an earnest young man in a new, neatly pressed suit, standing behind a bank of speakers. The young man kept glancing at the index cards in his hands, silently mouthing the words of an introduction. There was a slight glisten of sweat on his forehead.

"Douglas?" Wolfe spoke softly into his headset microphone and the young man on monitor three jerked as if stung by a bee. Douglas pressed one finger to his right ear, listening intently to Wolfe's instructions over his earphone. On the monitor, he grinned and gave a shaky thumbs-up.

"Oh, brother." Wolfe put a finger to his head and pretended to squeeze off a shot. "He's as ready as he'll ever be."

"Chin up, Jimmy. Let's do it."

As Wolfe faded the music, the nervous young man stepped up to a podium at stage right and leaned toward a microphone. His cough echoed through the tent like a rifle shot.

Wolfe smacked his forehead. "Don't get so close to the mike, Doug. Look, you're gonna do fine. Just take a deep breath and say the lines."

Douglas nodded to the unseen voice and did as he was told.

"G-Good evening. My name is Douglas Oliver, and it's my pleasure to welcome you all this evening to the first in a series of lectures on improving the potential of human life." Douglas took another breath. "Our speaker is a man I've long admired . . . a man who has devoted his career, not just to research into the secrets of the genetic code . . . and not just to the advancement of humankind and the enrichment of human life . . . but to making that knowledge available to us all." The young man looked out over the crowd. People were listening to him with rapt attention. This wasn't so bad after all. "He's a Graduate Fellow of the School of Genetic Study of San Mattese and a founder of the Ascendance Foundation. Will you please join me now in welcoming . . . Doctor Donald Jacobi!"

As Jacobi entered from stage left, the veteran website subscribers in the audience sprang to their feet, applauding wildly. The locals in the audience were surprised by the enthusiastic display. They glanced at each other, then at the out-of-towners, and slowly got to their feet, applauding politely. Jacobi paused for a few seconds at center stage and smiled, graciously acknowledging the applause. As he reached the podium, he shook Douglas's hand.

"Thank you, Douglas." Still grasping the young man's hand, Jacobi turned him toward the audience. "Douglas Oliver, ladies and gentlemen! Let's hear it for him as well!"

The applause level held steady, and Douglas grinned from ear to ear. And then, as the young man made his way off stage, Jacobi stretched both arms out before him, as if in benediction, and gestured for the faithful throng to be seated.

"Thank you! Thank you for that most gracious welcome, one and all. I have to say that Kansas hospitality is even warmer than I had been told it was. I am a stranger to this area, but tonight you have made me feel as if I have come home."

The audience responded with a second, more sedate round of applause, this time joined more readily by the locals.

Backstage, Wolfe was grimly amused. He had to give the

devil his due. "Onstage for less than a minute, and you already have them on your side." If Jacobi had been the one born with the cold, pale eyes, he might have had to find another line of work. Not necessarily honest work (Wolfe couldn't picture Jacobi toiling at any sort of nine-to-five grind), but not a slick con operation either. *If I had the looks, the voice, I could have been the top dog in this team. Team?* He shook his head. *No, if I had all that, I never would've needed to be part of any "team."*

Clipping a small microphone to his lapel, Jacobi moved away from the podium. "Lowell County feels like the end of a long journey to me, and perhaps for many of you as well. This area holds a legacy for us all, a legacy which was bestowed upon us twelve and a half years ago . . ."

Behind him, the starscape was replaced by an image of a billboard, surrounded by fields of corn. Jacobi turned to read it aloud.

" 'Smallville—Meteor Capital of the World!' No doubt, many of you saw this sign on your way here. Those of you who live nearby probably see it every day. It has become part of the scenery, as much a part of this area as the fields or the local LuthorCorp plant. The Meteor Capital of the World . . . something to brag about to your friends in other parts of the country. But no one was bragging back in 1989!"

Backstage, Wolfe hit another series of buttons. The ground began to pulse from the deep, subsonic bass rumble of the sound system. And over Jacobi's shoulder, the screen abruptly switched to an image of downtown Smallville, twelve years before.

"October 1989!" Jacobi's voice rang out, his volume increasing slightly to carry over the discomforting rumble. "It was a beautiful autumn day. The Smallville Crows had just won their homecoming game. It should have been a day to celebrate. But then the heavens opened up!"

Suddenly, the frozen image behind Jacobi began to move, panning shakily up into the sky.

"These images were captured on a handheld camcorder that day. I managed to acquire a copy of the tape from a Metropolis news agency. Apart from a few retrospectives, most of this footage hasn't been shown in over a decade. I'll warn you, many of these scenes may be too intense for some."

The audience sat mesmerized as bright, burning points of light streaked across the sky, leaving smoky trails in their wake. From just off-camera came a flash of light, a loud bang, and the whoosh of gasoline igniting. Startled shouts and cries echoed through the tent, some from the audience, some from the screen.

The picture became shakier, as the camera operator started running. The image abruptly swung skyward, just as a meteor blasted through a tall steeple. The screen seemed to explode in a ball of fire and a loud boom, and the audience jumped back, eyes wide.

"Heads up!" Wolfe's voice was an urgent electronic whisper in Jacobi's ear. "We've got a fainter! Row four!"

Jacobi rushed to the edge of the stage to see a woman in an aisle seat turn ghost white, her eyes rolling up into her head. An usher was already headed her way, but Jacobi jumped from the stage and reached her first. He caught her by the shoulders as she slid from her chair and gently lowered her to the sawdust floor. People started to crowd around, but Jacobi held them back with a wave of his hand.

"Stand back! Give her air! And clear that screen!" Wolfe had already blanked the screen and killed the subsonics, but no one in the audience had noticed.

Jacobi plucked a capsule of ammonia spirits from his

pocket and snapped it open under the woman's nose. She gave a little cough, and looked up, surprised.

"Are you all right, ma'am?"

"I-I think so. What . . . ?"

"Careful, don't sit up too quickly. You still look a little faint." People drew back, giving them room, as Jacobi helped her back into her chair. "Can we get some water here, please?"

An usher came on the run with a chilled bottle of spring-water and a paper cup.

"Thank you." The woman gratefully accepted the water and slowly sipped from the cup. "I'm terribly sorry. I'm not usually like this."

"Think nothing of it, dear lady. If anything, I should apologize to you." Jacobi knelt beside her. He refilled her cup, capped the bottle, and set it next to her. Jacobi took her hand and gazed into her eyes. "You were there that day, weren't you?"

She nodded. "I . . . saw my sister and her husband die in one of the first strikes."

"And I brought that horror back to you. I'm so terribly, terribly sorry. Can you ever forgive me, Ms. . . . ?"

"Potter . . . Nell Potter. Of course, I forgive you, Doctor. It wasn't your fault. You couldn't have known!"

"But I should have anticipated such a reaction. I appreciate your sentiment all the more, Ms. Potter. Thank you, so very much . . . !"

In a very soft voice, she corrected him. "Nell."

"Nell . . . yes. Thank you, Nell." Jacobi stood up, still holding her hand. "Let me assure you—let me assure all of you—that we won't be screening any more footage like that tonight. Now, let's all take a few moments to catch our breath before we continue." He gently squeezed Nell's hand. "That is, if it's all right with you, Nell?"

"Goodness, yes. Of course." Nell's face flushed, and she leaned closer to him. "I do want to hear what you have to say. That's why I'm here!"

Jacobi gave her his most beatific smile and returned to the stage.

Backstage, Wolfe pumped a fist in the air and began to bring up the music.

And in the middle of the tenth row, Ray Harrison sat perched on the edge of his seat, leaning forward, listening intently.

CHAPTER 7

Thursday morning, Lionel Luthor looked down over the city of Metropolis from his corner office on the ninety-sixth floor of the building that bore his name. The great city stretched out in all directions before him. Far below, millions of people scurried about on their way to work, and nearly half drew a salary directly from LuthorCorp or one of its subsidiaries. LuthorCorp had holdings worldwide, but the home office was still in Metropolis. Its citizens lived in apartments managed by Lionel Luthor's agents, bought homes built by his contractors. They were born in his hospitals, attended his schools, ate in his restaurants, and were interred in his cemeteries. Metropolis was his.

It still wasn't enough, of course, but it was a good start.

Lionel took a step back from the window, and caught a glimpse of his reflection in the glass. His beard was looking a little uneven. Time for a trim soon. His hair reached well below his collar. It was showing more gray these days, but there was still plenty of it, thank God. Men who started going gray at his age generally did keep their hair. The gray was a small price to pay, really.

He turned to his financial assistant. "Overnight summary?"

"Tokyo, Hong Kong, and Singapore are holding steady, sir. And trading is up on the European market."

Lionel stroked his beard. "Watch for a spike in share prices of TransNational. When it hits sixty, sell."

"Yes, sir." The little man bowed slightly as he backed from the room.

Lionel crossed the room to a massive oak desk and began to thumb through a thin manila folder. "Damian!"

A tall, powerfully built man emerged from the shadows.
"Yes, Mr. L."

"Nice job, the way you cleared things for our Keystone
City development project."

"Thank you, sir."

"The local Greens there had held things up far too long. I
knew I could count on you to break the logjam. Expect to
find this reflected in your quarterly bonus."

"Thank you very much, sir."

Lionel Luthor looked (for him) almost mellow as he
leafed through the rest of the folder. Damian Marco never
went to Mass anymore, but he said a silent little prayer of
thanks now. Placing the Keystone report at the front of the
folder was having the desired effect. *Now if only the good
mood holds steady through the last item in the folder.*
Damian added a quick prayer of supplication.

Sure is taking his time today. Damian tried to distract himself by looking at the framed testimonials and pictures in his
boss's office: Lionel Luthor with mayors, governors, and
presidents. With foreign heads of state. With other top business leaders. With Olympic-medal fencers. Lionel had been
a nationally ranked fencer in college, and he still kept up his
game. (He was half a head shorter than Marco, and at least
thirty pounds lighter, but Damian had resolved long ago to
never, ever, get into a fight with his boss. Not even if Luthor
publicly fired him.)

There was an interesting thing about those pictures. In the
ones from the 1980s, regardless of then-current styles, Lionel Luthor wore his hair relatively short. From 1989 on, his
hair was always longer.

Damian glanced back to his boss just as Lionel got to the
back of the folder. He lifted a sheet of pulp paper from the
folder. As he read it, his face darkened.

Uh-oh, thought Damian. *Here it comes.*

"Damian?" There was ice in Lionel's voice. "What is this?"

A thin film of sweat began to bead up on Damian's upper lip. "News story from Smallville, Mr. L. Off the wire. Came in too late to make the morning edition of the *Daily Planet*. Figured you'd want to see it."

"And why, exactly, wasn't I informed of this sooner?"

"It came across the wire just this morning—"

"I don't pay you to read and rip wire copy! I pay you to keep on top of things!" Lionel threw the folder back down on the desk in disgust. "I don't expect to find out, after the fact, that some quack is running a New Age dog-and-pony show on farmland outside Smallville."

Lionel came around the side of the desk, advancing slowly on Damian. "On the old Davis farm. The local S&L foreclosed on that property months ago. The asking price had been dropping lower and lower. I have plans for that property, Damian. Those plans are now compromised."

"Mr. L, I—!" The words caught in Damian's throat as Lionel fixed him with a stare.

"But even that isn't the worst of it." Lionel scooped up the wire copy and smacked it with the back of his hand. "If I'm to believe this exercise in journalistic drivel, this . . . 'Doctor' Jacobi . . . is preaching 'meteorite power.' I don't like that, Damian. I especially don't like that coming out of Smallville and making the national news wire."

There it is. I should have known it would come to this. Damian shifted uneasily. *It all gets back to Level Three . . .*

Well over a year ago, LuthorCorp had conducted a top secret experiment in the lower levels of its Smallville fertilizer plant. Lionel's scientists had developed experimental fertilizers from meteorite fragments. The results looked great at first. *That project could have been a big, big moneymaker for the corporation, if not for the damned side ef-*

fects. Animal test subjects went into convulsions and literally shook themselves apart. Lionel ordered the experiment shut down, the level sealed off, the failure kept secret.

No one currently working at the Smallville plant had even known that Level Three existed, not the plant's manager and certainly not its new general manager. No one would've ever found out about it, if not for one janitor who'd been exposed to the fertilizer. The man went off his nut, held a bunch of people hostage at the plant. It had taken all of Lionel's skill and guile to bury that story. But his son, Lex, had learned much of the truth.

He tries not to show it, but I know that drives the old man crazy. Not that I blame him. I wouldn't trust his kid either.

"Uh, sir? If this is about Level Thr—!"

"Damian!" Lionel's eyes narrowed. "That subject is never to be spoken of."

"Yes, sir. But this Jacobi guy is just some quack. Who's gonna believe—?"

"Apparently, some already believe." Lionel roughly jabbed at the wire copy. "The story says most of the attendees were from out of town. Many of them are camping onsite. And more are expected." He thrust the paper into Damian's hand. "I need to know more about this, Damian. There's not enough information here."

"That's all there was on the—!"

"Not enough, Damian." Lionel clamped a hand over Damian's shoulder. His voice was a harsh whisper. "I want to know all there is to know about this quack doctor and his 'Foundation.' He must be dealt with." Lionel began to squeeze the shoulder, hard. "Understood?"

Sweat oozed down the back of Damian's collar. "Completely, Mr. L."

"Good." Lionel released his grip and returned to the window.

He was the king of all he surveyed. It had taken much hard work to become the king. It was harder still to maintain that power.

It was a never-ending battle.

◆◆◆

Deep in the back of a storm cellar behind the Kent farmhouse, Clark pulled back a dusty old tarp to stare at the hull of the spacecraft that had brought him to Earth. *I still can hardly believe it.* He ran his hand over the pitted metal surface. *It's like something out of a dream . . . but it explains so much.*

Even as a toddler, Clark could lift Martha's old rosewood table with one hand. That early show of strength had been enough to convince Jonathan that they shouldn't enroll the boy in preschool. *I must've given the folks plenty to worry about, just keeping secret how strong I was. When I finally went to school, they were always warning me not to "show off."* He grinned. *I'll never forget the first time Mom caught me lifting up the back end of Dad's old pickup.*

It was the year he turned eleven. His ball had rolled under the truck, just out of reach, and he'd been sure that no one was around to see. Martha had come out the back door to call him in for lunch, and found him crouched under the back of the truck, holding it overhead by the rear axle.

Clark smiled at the memory. *I don't know which of us was more surprised.*

"Son? You down there?"

"Yeah, Dad." Clark turned as Jonathan descended the steps into the cellar. "I was just . . . checking things out."

"Yeah, well, I guess you're entitled." Jonathan stared

down at the spacecraft. "Ya know, when I was your age, your grandfather was still keeping things from me. And I didn't like being in the dark any more than you do. I swore that if I ever had a son, I'd never keep secrets from him— not the important things." He looked up at Clark. "But I did. For twelve years your mother and I kept this from you. I'm sorry for that. I guess I was just waiting for the right time."

"I know, Dad. I was really angry at first, but—looking back—I'm not sure if there *was* ever a better time. If you'd told me when I was six, I'd have probably brought all the guys down here to check out my cool rocket ship. When I was twelve, I'd have been down here monkeying with it every day, trying to get it to fly!"

Jonathan started to chuckle. "That's what I was afraid of."

Clark ran his hand over the metal hull once more. "Dad . . . last week, I had another one of those dreams."

"A flying dream?"

"Yeah. This time I woke up in the loft. I don't know for sure that I floated out there, but I'm afraid I might have."

"Maybe I should sit down for this. Maybe we both should." Jonathan pulled an old milking stool out from the wall and motioned his son toward a plank bench along the cellar wall.

Clark sat down, took a deep breath, and recounted his nightmare of the previous Monday. ". . . so now I have something else to worry about! What if I *do* take off for outer space? Or maybe even worse, what if I wake up floating over Metropolis? With my luck, I'd wind up drifting past some factory just as the night shift was taking a break." He folded his arms and stared down at the floor. "I just wish I knew what was happening to me . . . and how much more is still ahead."

"I know you do, Clark. And I wish I had the answers." Jonathan leaned forward on the stool. "We'll just have to keep dealing with these gifts of yours as best as we can." He thought for a minute. "If you're really worried about floating off, there is a way to deal with that."

"There is?"

"Uh-huh. We can install some motion sensors at your window. I know I saw some in at Kirk's Hardware. They're not too expensive. Just wire 'em up to a buzzer, and the problem's solved. Better to have an occasional wake-up call than take the risk of becoming a public spectacle."

"That should work." Clark looked at his father, impressed. "And it's so simple."

"Well, you know me, Clark. I tend to go for the down-to-earth solutions."

"Oh, yeah?" Clark arched an eyebrow. "Then why did you and Mom adopt a kid from outer space?"

"You know, I've asked myself that very question many times." Jonathan grinned, looked at the spacecraft, and shrugged. "Seemed like a good idea at the time."

"Very funny, Dad." Clark tapped the hull, listening to the deep, metallic echo. "You know, I used to surf the Web, looking for stories of other kids with unusual abilities. I still check, from time to time. But I was never able to find anyone as strong as I am. Now I know why. For all I know, I may be the only one of my kind . . . at least, the only one on Earth."

He rapped on the hull again, more impatiently this time. "I know *how* I got here, but I still don't know *why*. Was I sent here deliberately, or did I land on Earth by accident?"

"Son . . ."

"I might have been the 'guinea pig' in somebody's weird experiment. Or part of some, I don't know, ritual sacrifice." Clark dropped his voice an octave. "'I command you to send your firstborn son into the vastness of space.'"

"Anything's possible, Clark." Jonathan laid a hand on the

ship. "But did you ever consider that this might be an escape craft? Maybe you were put in this ship to *save* you from something."

"Yeah, or maybe I was the *last*-born son. Maybe I was just 'dropped off' the way some people dump unwanted pets out in the country."

"Clark!"

"It happens, Dad! It happens a lot. How many dogs and cats have been dumped right here, right on our farm?"

"Too many. I know it happens, Son. What we don't know is whether that's what happened to you. We don't know if any of our guesses are correct. There's no need to torture yourself—"

"Dad, we might *never* know." Clark got to his feet, shuffling about nervously. If there had been more room in the cellar, he would have started pacing. "What if 'my people' come looking for me someday? What if they want to take me back?"

Jonathan stood up. "For your first few years with us, I don't think a day went by without your mother and me wondering about that. But a body can't worry like that every day, Clark. It takes too much energy. We eventually decided that, if it ever happened, we'd deal with it then."

He put a hand on his son's shoulder. "And if it does happen—if your people show up and turn out to be decent folks, and you really want to get to know them . . . well, that's one thing. Your mother and I could live with that. But if they're not, if they just want to take you away"—Jonathan's eyes narrowed and the muscles around his jaw tightened—"they better come prepared. Because we are not giving you up without a fight."

Clark had an instant flash of Jonathan and Martha facing off against an alien starship, shotguns in hand. *They'd do it, too.* He blinked back a tear. It was a long moment before he could speak. "I hope it never comes to that, Dad, but . . . thanks."

Jonathan nodded. "So . . . you going to put aside all those worries?"

"I'll try." Clark looked down at the craft and half smiled. "Some of them weren't exactly *worries*. This sounds stupid, but I sometimes wonder if I started up the spaceship myself . . . by accident. You know, like the stories you hear of toddlers accidentally starting up the family car?"

"It doesn't sound stupid at all. In fact, if that is the case, then you *really* were meant to be my son."

"What?" Clark's half smile widened into a full grin. "Don't tell me you . . . ?"

"Ohhh, yeah." Jonathan smiled wryly. "My dad's pickup, when I was four or five. Lucky I didn't break my neck." His voice grew more serious. "But I want you to understand something. Whatever the reason you wound up here—and whether or not we ever learn why—it's their loss. Don't ever forget that. Their loss, and our gain.

"And something else you should keep in mind. Life did not begin here in Kansas or anywhere else in these United States. Go back far enough and you'll find that we're all immigrants here. You just came from farther away than most."

" 'Just'?"

"Okay, a lot farther away! Clark, what matters is what you make of yourself, not where you're from."

"I know, Dad. I . . . it's just . . . it's not easy, knowing that I'm a freak from outer space." Clark pulled the tarp back into place. "But before, I thought I was a freak of nature. At least now I have a better notion of why I'm the way I am, even if I still don't know where I'm from."

"Hey, you're not any kind of freak—you're my son!" Jonathan reached out and tousled the boy's hair. "And your mother and I love you very much."

Clark smiled at that, but it was a distracted smile that quickly faded. He stared at the tarp, brooding. "Dad . . . why *did* you and Mom adopt me?" He gestured to the covered spacecraft. "I mean, you guys knew right from the start, but you kept me anyway. Why?" Clark looked back at his father. "And no jokes about how it 'seemed like a good idea at the time.' I need to know the answer to at least *one* of these questions."

"Clark, this may sound strange—and I swear I'm not pulling your leg—but the fact of the matter is, you made a great first impression."

"Dad . . . !"

"That's the truth, Son. The plain and simple truth. Besides, your mother and I didn't know *right* from the start."

"Oh, sure, when did you find out?" Clark raised an eyebrow again, frowning this time. "A whole five minutes later?"

"I couldn't say to the second, but it was time enough. More than time enough." Jonathan put a hand on Clark's shoulder. "What's going on here, Son? We've been over all this."

Clark looked away, exasperated.

"Right." Jonathan nodded thoughtfully. "Your mother and I have been living with this for years. You've known for just the past few months." He gave Clark's shoulder an easy shake. "Tell you what. How about we continue this discussion after dinner? I strongly suspect that your mother would have a lot to contribute to it."

"Yeah. Yeah, let's do that."

"Great. Because I also suspect that she has dinner almost ready!"

Martha stood by the stove, her attention divided between a skillet of peppers and onions and that day's edition of the

Ledger. She barely glanced up as Clark and Jonathan came in the back door. "It's about time. Where have you two been?"

"Down in the storm cellar." Jonathan shot Clark a quick wink. "Clark and I have been working on his spaceship."

"What?" A fork fell from Martha's hand, and a slice of green pepper went flying.

Clark's hand darted out, catching the airborne slice before it could fall. He leaned back against the wall, happily munching the sizzling pepper.

"I think we finally got all the bugs out of that engine. Don't you, Son?"

"Yeah, she's purring like a kitten. Now I'll never be late to school again." Clark looked at Martha. "Want to go for a ride, Mom?"

Martha cast a fishy eye on her men. Both grinned like Cheshire cats. She pointed the fork in Jonathan's general direction. "You are terrible! And you"—the fork swung around toward Clark—"do not get your sense of humor from anyone strange. At least, not from anyone stranger than your father."

"Thank you, dear." Jonathan gave his wife a quick peck on the cheek. "I live for your acknowledgment. Anything good in the paper?"

"I don't know how good it is. There's a big write-up on that tent meeting last night."

"Hmm? Let me see that." Jonathan quickly skimmed the front page article, as they settled around the table. "Oh, this is just what the county needs! Some slick character trying to sell meteorites as the cure for everything."

Caught in midswallow, Clark spit half a mouthful of water back into his glass. "He's selling meteorites?" He grabbed the paper from his father.

"Not literally, Son. According to the *Ledger*—which

should always be taken with a grain of salt—this Jacobi fella is touting 'self-fulfillment and total realization of human potential.' Looks to me like the meteorite angle is just window dressing for some crazy New Age scam."

"I don't know, Jonathan." Martha shook her head. "Evidently, that Dr. Jacobi showed actual video footage of the meteor shower. Freida Wilson was at the meeting, and she said that a lot more went on last night than was covered in the paper."

"Freida said that, did she?" Jonathan rolled his eyes for Clark's benefit. *That Wilson woman could gossip faster than the speed of sound.* "I don't suppose she passed along any other 'inside information' about the talk?"

Martha ignored her husband's sarcasm. "Just that Dr. Jacobi talked a lot about the weird effects the meteorites have had on people around here." *And Nell Potter made a perfect fool of herself over him.* "He seemed to know all about them."

"So, the man's read up on the area. These days, he could probably find all he needed to know on the Internet."

Clark remembered Chloe's website. "Yeah . . ."

"Trust me, hon, this guy is running some sort of con. He's like the rainmakers who used to fleece this county, back when my dad was a boy—just a little more sophisticated, that's all."

"I hope so." Martha still wasn't certain. "I'm just concerned that his lectures might lead people around here to poke around and learn the truth about Clark."

"I wouldn't worry too much about that, Mom. From what it says here in the paper, all the footage Jacobi showed was of the meteors hitting downtown. It's not like he had pictures of my spaceship or anything."

"And thank heaven for that!" Martha sipped her coffee, her eyes becoming distant. "I'll never forget the day the meteors fell. When I think back, I can still smell the burning corn."

Clark sniffed the air. "That's not corn. The broiler—!"

Flames licked up from beneath the oven, and the kitchen smoke detector started to blare. Before either of his parents could get up from their chairs, Clark was across the room, turning off the gas. He pulled the broiler door open and quickly patted out the flames with his bare hands.

By the time Jonathan and Martha had risen, the fire was out and Clark stood facing them, licking some hot grease off his thumb. "Relax, it's taken care of."

"Are you all right?" Even as she said it, Martha knew he was, but she still took his hand and turned it over, just to be sure.

"No problem, Mom. See?"

"I have to check, Clark. It's part of the job." Martha winked at him, and he smiled back at her. Then she frowned. "Could've sworn I turned that broiler off. I must've been too distracted by the paper."

"Well, no harm done." Jonathan lifted the warming cover off a platter on the table. "You remembered to get these chops out of there, that's the important thing." He started moving the chops to their plates. "What do you say we forget about all that tent show nonsense and enjoy this fine dinner?"

"Sounds good to me, Dad." Clark turned to Martha. "But, Mom . . . about the day of the storm? Hang on to that thought for later, will you?"

◆◆◆

Afternoon was fading into evening, when Lana turned her key in the lock and pushed open the front door of the big, rambling country house she shared with her aunt Nell.

"Hello, I'm home!"

"Oh, good!" Nell's voice came echoing down the stairs. "I was just about to leave you a note. You're running late, dear."

"I had to stop at the Talon. I went over the receipts, and made sure all the shifts were covered for tomorrow and the weekend." Lana dropped her books on a side table. "Lex may own the building, but we manage the place, remember?"

"Of course, where's my head?" Nell came down the stairs, her heels clicking on the steps as she adjusted her earrings. "There's dinner in the 'fridge. I'm not sure how late I'll be."

"Okay." Lana surveyed her aunt's outfit. "Are you driving in to Metropolis for dinner and a show or something?"

"No, I signed up to take a seminar at the Foundation Compound tonight. I told you about that, didn't I?" She noticed the look her niece was giving her. "Why? Too dressy?"

"For Thursday night in Smallville? Maybe a little."

"Strictly speaking, it's *outside* of Smallville." She checked her makeup in the hall mirror. "Besides, the other attendees will mostly be from out of state. It won't hurt to show them that we're not all hicks around here."

"You're really buying that whole 'cosmic ladder' consciousness?"

"I wish you wouldn't use that tone of voice, Lana. You make it sound like I'm joining some sort of cult." Nell paused to touch up her lipstick. "It's really a very interesting line of study. I'm finding it quite useful. I think that Donald—that Dr. Jacobi can help me deal with a lot of issues I've kept buried."

"Donald, huh? Is he handsome?"

"He's distinguished-looking, but that has nothing to do with it!"

Lana looked at her aunt skeptically.

"All right, he's very handsome. He has dark blond hair and the most amazing eyes. But this is about much more than just his looks. The way he talked . . . !" Nell actually blushed a bit. "I wish you could have been there last night. The doctor showed us an entirely new way to look at that terrible meteor storm. He's already given me a whole new perspective on life in general."

"He talked about the meteors? You didn't say anything about that this morning."

"I didn't? Well, I've had so much on my mind. In a way, the meteors are what brought Dr. Jacobi to Smallville. There's a little piece about it in today's paper." She reached out to stroke Lana's hair. "Don't frown so. This will be good for us."

"If you say so."

"You'll see." Nell checked the mirror one last time, adjusting the string of pearls that hung at her throat. "Lana . . . ? I haven't seen you wearing your necklace lately."

"Oh, that? I kind of got out of the jewelry habit when I took that first waitressing job at the Beanery. Dress code and all."

"It's been months since you worked at the Beanery." Now it was Nell's turn to look skeptical. "And we control the employee dress code at the Talon."

"Actually, it's something like what you were just saying . . . about new perspectives? It was time for a change." Lana gave her aunt a reassuring smile. "Don't worry, Nell, I still have the necklace. I'll never forget what it meant to you . . . to us. I just don't feel like wearing it all the time anymore."

"All right, I can see that. You've become such a young lady, taking on all these new responsibilities. There's so

much of your mother in you." Nell gave her a hug. "Well, I
have to go. Don't wait up for me!"

With a wave, Nell was gone. Lana locked the door behind
her and went upstairs to her room. *Sometimes, I wish I really
could find a new perspective on things.* As she put her jacket
away, she stared into the big, double closet. *Too many
clothes.* Lana closed the doors and looked around the room.
Too much stuff! She began opening bureau drawers, sorting
through a seemingly endless assortment of socks and
sweaters. *I don't even wear half of these things anymore. I
should give them to Goodwill!* Lana started making a small
pile of clothing on her bed. Then she pulled open the big,
bottom drawer.

Lana knelt on the floor, pondering the drawer's contents.
Here was the tiara she'd worn at the last Homecoming
Dance, the trophy she'd won in the middle-school cheerleading competitions, the ribbons from all the "Little Miss"
pageants her aunt had enrolled her in. *Way too much stuff.
And this is only about half of it. All the equestrian awards
are in that display case Nell hung up in the stable.* Lana
poked through the mementos. Would Goodwill have any use
for a drawerful of old ribbons and trophies? They all seemed
so meaningless now.

Finally, down in one corner of the drawer, Lana's hands
fell upon the ornate little metal case that Clark had given her
to hold her necklace. "It's made of lead armor," he'd told
her. "I want you to have it. I figure that way it can protect
your memories." She opened the lid and looked at the necklace. Its chain sparkled in the green glow of its gemstone.

The stone in Lana's necklace had come from the meteorite that struck her parents' car, all those years ago, killing
them before her eyes. Nell had raised her since that horrible
day. Her aunt had given Lana the necklace on the day the
adoption was finalized. It was Nell's own eccentric way of

helping the girl come to terms with her parents' deaths. She knew her aunt's words by heart: "Life is about change, Lana. Sometimes it's painful, sometimes it's beautiful. But most of the time it's both."

Lana put the necklace back into the case, and decisively snapped it shut. *Well, there's a time to wear the symbols of the past, and a time to put them away. And if that isn't in Ecclesiastes, it ought to be!* She slid the drawer back into the bureau and returned to her sorting.

◆◆◆

One of the cardinal rules in the Kent household was: "Whoever cooks, does not have to do the dishes." But there was never any mandate that cleanup had to begin immediately after the last bite. Generally, the family would linger a bit at the table after the meal.

But this evening, the instant dinner was over, Clark leaped up, cleared the table, loaded the dishwasher, refilled his parents' coffee cups, and was back in his chair—all in under five seconds.

"Clark . . . ?" Martha looked around, taken aback. "Is something on your mind?"

"I asked Dad earlier, and he said I should ask you as well." Clark cupped his hands around his glass and looked at her earnestly. "Why did you adopt me?"

"What a thing to ask!" Now Martha looked distressed, as well as taken aback. "How could we *not* adopt you! You were so adorable—!"

"But I'm an *alien*! And not just from another *country*, but—!"

"You obviously needed a family—"

"I arrived here in a *spaceship*—!"

"—and we'd been wanting a child for so long—"

"Mom, are you even listening to me?"

"I've heard every word, dear." Martha reached across the table and took his hand. "Seriously, Clark, when you came into our lives, it seemed like fate. We'd wanted a child of our own for so long, but it just didn't seem to be in the cards. We tried everything."

Jonathan cleared his throat. "Well, not everything. We drew the line at the fertility clinic. I wasn't about to have your mother poked and prodded like some kind of—!"

"I get the picture, Dad." Clark stared into his glass. "That's maybe more information than I really needed."

"Anyway," Martha continued, "we were just starting to look into foster programs and adoption, when you came along and settled things for us . . ."

◆◆◆

She and Jonathan had been driving home from town, when the sound of the first meteors boomed over Smallville. As their pickup truck sped along Route 5, a small meteor crashed into the field alongside the road, less than twenty-five feet away from them. Then another meteor tore through a billboard, blasting it to smithereens, just seconds after the truck passed it. They peered back, terrified to see the smoke trails streaking down over the fields of corn.

"What's happening, Jonathan?"

Before he could respond, something streaked across the road not a hundred feet ahead of them. It seared a huge gash into the blacktop, igniting the asphalt and plowing into the adjacent field. Jonathan frantically hit the brakes and held tight to the wheel, fighting for control, but it was useless. The truck plowed into the billowing, black smoke. Its front wheels hit the edge of the ditch, and it flipped over, spinning

around and coming to rest upside down in the new ditch that
had been created in the middle of the road.

". . . That's when we blacked out. I'm still not sure how
long we were unconscious, but when we came to, we were
both upside down, held in by our seat belts."

"Yeah, that was pretty disorienting." Jonathan stirred his
coffee. "It took us a minute or two to figure out what had
happened and where we were. That's when I saw something
moving out of the corner of my eye, something outside the
truck."

Martha smiled. "It was a little boy, not more than three or
four at the most."

"Yep. And naked as a jaybird."

"Dad!"

"What, did you think you were wearing a little space suit
when we found you?"

"You had the cutest smile, Clark." Martha tilted her head
fondly at the memory. "And such a heavenly laugh."

"Mom . . ."

"Well, it was!"

"Your mother's right, Clark. I ought to know, I'm the first
one you laughed at." Jonathan rubbed the back of his shoulder, as if trying to ease an old injury. "I just about broke my
neck, trying to get out of that truck . . ."

Jonathan braced himself against the wheel with both
hands, while Martha unfastened his safety belt. Slowly, he
let himself slide down out of the seat until his back was just
a few inches from the floor. Then he let go and fell onto the

top of the inverted cab. Outside, the little boy clapped his hands together and giggled.

"Come on, Martha, you next." Jonathan looked up at her. "It's just like tumbling in high-school gym . . . except I'm here to catch you. Just unbuckle yourself and slide."

It was as easy as that. Jonathan made sure her landing was softer, if not more graceful than his. They crawled out of the truck, and Martha held out her hands to the little stranger.

"Are you all right, sweetheart? Don't be afraid . . ."

He was anything but fearful. Again he replied with a gurgling laugh, as he took hold of her outstretched hand.

"Oh, Jon, he'll catch his death out here."

Jonathan reached back into the truck cab and pulled a blanket out from behind the seat. He wrapped it around the boy, and Martha picked him up, cradling him in the crook of her arm. They looked around them. They, the boy, and the truck were in the bottom of a huge gash in the earth, topped by lines of burning asphalt. Thick smoke still billowed all around them. They turned and followed the gash out into the field.

Jonathan led the way, with Martha following close behind, talking to the boy.

"What's your name? Where are your parents?"

The boy cocked his head and tried to mimic her. "Payy-rennz?"

"Maybe he doesn't understand English." Jonathan smiled encouragingly at the boy. "*¿Habla Espanol?*"

The boy looked from Jonathan to Martha, his lips pursed.

"Jonathan, stop. You're confusing him."

"Sorry."

◆◆◆

"It made sense at the time." Jonathan told Clark. "You were walking . . . you should have been talking. And with that thick thatch of dark hair, I thought you could have been Hispanic, maybe the kid of a migrant worker."

"We still didn't know how you'd gotten there, dear. You were such a beautiful little boy, just like a little angel."

"Mom . . . !"

"Well, you were. I still have the pictures to prove it!"

"Don't roll your eyes at your mother, Son." Jonathan paused. "Actually, on second thought, go right ahead."

"Jonathan!"

"No, Martha, I think it's fine. Proves that it doesn't matter where he came from. He still reacts the same way any teenage boy would. I know I wouldn't have wanted to be called an angel at his age. Not that anyone ever did." Jonathan caught Clark's eye, and they both started to snicker.

"All right, you two!" Martha turned to Clark. "I thought you wanted to hear about this?"

"I do!" He straightened up. "Dad was trying to speak to me in Spanish, which I didn't understand any better than English."

"Yes, but you were so bright and cheerful, you didn't seem to have been neglected. And I couldn't believe anyone would abandon such a healthy, good-natured child."

Jonathan nodded. "Remember, we'd just crawled out of that overturned truck. In the back of our minds was the fear that there'd been another accident nearby, that you'd somehow survived while your parents—! Well, I was afraid that any second we'd come upon a horrible car wreck . . ."

◆◆◆

Martha had begun to hum a little tune to the boy she carried, as Jonathan kicked clumps of smoldering cornstalks from their path.

"Kids . . . don't just fall out of the sky, Martha."

"Then where did he come from?"

"I don't know, but he must have parents."

They suddenly came to the end of the trench, and froze in shock. There was a strange metallic craft embedded in the ground just ahead of them.

She hugged the boy to her. "Well . . . if he does, they're definitely not from Kansas."

The longer they stared at the strange craft, the more accurate Martha's reaction seemed. Near one end of the vessel, a small hatchway gaped open, and in the raw earth alongside it were tiny footprints . . . just about the size of the boy's. The craft itself bore no familiar markings, nothing recognizable beyond the telltale scorch marks left by its fiery descent through the atmosphere. There were no flags or insignia of any nation on Earth, no logos from any military force or space agency.

They watched apprehensively for a while, wondering whether something else might emerge from the craft, something less innocent. All remained quiet. That was reassuring, but this was still a much stranger First Contact than from any science fiction movie that Jonathan and Martha had ever seen. There were no tentacled blobs, no giant insects, no big-headed humanoids with saucer-shaped eyes.

Just an utterly alien ship and a perfectly human-looking little boy.

Martha looked from the craft, to the boy, to her husband. Then she began gently rocking the child in her arms. Jonathan didn't have to ask what his wife was thinking. She didn't care one bit where the boy had come from, not really. The bond between Martha and the child was growing stronger with every passing second.

Jonathan felt drawn to the boy as well, but a more down-to-earth question gnawed at him. "Sweetheart, we can't keep him. What're we gonna tell people? 'We found him in a field' . . . ?"

Martha stared into the boy's eyes, convinced that they shared a destiny. "We didn't find him . . . he found us."

Jonathan looked up into the sky, as if looking for a sign, and the smoke seemed to part before them. He shook his head slightly, then started to smile. Maybe Martha was right. Maybe the boy *had* been sent to them.

◆◆◆

"Wow." Clark sat back in his chair. "So what *did* you tell people about where I came from?"

Jonathan looked a little sheepish. "Actually, Clark, we wound up telling them that we found you wandering in a field. The whole area had been thrown for a loop by that meteor storm. Emergency services were taxed to their limits. County welfare was happy to let us provide foster care while the Sheriff's Office tried to match you against the missing persons files."

"We knew there was no one on Earth who could claim you, dear. Getting the approval for your adoption was complicated"—Martha took Jonathan's hand—"but we managed to get through it."

"And the spaceship? How did you ever get it out of that field without anyone noticing?"

"With great difficulty and a lot of luck! Under cover of darkness." Jonathan shook his head at the memory. "I burned out a good winch engine getting that thing out of the ground and onto a wagon. We hid it under hay in the barn until I could enlarge the storm cellar."

Clark pushed his chair back from the table and stared off into space. Jonathan and Martha fell silent, giving him time to take it all in. The only sound in the kitchen was the soft whir of the refrigerator's compressor.

"Well . . ." Clark slowly turned back and looked at his parents. ". . . I have to say, I'm very glad I found you. A lot of people would have turned around and sold me to the *Enquirer* or something."

"Sell my little angel? Clark, have *you* been listening? You were the answer to all our dreams!" Martha went over and hugged him. "You still are."

"That's right, Son. We've never regretted adopting you." *Son.* Jonathan rolled the word around in his head. It triggered an old memory that made him grin. He leaned back and raised his cup. "In the words of the great Bill Cosby: 'You are my son. You will always be my son. And you can live here . . .'" Jonathan paused for effect "'. . . as long as you have a job.'"

Clark sighed. "Great. So the answer to all my questions ends with a sitcom punch line."

"Oh, that bit wasn't from one of Cos's TV shows, that was from a story about his father, from his old stand-up comedy routine."

Clark's jaw dropped. "*Bill Cosby* used to do stand-up?"

Jonathan looked from his son to his wife and threw up his hands in mock resignation. "Now this is what parenthood really comes down to: I try to reassure him, and he tries to make me feel really old."

"What can I say?" Clark looked at Martha and grinned. "It's my job!"

"Then I guess you get to stay!" She returned the grin, and Jonathan began to laugh.

CHAPTER 8

No sooner did Clark step onto the bus Friday morning than Pete hailed him. "Clark! Back here."

Clark strode up the aisle and slid into the seat next to Pete, as the bus started to roll down Hickory Lane. He looked around.

"Where's Chloe?"

"Don't know. She wasn't waiting for the bus this morning. Was I surprised! I expected her to hand me a bunch of errands to run for her publicity stuff for the benefit concert. It's been, what, a week since you guys had that first meeting?"

"I know, but nothing's been nailed down yet. The committee's still contacting groups and trying to settle on a day." Clark leaned back into the seat. "I hope Chloe's not sick."

"She seemed fine yesterday." Pete grinned. "Hey, maybe she's out chasing down a hot story!"

"Stop the presses! Tear out page one! 'Scoop' Sullivan has a new exclusive!"

Pete removed an imaginary cigar from his mouth. "Egad, 'Scoop,' you've done it again!" He tapped an imaginary ash from the "cigar" and bugged his eyebrows, Groucho-style.

Clark began to snicker. "Ya know, we'd better stop this. It's not right to rag on Chloe behind her back."

"You're right. Much better to do it to her face."

"Oh, yeah? Well, if we keep this up, sooner or later one of us is going to slip and call her 'Scoop' to her face. And then we'll both be toast."

Pete's face fell. "Whoa, I hadn't thought of that. Let's talk about something else, quick!" He snapped his fingers. "Hey, did you see that write-up in yesterday's *Ledger* about that wacko doctor and his amazing meteorite show?"

"Yeah, pretty crazy, huh?"

"Crazy? Let's talk Looney Tunes! Chloe told me that she and you saw part of his website—what was it, the 'cosmic ladder'? I didn't think there were enough old hippies still alive who'd buy into that cosmic b.s."

"People believe all kinds of things, Pete."

"Yeah, but I can't believe the *Ledger* wasted paper on that guy."

"They have space to fill, and the guy has lured in a lot of out-of-towners who are spending money in the county. And the meteorites give it even more of a local angle."

"Now you're sounding like Chloe."

"Well, it is the sort of story that she'd . . ." Clark stopped. He and Pete looked at each other. "She wouldn't."

"Five bucks says she would."

◆◆◆

Jacobi came down the back stairs of the old farmhouse to find Wolfe seated at a long table in the kitchen, crunching numbers on his laptop.

"Good morning, Jimmy. How're we doing?"

"Not too bad, all things considered. I'm a little worried about the central projector. The calibration on the lasers was a little off Wednesday night. One of them was highlighting the edges of the display screen. I think I can nurse it along, but we may need to send to Metropolis for a backup element." Wolfe reached over to a side table and filled his Styrofoam cup from a steaming coffeemaker. "Don, my hat's still off to you for the way you handled that fainter. That couldn't have gone better if we'd rehearsed it."

"Nell Potter? Well, it helped that she was attractive and

still relatively young. Her type is almost as receptive to my charms as the kindly old grannies."

"I'll say. She not only showed up for last night's seminar, she enrolled for the whole series. I suppose you got her phone number?"

"And address. Nell gave me her card. I scanned it onto our mailing lists." Jacobi's smile turned wistful. "She was lovely, wasn't she? But it wouldn't be wise to get romantically involved with a local."

"That's my boy." Wolfe leaned back and cracked his knuckles. "Okay, here's how things now stand. Our devoted out-of-towners are currently renting thirty-seven of the campsites in the east acreage. And we've already received Web and phone reservations for another fifty-four. And, adding in the donations we received at the end of the first lecture"—Wolfe leaned over the keyboard and tapped a couple of keys—"we've so far grossed nearly seven grand. We're still a long way from recouping expenses, but seeing as how that was the first night, and a Wednesday . . . we're way ahead of where I thought we'd be."

"Just wait until the weekend." Jacobi looked over his shoulder and smiled. "Have you checked to see if our website has gained any new subscribers? A hundred bucks says we picked up at least five from last night's crowd."

A knock at the door interrupted the wagering, and an orange-vested security volunteer opened the door just enough to allow her head and shoulders into the room. "Pardon me, but there's a young woman out here who wants to speak with Dr. Jacobi. She claims to work for a newspaper."

"'Claims'?" Wolfe cocked an eye toward the volunteer. "Did you ask to see her credentials?"

"Uh, yes." The volunteer looked uneasy. "And she has a press pass for something called the *Torch*. But she seems awfully young."

"It's all right." Jacobi smoothed back his hair. "Show her in."

As Wolfe cleared their financial reports from his laptop, the door swung wide and Chloe Sullivan entered the room.

Chloe's appearance would have surprised her high-school friends. She wore a conservatively tailored dark gray suit and flats. A stylish black bag hung over one shoulder. There were no plastic flowers or barrettes in her hair, just a hint of styling gel.

"Dr. Jacobi? I'm Chloe Sullivan of the Smallville *Torch*."

"How do you do? This is my associate, Mr. James Wolfe, and . . . wait a minute! Sullivan . . . ?" Jacobi's eyes seemed to light up at her name, and he warmly shook her hand. "Young lady, I am very much in your debt!"

"You are?" Chloe looked surprised.

"I am indeed! You are *the* Chloe Sullivan? The one who established that remarkable website, about the 'mutants of Smallville'?"

"Uh, yes. Yes, I am."

"My dear, I have devoted much of my life to unlocking the mysteries of the genetic code. And you have given me a vitally important key!"

"I have?"

"You most certainly have! Ms. Sullivan, you are, of course, familiar with the hypothesis that comets seeded our world with the biochemical building blocks necessary for the development of life?"

"A little . . ."

"For years, I have studied meteorite fragments and their effects upon the human genotype. I believe that they—like the comets before them—have given life on Earth a periodic boost up the ladder, so to speak. I found your website a godsend!"

"Really?" Such a rave review was foreign to Chloe. She

was used to her ideas being, at best, tolerated. "You really like it?"

"Like it?" Jacobi pulled Wolfe's laptop around and called up the Foundation homepage. "My dear, I have linked our Foundation's website to it." Clicking on "Links" brought up a long listing of related sites. And there, right at the top of the list, was a new entry for "Smallville, Land of the Weird, Home of the Strange."

"I . . . you . . . wow!" Chloe could hardly believe her eyes. "May I . . . ?" Jacobi nodded, and she clicked on the link. The homepage of her cyberarchive opened on the screen. "No one has ever linked to a site of mine before. This . . . this is beyond anything I ever—!" Chloe stopped herself. *Get it together, Sullivan! You're gushing! Keep it impartial, remember?* "I mean, this is all very unexpected. I'm flattered that you think so much of my site, but I didn't come out here for an ego boost." She pulled a microcassette recorder from her bag. "You've started attracting a lot of new attention to Smallville, and my readership would like to learn more about you and the work of the Ascendance Foundation."

Wolfe clamped his jaws tight, choking off a laugh. *I don't believe it. An interview for a high-school newspaper?* "We . . . uh . . . try to help the media whenever we can, Ms. Sullivan, but you've caught us at a very busy time. Dr. Jacobi has a radio interview in less than an hour. Why don't you come to the doctor's lecture tonight? You could learn much more there."

"Yes, well . . . I'd like to attend, but my paper has a limited budget, and . . ."

"James, we can provide complimentary tickets to tonight's lecture for Ms. Sullivan and some of her friends, can't we?" Jacobi nodded pointedly to Wolfe and returned his attention to Chloe. "Mr. Wolfe will take care of everything. You really should experience the program for yourself, Ms. Sullivan. It would provide excellent background for your article. And in the meantime, I think I can spare a few minutes to answer a couple of questions before I have to leave." He turned up the wattage on his smile. "What would you like to know?"

◆◆◆

Shortly before nine, Lex turned his Lamborghini onto an old gravel lane and drove past a row of ancient poplars to an isolated old farmhouse and barn. Parking out of view of the road, Lex got out of the car, casting an eye around him. The house appeared deserted, and that was close to the truth. The man he'd come to see spent most of his time in the larger building.

Lex pushed open a small side door and entered the barn. The makeshift laboratory within was as cluttered as ever. There were a number of experiments in progress, scattered across a series of lab tables, and each experiment involved a glowing green chunk of meteorite. But there was no sign of the experimenter. Lex looked around, noting with some satisfaction a shiny new centrifuge and a new computer terminal. *At least Hamilton's starting to put some of my money to good use.*

An angry curse suddenly erupted from behind a partition wall.

"Dr. Hamilton? Are you over there?"

"Just a minute!" Something slammed shut with a loud boom, and Dr. Steven Hamilton stormed out into the main part of the laboratory. "Luthor! Should have known it would be you!"

"Who else?" Lex briefly surveyed the scientist. Hamilton had put on a bit of weight since their initial meetings, a good development, and he looked considerably more kempt.

Good to see he's taking better care of himself. Hamilton's jeans and lab coat looked new, the white coat gleaming against the man's dark brown skin. His T-shirt, also new, was emblazoned with an image of Albert Einstein wearing a police officer's cap, and the slogan: "186,000 MILES PER SECOND—IT'S NOT JUST A GOOD IDEA, IT'S THE LAW."

Lex had to smile. *He's on his way back up.*

Hamilton had once been one of the nation's most respected mineralogists, until a scandal had cost him his research fellowship. For years, he had worked in virtual anonymity, studying the meteorites of Smallville from the laboratory he'd cobbled together in the old barn. Recently, Lex had become his patron; he found the scientist's research a neat fit to his own curiosity about the meteorites. Funding Hamilton under the table satisfied that interest while concealing it from his father.

"Well?" Hamilton waved his arms, as if trying to engender comment from his visitor. In one hand he clutched a bottle of aspirin, in the other an old transistor radio. A thin wire snaked from the radio to his left ear. "What do you make of this?"

Lex looked at him quizzically. "An aspirin bottle and an old radio? I give up, what? A death ray?"

"No, no, no!"

"You'll have to give me a better clue. I never saw myself as the mad scientist type." Too late, Lex realized what he'd just said. "No offense."

"None taken. I meant, what do you make of what's on the—? Oh, hell!" Hamilton yanked the earphone jack from the radio, and its tiny speaker instantly blared to life.

". . . currently twenty before the hour on K-T-O-W, the news voice of Lowell County. And we're talking with Dr. Donald Jacobi, noted geneticist and founder of the Ascendance Foundation."

" 'Noted geneticist,' my ass!" Hamilton handed Lex the radio and began rummaging through the drawer of a lab table.

The radio droned on. "Doctor, the second of your lectures is tonight. I understand that there is an admission fee?"

"That's right, Cassie. A small charge of seven-fifty. I wish we could present our entire series free of charge, but expenses being what they are . . ."

"Say no more, Doctor. That's still cheaper than a movie in Metropolis. Now . . . from what I've been reading, the meteors of Lowell County play a big part in the work of your Foundation, is that right?"

"Yes, Cassie. In fact, they are absolutely crucial to our research. It's hard to explain in such a short time. Those of your listeners who are interested are invited to attend our lectures and visit our website at www.cosmicladder.com."

"I'm sure they will, Doctor. We'll be right back with the times and location of that lecture series after this word from Pleasant Meadows Homes—making America a better place to live!"

Lex switched the radio off, as Hamilton pulled a glass beaker labeled "Beverage Use Only" from the drawer and began filling it with water from the tap on a nearby sink.

"I take it that Dr. Jacobi's work fails to impress you?"

" 'Doctor'? Hah!" Hamilton tossed back a couple of aspirin and downed the beaker of water. "He got his doctorate at one of those Caribbean diploma mills. And if his Foundation exists for any reason other than to make money, I'd be deeply shocked."

"Are you saying his reputation is worse than yours?"

"At least I once had a reputation." Hamilton perched on a stool. "No, Jacobi is very charming. He talks a good game. But as far as science goes, he's a lightweight. He has few credentials, and he's never published anything of significance. His biggest claim to fame is his website. That alone probably nets him over $100,000 a year." Hamilton paused, remembering—that had been the sum on the first check Luthor had given him. "No offense."

"None taken." Lex grinned. "We both know that what I gave you was just a retainer for your services. There'll be more to come, much more." He leaned back against a cabinet. "So, aside from offending the standards of science, what bothers you most about Jacobi?"

"Just that he might lure a bunch of yahoos to the area and get in the way of our research."

"Is that really likely?"

Hamilton looked up at his young patron. "You seem to know everything that goes on in and around this town. You tell me."

It wasn't until noon that Chloe finally met up with Clark and Pete. They were midway through lunch in the high-school cafeteria when she came running over to them.

"Hey, guys!"

"Talk about fashionably late." Pete put down his sloppy joe, and looked her over. "And speaking of fashion, what's with that outfit? Who died?" He abruptly slapped a hand over his mouth. "Omigod, did Stuart—?"

"No, he's still hanging in, the last I heard." Chloe lowered herself into a seat next to Clark. "And there are reasons other than funerals to dress nicely, you know."

"Let's see . . . too early in the day for a wedding. Job interview?"

"You're close."

"I don't want to play this game." Pete picked up his sandwich. "Where were you this morning?"

"Yeah," Clark asked, "what's the scoop?"

It wasn't so much what Clark said, as his totally innocent delivery, that made Pete drop his sloppy joe. He pounded the table, faking a cough to cover his laughing jag.

Chloe looked at him, startled. "Are you okay?"

"Huh . . . yeah." Tears were coming to Pete's eyes. "Something just went down the wrong pipe."

"Well, stay alive! I'd hate to lose you, especially now." Chloe leaned in closer. "You guys are not going to believe this! I went over to interview Dr. Jacobi this morning!"

"You skipped your morning classes to talk to the tent-show guy?" Clark exchanged a knowing glance with Pete. *Good thing I didn't take his bet.*

"Just first period, and I had a valid excuse. I was working on a reporting assignment given me by the editor of the *Torch*."

"Chloe, you *are* the editor of the *Torch*." Clark shook his head. "I don't believe you'd waste your time on that guy, not after what we saw on his website."

"I know, at first glance, it did look pretty whacked out. But when I found out that Dr. Jacobi was involved in meteorite research, I just had to check him out. And I'm so glad I did." Chloe gazed longingly at the french fries on Clark's plate. "Would you mind if I . . . ?"

"Help yourself."

"Thanks." She snagged an especially long fry and waved it about. "It was so great. Dr. Jacobi *totally* agrees with my weirdness theories. He's even linked his website with mine!"

Pete looked skeptical. "And this is good—how?"

"It validates all my efforts to make people wake up and pay attention to what's going on around here. A national expert with a major lecture series is saying what I've been saying all along. This is even better than selling a story to the *Ledger*!"

"Chloe . . ." Clark searched for the right words. "I wouldn't be so sure about that."

"Yeah, my pop thinks this guy is some kind of snake-oil salesman."

"Pete!"

"Mine, too."

"Clark!" Chloe gave them both her sternest look. "Has either of your fathers heard him speak?"

Clark looked at Pete, who shook his head. "No, but—!"

"Has either of *you* ever heard him speak?"

"Well, no."

"Good. Then we can all judge for ourselves!" Chloe was all smiles as she pulled a handful of tickets from her bag.

"Wha—? No way!"

"What's the matter, Pete? Afraid to find out that your father could be wrong?"

"Hey, I don't think Pop's off base about this. He can be wrong about some things, maybe even a lot of things, but—"

"There's an easy way to find out." Chloe fanned the tickets out, waving them under his nose. "Don't tell me you're busy tonight!"

"Me? Of course, I'm . . . it's just that . . ." Pete faltered. "Okay, I got nothin'."

"Clark?" Chloe fanned him from across the table.

"Well, I am curious, but . . ." Clark took a closer look at Chloe's fan. "How many tickets do you have there?"

"One-two-three . . . four-five! That's funny. I told them I had a couple of friends . . ."

"Maybe they thought you'd want two for your parents."

"Going out on a Friday night . . . with my parents?" Chloe's nose crinkled as she frowned. "I don't think so.

They must have thought I was the most popular girl in school."

"Chloe . . . Clark!" Lana called out to them as she crossed the cafeteria. "I'm so glad I found you here. I'm trying to set up a time for another planning meeting."

Clark rose from his seat. "I'm pretty flexible."

"Me too." Chloe smiled. "Any time is fine for us, as long as it's not tonight."

"Okay." Lana pulled out her daily planner. "You two have a date—?"

"No, not a date!" Clark was quick to correct her. "A bunch of us are going to hear the Ascendance Foundation lecture out at the old Davis place. Chloe scored some tickets. We have a couple extra, maybe you'd want to come along?"

"To hear the tent-show guy? Weird!"

"Hey!" Chloe's stern expression instantly returned. "What's so weird about him?"

"Sorry. Weird timing, I mean. My aunt went to Wednesday night's show, and now she won't stop talking about 'the great Dr. Jacobi.' She even went to a special seminar the Foundation held last night, and that cost her over a hundred dollars." Lana shook her head. "I can't get over it. Nell is always so smart about her money. Now she has posters for his show up in the window of her flower shop and everything. She's already made plans to attend the entire series."

"I guess you wouldn't be interested in going then." Chloe started to stuff the tickets back into her bag.

"Actually, I have to admit, anything that could get Nell so worked up does make me curious. It all sounds so wacky, it might just be fun . . . I mean, as long as we didn't have to sit beside her."

"What's wacky fun, babe?" Whitney came up behind Lana and gave her shoulders a gentle squeeze. "And who aren't we sitting beside?"

Lana put her hand on his and squeezed back. Clark could have sworn he felt that squeeze all the way to the pit of his stomach.

"Chloe has a couple of extra tickets to the Foundation lecture tonight."

Whitney seemed confused. "Foundation . . . ?"

"You remember, that one Nell was going on about?"

"Oh, the tent-show guy!"

"His name is Jacobi." Chloe's face began to redden. "Dr. . . . Donald . . . Jacobi!" She took a breath to compose herself. "It's tonight, though. You're probably busy."

"Nope. For once, I'm free." Whitney gave Lana another squeeze. "One of the store's salesmen came back from vacation early. I have the night off. I was gonna suggest burgers and a video, but if you want to go to this show, that's cool, too."

"You wouldn't mind . . . ?" Lana turned to Chloe. "That is, if you really have enough tickets?"

"Oh . . . sure." Chloe forced a smile and held up the two extra tickets. "Be my guest."

"Thanks, Short Stuff!" The tickets vanished into Whitney's hand. "This oughtta be a hoot!"

"See you all tonight then." Lana gave a little wave, and she and Whitney disappeared across the lunchroom.

Chloe's teeth were clenched as she waved back. "'Short Stuff'? 'Oughtta be a hoot'? Thank you *so* much for mentioning the extra tickets, Clark." *And did you have to fall all over yourself, telling Lana we weren't on a date?*

"Sorry, Chloe." Clark sank back into his seat. "I just thought—"

"Clark, it's reserved seating. They're all in a block!" Chloe started flipping through the remaining tickets. "I could wind up sitting next to that big Jock Strap!"

"It's okay, Chloe." Pete patted her hand. "Clark and I'll sit between you and the Whitster, if it comes to that."

"'Short Stuff'!" She angrily chewed a french fry.

"I'm sure he meant it affectionately."

"Makes me sound like a sandwich cookie!"

Pete grinned. "Well, you'll always be 'Double Stuff' in our book."

"What?" Chloe pulled away from him. "Oh, so now I'm fat, as well as short?"

"No! No way! I just meant—" Pete felt himself sinking in deeper and deeper. "Clark, help me out here!"

"Chloe, you're twice as lovable as Pete."

"Well, I should hope so." She smiled back at Clark. "All right, you're forgiven."

"*He's* forgiven? What about me?" asked Pete. "Didn't I volunteer to use my own body to shield you from Toxic Jock Syndrome?"

"Well . . ."

"Tell you what, I'll even provide the transportation for us tonight."

"You're on." Chloe's stomach began to make soft rumbling noises. "Pardon me. Thanks for the fries, Clark, but I think I'd better grab a sandwich or something, if I'm going to last through the final bell." She rose from the table. "Pick me up a little before seven, Pete. We want to get there in plenty of time."

"I'm on it!"

Clark looked over at Pete as Chloe passed out of earshot. "Are you sure you can get your father's car on such short notice?"

"Nothing's ever sure, Clark. But I'd rate my chances at a good eighty-five percent."

"And what if you wind up in the fifteen percent group?"

"Well, I didn't say what kind of transportation." Pete

looked thoughtful. "Though Chloe probably wouldn't want to ride double on my bike, would she?"

"No. Especially not since there's rain in the forecast." Clark put a hand on Pete's shoulder. "When you talk to your dad, I suggest you lay on the charm."

◆◆◆

Five hours later, Pete breezed into the living room, where his father sat reading the paper. "Hey, Pop! Okay if I borrow the car tonight?"

Dale Ross peered over the edge of his newspaper. "That depends, Peter. How late are you going to be out, where are you going, and with whom?"

"I'm taking in a lecture with Chloe and Clark, and I sort of promised that I would provide the transportation. It shouldn't run too late. I want to be home in time to catch Leno."

"Okay then." Dale folded the late edition of the *Daily Planet* and fished out his car keys. "Chloe, huh? Just how are things between you and your little blond friend? You two getting serious?"

"Serious? Chloe and me?"

"Well, as I recall, you two did go to the Homecoming Dance together."

"Not as a date. We hung out together 'cause neither of us had real dates. We're buds, Pop. She's my friend, just like Clark is my friend."

"Okay, I'm cool with that." Dale handed over the keys. "Just keep it on the road, keep to the speed limit—"

"'—and don't bring it home with the tank on empty.' No problem!" Pete gave the keys a kiss and tossed them into the air. Then he spun around and pulled his jacket out wide to catch them in his pocket as they fell.

Dale couldn't help but laugh. Pete always cracked him up. In a family of rather serious overachievers, his youngest son had carved out a niche as the one who was smart but funny. Still, Dale worried about the boy. "You know, Peter, when I was your age—"

Uh-oh, thought Pete, *here it comes.*

"—even being 'just friends' with a white girl would've gotten me a lot of dirty looks, and maybe a threat or two. Your granddad would've gotten a cross burned on his lawn—or worse!"

"Times have changed, Pop. Things are better now."

"And thank God for that. But they still *haven't* changed for a lot of people, even in Smallville. I just want you to be careful."

"I always am, Pop!"

"I hope so, Son. I dearly hope so. Drive carefully, it looks like rain."

CHAPTER 9

That evening, Pete picked Chloe up at about 6:45, then swung around to Hickory Lane. There, Chloe vacated the front passenger's seat for Clark.

"I'll just hop in the back. You need the leg room more than I do." She turned to Pete. "And don't even think about pulling any 'Short Stuff' gags."

"Never even crossed my mind."

"Good." Chloe settled into the backseat and fastened her safety belt. "This lecture is a really big deal. Promise me you'll both be on your best behavior."

Clark raised his right hand, as if taking an oath. "I promise."

"Yeah, yeah. Me too." Pete glanced in the rearview mirror at Chloe. "But don't you think you're going just a wee bit overboard?"

"I just want to have a nice evening out with my friends." She checked her watch. "Better get going now, we don't want to be late."

"Yes, Miss Daisy!"

"Ho-ho! Just drive."

In just a few minutes, Pete joined a line of cars heading onto the Foundation Compound. He tailed the others along a new gravel drive, following the signs to the parking area. The car was moving at a crawl when they were stopped by a man in an official-looking orange vest, wielding a flashlight.

Pete rolled down his window. "Hi, we're here for the lecture."

"Tickets?"

"Already got 'em, right here." Pete produced the three tickets Chloe passed him from the backseat.

Orange Vest checked the tickets out with his flashlight, nodded, and passed them back. "Okay. Hang on to those and give them to one of the ushers as you enter the tent. No cameras or recording devices are allowed inside. Parking is five dollars."

"Say what?"

"Pete!" Chloe hid her face in her hands. "Don't embarrass me! Pay the man!"

Clark reached into his pocket. "If you're short, I can cover you."

"Never mind." Pete produced a well-worn five from his wallet. "Here ya go."

"Thank you, sir." Orange Vest pocketed the tattered bill and waved them on. "Park it anywhere straight ahead."

"Five bucks for parking!" Pete put the car into gear and rolled on toward the nearest free space. "What do they think this is, Metropolis?"

"Actually, five dollars would be a bargain in Metropolis."

"Chloe's right. Last time I was there, the cheapest parking lot I saw charged at least six-fifty."

"All right, all right!" Pete pulled his father's car in between a vintage Mustang with Texas plates and a new Beetle. "And here, I thought this evening wasn't gonna cost me more than half a tank of gas."

Chloe was all smiles as she emerged from the backseat. "Thanks, Pete. I owe you!"

"Darned right you do!"

As Clark got out, he reached into the backseat and pulled out an umbrella. "Wait up, Chloe, you forgot this."

"Oh. Thanks, Clark, but do you really think we'll need it?" She looked up into the sky. "Those clouds don't look that threatening."

"Not now, but you never know what might blow in later."

As the three friends neared the tent, they found themselves passing ever-more-expensive cars. Many of them sported FULFILL YOUR DESTINY bumper stickers.

"Look at this!" Clark gestured at the lines marked off on the ground. "These cars got to park in extralarge spaces. There won't be any dings from opening car doors here. This had to be planned."

"That's correct." A woman in an orange vest confirmed Clark's suspicions. "This is our VIP parking section, for Foundation members and attendees who made special arrangements."

"Lincolns, Caddies . . ." Pete let out an appreciative whistle. "Look, there's a Prowler! Whatever this Jacobi dude is preaching, he's sure attracting a high-rolling congregation."

A familiar horn sounded, and a gold Lamborghini pulled into a reserved spot less than a yard away.

"Hello, Clark. Chloe . . . Peter."

"Lex!" Clark sounded surprised. "I never would've expected to find you here."

"Same here." Lex glanced over at Chloe. "Well, perhaps I should have."

"We'd better be going in." Chloe checked her watch impatiently. "The lecture will be starting soon. Clark . . . ?"

"Go on ahead. I'll catch up to you."

Chloe grabbed Pete by the arm and pulled him after her. Pete looked back over his shoulder at Clark and Lex. *The guy drives a freaking Lamborghini. That thing costs more than my folks see in a year. How the heck can any of us compete with that?*

Clark and Lex strolled along at a more leisurely pace. "So, have you learned anything new about this Jacobi guy?"

"Not as much as I'd like. He does appear to possess a

doctorate—courtesy of some island college of dubious repute."

"So getting back to my original question, what are you doing here? Do you think you can learn anything valuable in person?"

"One never knows. But it's worth a try."

"Why are you putting so much time into this?"

Lex stopped short. "Clark, everything that happens in and around Smallville is my concern." There was a driven, implacable tone to his voice. Then he smiled. "Besides, I could use an evening's entertainment. I assume that you came here with the rest of the Mod Squad to back up Ms. Sullivan?"

"Yeah, somebody has to keep her out of trouble."

Lex's eyebrows rose a bit. "Are you sure that's the only reason?"

"What do you mean?" Clark suddenly realized that Lex was staring back at the parking area behind him.

"Well, hello, Lana." There was just the hint of a smirk in Lex's grin. "Fordman."

"Hello, Lex . . . Clark."

"I was just suggesting to Clark here that there are any number of reasons to take in this lecture tonight. Don't you agree?"

"I suppose." Lana looked from Lex and Clark to Whitney. "I'm here mainly out of curiosity."

"I just think it'll be good for a few laughs." Whitney shrugged. "And I hear there's a pretty good light show."

"Well, I shouldn't keep you three from your fun. Enjoy the show." Lex handed his ticket to an usher and was conducted to a seat near the rear of the tent.

Another usher took one look at the tickets Clark, Lana, and Whitney presented, and started leading them toward the front of the tent. Midway down the aisle, Nell caught Lana's eye and waved. "I can't believe this," whispered Lana.

"We're farther down front than my aunt? Than Lex? How did Chloe pull that off?"

"Hey, they'd better be good seats, after what they charged us for parking," Whitney muttered.

"Here you are." The usher finally stopped alongside the second row. Chloe and Pete waved from their places, one seat in from the aisle. The usher handed Lana and Whitney their ticket stubs. "You two are in seats four and five. And you, sir," she gave Clark his, "are in seat one, right here on the aisle. We hope you all enjoy the lecture."

"Nice seats, Chloe!" Clark looked around. There were at least a thousand people seated under the big canvas canopy. "I haven't seen a bigger crowd in these parts for anything less than a football game."

"What . . . ?" Whitney looked around as instrumental music began to build over the tent's sound system. "Aw, man, don't tell me we have to listen to this John Tesh stuff!"

"Whitney, please!" Lana shushed him. "Let's at least give this a chance."

Pete looked up at the back of the stage. "What's with the swirling stars? Looks like some big computer screen saver."

"Shhh!" hissed Chloe. She glanced from Pete to Clark.

Clark held up his hands, palms out. "Hey, did I say anything?"

"You'd better not!" She checked her watch and looked back up at the stage. "I think it's about to start."

As he had on Wednesday night, Douglas Oliver stepped up to the podium. Tonight, he showed no sign of nerves, and he no longer needed his index cards to prompt him. His introduction was measured, heartfelt, and sincere, and Dr. Jacobi stepped on stage to thunderous applause.

The crowd rose to its feet, pulling any confused newcomers along with it. Their applause was deafening. Clark glanced back up the aisle. It didn't seem possible that even this many people could generate so much noise. *I could almost swear it's being amplified by the sound system.*

Tonight, Jacobi allowed the ovation to go on for nearly two minutes.

"What's with these people?" Whitney had been cheered on the football field, but this was beyond his understanding. "He hasn't even *said* anything yet."

Lana silenced him with a look, but she, too, was perplexed by the doctor's apparent hold on the crowd.

"Thank you, friends, thank you!" Jacobi held his hands up high and then slowly lowered them, quieting the crowd. "I see many familiar faces out there tonight. But I see many more newcomers. Welcome! Welcome one and all!"

He paused for the length of two breaths, letting the crowd's anticipation build, before he went on. "I know that many of you have never attended one of my lectures, and you are curious as to what our Foundation does, and just who I am."

"You can say that again," muttered Pete, earning a poke in the leg from Chloe's umbrella.

"I have devoted much of my adult life to the study of the stuff and substance of humanity"—Jacobi swept his arms wide, taking in the entire audience—"to understanding the linked causes of disease and disharmony in our lives . . . to recognizing the complex physical and metaphysical interactions which make us the cosmic beings that we are . . ."

Clark sat up with a start. *Did he just say "cosmic beings"?*

". . . and to developing integrated techniques to answer the questions, not just what we are, but of what we can be . . . and what energies exist that can make us greater still."

Suddenly, someone in the middle of the audience shouted, "GOD'S LOVE!"

Jacobi rushed to the front of the stage and thrust out an arm, pointing in the direction of the shout. "I don't for a second discount the power of spirituality, my friend! There is indeed a spiritual level to our being, just as there is an emotional level, a mental level. They all reside within our physical being. For all I know, the spirit is what moved you to come here tonight!" He smiled. "There are some who would pit faith in God against belief in science, but I am not one of them. After all, God gave us brains to think, eyes to see, voices to wonder. And the study of science has revealed so many amazing and wondrous things about this world and those in the cosmos beyond!"

The lights dimmed and the onstage screen behind Jacobi suddenly displayed the famous image of the Earth as seen from the surface of the Moon.

"Science, my friends, has allowed us to study other planets, to walk on the Moon. But it has also allowed us to turn inward, to study the very building blocks which make us who we are. Behold!"

A swirling column of light suddenly appeared alongside Jacobi at center stage. Slowly, the swirling light turned into a rotating image of a DNA helix, as big as a man.

"All *right*!" Whitney was finally impressed. "Check it out!"

Lana's eyes grew wide, her mouth forming an "O."

"Sweet." Pete turned to Chloe and Clark. "What is that? Some kind of hologram?"

"But *how*?" Chloe sat transfixed by the display. "It's like a special effect in a movie!"

"They must have a multilaser projector around here." Clark glanced upward, and his eyes caught a telltale glimmer in the trusswork high overhead. "See, the laser projects a regular video image into the display medium. That gives the illusion of a 3-D projection."

"Display medium?" Chloe looked at Clark. "*What* display medium?"

"Must be a kind of transparent screen in the middle of center stage. Yeah, there it is . . ." He pointed to an edge glowing softly alongside the rotating image. "You can hardly see it. It probably slid up out of the stage when the lights dimmed."

Now Pete was staring at his friend. "How do you come up with that stuff?"

Clark shrugged. "It's all on the Web."

Jacobi walked around the rotating helix, allowing his audience time to ooh and aah before going on. "Deoxyribonucleic acid . . . DNA . . . the molecular double helix of chromosomes within the nucleus of every living cell in our bodies." He waved an arm toward the turning hologram. "This is our own personal instruction book. The bits and pieces of these strands determine our physical being . . . whether we shall be short or tall, dark-haired or fair, blue-eyed or brown. Though microscopic in size, it is macroscopic in its impact. This is the great cosmic ladder that lifts us up from the primordial ooze to the heavens themselves. We have just begun to understand how this twisting ladder works. When we fully understand it, we will have a golden age the likes of which humanity has dreamed of for millennia. And the key to that understanding—the catalyst which will enable us to reprogram our DNA—waits all around us!"

The holographic helix flickered slightly as it faded away. The display medium slid back down into the stage, the lights brightened slightly, and the screen behind Jacobi again displayed the Smallville Meteor Capital billboard. Whispers of recognition ran through the crowd.

"Yes, we've all seen the sign, haven't we? Again and

again! The Meteor Storm of 1989 is this area's greatest claim to fame. At the time, it was regarded as a terrible calamity. But I believe that it was also a wondrous gift from the heavens . . . the harbinger of our new golden age!"

Lana fidgeted in her seat, and her fists clenched in anger. *That "gift from heaven" killed my parents.*

Lana was not alone in her feelings. Others in the crowd began to mutter angrily.

Backstage, Wolfe set down his cup and whispered into his microphone, "Better watch your step out there. Some of the locals are getting ugly."

Onstage, Jacobi was already playing to the anger.

"Yes, the meteors took a horrific toll on this land. They rained catastrophe upon this area, causing death and suffering . . . and we must never forget that! However, neither should we ignore the gift that was left us in the storm's aftermath!

"My friends, the great storm of 1989 was just the latest in a series of events—cosmic events—which have helped mankind emerge from the darkness of the caves. It is my fervent belief that the meteorites can provide a new boost up the great cosmic ladder. They will enable us to ascend to the next great level of humanity!

"There have been many such meteor storms over the eons . . . many impacts of nonterrestrial bodies on our world. Some may have made life on Earth possible. Others are now thought to have caused the extinction of the dinosaurs and other, earlier species . . . clearing the way for the rise of humankind. There are those who worry that further strikes could one day cause our own extinction, as well. I don't discount that danger. But don't all of us live with danger daily? Smallville is still very much a farming community, and farming can be *very* dangerous work. Existence itself is uncertain. And life, like old age, is not for sissies!"

That earned Jacobi a ripple of gentle laughter from the audience, and he smiled. They were his again.

From the back of the tent, Lex watched Jacobi play to the crowd. *Yes, he's good.*

"My friends, I am an optimist." Jacobi placed his right hand over his heart. "I am confident that an ascendant humanity will find a way to protect us from such dangers. And, as I said, we have within our reach the key to that ascendance."

Backstage, Wolfe pushed a button, and the onstage screen changed to show several meteorite fragments, studded with glowing green crystals. In the second row, Clark shifted uneasily in his chair.

"There they are, my friends." Jacobi half turned to gesture at the screen. "The seeds of our cosmic legacy . . . the key to the rise and advancement of mankind. In the aftermath of the '89 storm, the great institutes of science and learning combed the county, scooping up the largest meteorite fragments and carting them away for study. And what was the chief result of that study?" He faced the crowd, a look of indignation on his face. "I'll tell you what it was—*nothing*! Absolutely nothing.

"They gave those samples, at best, a cursory examination. The public was assured that any minor space rocks left behind posed no danger to public health. We were told that there was nothing out of the ordinary about the meteorites. Oh, there was some minor radiation, they told us, but nothing to worry about . . . no more exposure than you'd get from the luminous dial of a wristwatch. And, technically, they were right. But in a larger sense, they were very, very wrong.

"Because I say to you now, those scientists . . . no, I shouldn't dignify them with that title . . . those *bureaucrats* failed us! We did have something to worry about . . . a great boon to humanity was being ignored, *discarded*. Yes, there was some danger . . . it was the danger of that great tool being improperly used! In recent months, we have seen many examples of the consequences of this bureaucratic incompetence."

The meteorite fragments faded from the screen, to be replaced by a high-school yearbook picture of a young man, about fifteen to sixteen years of age.

"Take the case of young Jeremy Creek. He was institutionalized twelve and a half years ago after he suffered a major trauma from exposure to a near impact of one of the largest meteorites. Comatose, suffering an extreme electrolytic imbalance, he has not aged a day in over a decade! The experts are baffled. But Jeremy's case is far from unique."

Jacobi began to pace back and forth across the stage. "One local boy recently disappeared following the death of his mother under suspicious circumstances . . . her body was found encased in a sort of cocoon, as if spun by a giant insect. The bodily tissue of one girl apparently became so malleable that she could alter her appearance enough to impersonate other people. Another young lady fell victim to a runaway metabolism, endangering herself and others." He stopped and faced the audience. "These cases are proof of the power of the meteorites. Local citizens can tell you . . . they all occurred in this area in recent months. Young people have been institutionalized. Tragically, there have been some fatalities. This is cause for concern . . . but not for fear!

"The majority of these cases have involved teenagers, those who were children at the time of the meteor storm . . . those who have lived their whole lives in this environment. What happened to them was not their fault." Jacobi's voice grew softer. "My friends . . . we should not live in fear of our children. Meteorite exposure was only one factor out of many which led to this handful of extreme cases. Those unfortunate few are just a tiny fraction of the population. The vast majority of young people in these parts are healthy, normal individuals."

Chloe squirmed uncomfortably. *He cited all those cases, but didn't credit my website. Don't I at least rate a mention in passing?*

"Earlier, I referred to the potential for danger. Well, a power saw, used improperly, can cause injury, even death. But if you use that saw carefully, as it was meant to be used, you can cut and trim the lumber to build a fine, sturdy home. There's a proper use for the meteorite fragments, as well." Jacobi turned to stage left. "Douglas?"

Douglas Oliver approached, pushing a wheeled cart. On top of the cart was a small metal case.

"Thank you."

As Douglas departed, Jacobi snapped open the latches of the case. The lights began to dim again, and a hush fell upon the crowd. "Think what we could do, if we could harness the power of the meteorites as a force for good!" Jacobi opened the case, and his face was bathed in a soft green light.

Clark began to get a queasy feeling.

Jacobi lifted his meteorite from the case.

Clark gripped the sides of his chair, and felt the metal start to deform in his hands. He quickly bent things back into place as best he could. *Relax, Clark . . . keep it cool. As long as he doesn't come down off the stage with that thing, you ought to be okay.*

"This is my own personal space rock." Jacobi balanced it in one hand. "I have kept it close by my side for approximately three years now. I bathe in its soothing rays daily, and—I can assure you—I have experienced no ill effects. On the contrary, I haven't suffered so much as a cold in all

that time. My studies are not yet complete, but I do not believe this is a coincidence." He smiled. "But I am talking
about more than just a cure for the common cold, welcome
as that might be. I'm talking about the eradication of virtually *all* disease . . . the extension of the human life span . . .
the advancement of humanity to its next level . . . the fulfillment of our destiny as citizens of the cosmos! I believe that
these meteorites, if they are utilized properly in a controlled
environment, are the key!

"Just imagine the possibilities: The energies that could
halt the aging process for over a decade could arrest—perhaps even reverse!—mental and physical deterioration! A
mineral that could make living human tissue as malleable as
plastic, could promote levels of healing we can at present
only dream of. Missing limbs might be regenerated! Injuries
could heal without scars!

"This is all within our grasp if we but seek it out. Is there
danger? Yes! But the greater danger is in not continuing to
strive and better ourselves! None of our hopes and dreams
will be realized if we do not soldier on!" He held the meteorite aloft. "I promise you—I will not shirk my responsibility to you. I will continue to study these meteorites. And,
unlike other institutions, the Ascendance Foundation will
not keep any discoveries under lock and key! All our discoveries will be shared with others. We cannot rest until we
master this great tool! I believe that I am very near to a great
breakthrough . . . very near to discovering potent new therapies that can improve the quality of life. We can do it, and
we *will* do it, thanks to the generous help of all who have
joined and contributed to the Foundation!"

"Doctor, I want to help!" Heads turned toward the voice
from the audience. A spotlight swept across the crowd, coming to rest on a modestly dressed man in the tenth row. An
usher rushed over to him, pointing a wireless microphone in

his direction. "My name is Herb Langley, and I've been a subscriber to your website for over six months. I agree with you one hundred percent. We all have to do our part to make this happen."

"Thank you, Herb. The money you've already contributed through your subscription has helped underwrite our work."

"Thank *you*, Doctor! But I want to do *more*." He pulled a wad of bills from his pocket. "I'm not a wealthy man, I'm just an average working stiff. But I have a hundred dollars here that I want to contribute to the Foundation!"

"Herb, I don't know what to say." Jacobi's voice seemed to crack, and his eyes grew misty. "Members often make additional contributions and bequests to the Foundation, but I've rarely received such a heartfelt—!"

"I want to contribute, too!" A second spotlight picked out a woman standing another two rows back. "I attended your seminar last night."

"Ah, yes. I remember you, dear. Ms. Carney, isn't it?"

"Yes, Doctor . . . Elaine Carney. I've suffered from bursitis in my shoulder for a very long time. But during that seminar, I had an opportunity to sit close to your meteorite, concentrating on its power like you told us to—and look at me now!" She raised her hands high above her head, moving her arms gracefully. "There's no pain at all!"

"That is absolutely remarkable, Ms. Carney. But we can't be certain the meteorite was solely responsible for ending your pain."

"*I'm* certain!" There were tears in her eyes. "I haven't felt this good in years! There's not enough money in this world to repay you, but I have to make a start. Here's three hundred dollars to put towards your work!"

Then another member of the audience stood up, and another. Suddenly, ushers were dashing back and forth with buckets to collect the contributions, and people were fumbling

with wallets and purses, trying to contribute something—
anything—as the buckets went past.

"What is going *on* here?" Chloe whipped her head around
as another usher breezed past, bucket in hand. "How did this
suddenly turn into a revival meeting?"

"Well, they better not pass the hat to me." Pete crossed his
arms. "I gave at the parking lot."

Whitney snorted. "Same here."

"Oh, my God." Lana tried to disappear into her seat.
"Now Nell is getting up!"

"DOCTOR! I NEED YOUR HELP!" From the back of
the tent, a man came striding up the aisle, hat in hand, a
woman and a teenage boy following close behind. "My
name is Ray Harrison, and my son is sick."

Backstage, Wolfe caught a glimpse of the Harrison family
on one of his monitors, and cursed silently to himself. "Bas-
ket case dead ahead and closing fast." He started to bring up
the music, and thumbed a switch to warn his ushers.

Ray grabbed a microphone from one of the ushers, but it
went dead in his hand. He handed it back, pushed the usher
aside, and kept coming. His voice was a hoarse bellow,
fighting to be heard over the music. "Doctor, my boy has a
TUMOR!" A couple of ushers tried to turn Ray aside, but he
bulled right past them, too. "His doctors say they can't do
anything for him! Doctor, you gotta HELP US!"

The crowd grew silent. Sweat poured off Wolfe's brow as
the Harrison family filled the screen on one monitor.

"Stu . . . ?" Ray pulled his son forward, hugging him to
his side. "This is my son, Stuart." Ushers who were moving
in to block the Harrisons got a good look at Stuart and
stopped in their tracks.

Stuart Harrison's skin was as white as parchment, and he
was almost skeletally thin. Stuart's balance was uncertain,
and he leaned heavily against his father to steady himself. A

soft cloth cap clung tight to his head, as if shielding it from the night air. Sick as he was, Stuart looked embarrassed, and just a little angry, at the stares he was getting.

The ushers stepped back to let the family pass.

Up on the stage, Jacobi set his meteorite down atop the case, and looked out over the audience. Half of the people in the crowd were staring at the Harrisons. The other half were staring up at him.

"Doctor, I don't have a lot in this world, but it's all yours—my house, my car, every last bit of it—if you'll just help my son! PLEASE!"

Shouts of "Do it!" and "Help them!" erupted here and there, as the music swelled.

Jacobi thumbed his main microphone off and whispered into a smaller closed-circuit mike hidden in his collar. "Kill the music."

"Are you crazy?" Wolfe's voice buzzed in his earphone. "That kid's at death's door. We've gotta get out of this fast!"

"It's too late for that. I have to deal with this! Kill that music. Now, dammit!"

Wolfe punched a button and sank back into his chair. The music died out.

Jacobi held his right hand up high. Except for scattered murmurings, the tent grew quiet.

"I hear you, Mr. Harrison. I don't want your property. I wish with all my heart that I could help your son, but our research is still ongoing. I'm afraid we're still a long way from being able to—!"

"I thought you said you were close to a breakthrough!" Weak as Stuart was, his voice still carried. He took a swaying step forward and yanked off his cap. His hair was cut close to his scalp, and a tight, puckered scar snaked across the crown of his head. "You're full of it! That miracle rock of yours can't do squat!" He flung his cap with a sweeping sidearm throw, and it sailed down the aisle like a Frisbee, landing on the stage at Jacobi's feet.

Stuart turned to his father. "I told you this was a waste of time."

"STUART!" The audience jumped as Jacobi's amplified call echoed from the speakers. "I never promised that I could perform miracles. That's the stuff of faith, not science." Jacobi moved to the edge of the stage and knelt, picking up the cap. "I don't know if I can help you or not. All I can really offer you is hope." He stretched out a hand. "Are you willing to take a chance?"

The boy stared at Jacobi. The crowd hushed, waiting. Barely breathing.

Stuart shuffled forward and took Jacobi's hand. The crowd roared, and two ushers rushed forward to help boost Stuart up onto the stage.

Pete looked over at Chloe and Clark. "What are they doing?"

James Wolfe just stared at his monitor screens, dumbfounded. "What the hell are you *doing*? We are *screwed*! You can't help that kid!"

Jacobi clasped both hands around Stuart's. "We never know what we can accomplish until we try. Are you willing to try a little experiment with me, Stuart?"

"Why not? What do I have to lose?"

"My thoughts exactly!"

Jacobi handed the meteorite to the boy. "Could we dim the lights, please?"

Numbly, Wolfe did as requested.

"All right, if everyone could remain seated and quiet . . ." Jacobi put his hands under Stuart's forearms, steadying the boy and helping him support the meteorite. "Stuart, I want you to grasp the sides of the meteorite—yes, just like that—

let its light shine upon you. Now, close your eyes and relax . . . relax . . ."

"Son of a—!" Wolfe ran a handkerchief over his sweat-soaked head. "You're going to try the hypnotherapy? *Now?* Under these conditions?"

". . . nothing else matters . . . just relax." Jacobi's voice was soft, soothing. "Relax. Let the tension drain from your muscles. Picture the power of the meteorite flowing through you. Let it wash over you . . . washing away the toxins, cleansing your body and mind. Tell me . . . how do you feel?"

"Better . . ." Stuart's response came slowly. His voice sounded lighter, a little surprised. ". . . good."

"Yes . . . good. Relax and feel all tension and fear subside. Let the power replace it. Picture yourself growing stronger . . ."

Backstage, Wolfe bit his nails. "You've got more nerve than sense!" He switched his mike to channel three and gave his ushers a new heads-up. "Okay, people, it's important that we not interrupt the Doctor's experiment. But some members of the audience may become a little . . . overly excited when it's over. I want you to start edging, slowly and quietly, towards the stage."

Wolfe leaned against the console with both hands, and his cup began to tip precariously. He grabbed for it—too late—and it toppled over, spilling his sports drink down into the lighting control bay. There was a sizzle, a pop.

High above center stage, the hologram projector's lasers suddenly blazed to life. One of the beams pulsed—full power—directly down into the heart of the meteorite. Green light flooded the stage, blazing all around Jacobi and the boy.

Stuart Harrison began to convulse. He shook so violently that Jacobi was thrown back from him.

A few yards up the aisle, Mary Harrison began to scream.

"No! NO!" Wolfe slammed his hand down on an emergency switch and the laser went dead.

Stuart collapsed onto the stage, dropping the meteorite.

Clark was out of his chair in an instant, but as he reached the edge of the stage, his knees began to buckle.

"STU!" Ray Harrison bolted down the aisle, Mary close behind.

Clark gritted his teeth and strained, managing to pull himself up onto the stage.

Two ushers grabbed Ray by the arms, trying to hold him back. He flung his arms wide, knocking the ushers aside, and charged ahead.

Trapped in his row, Whitney vaulted over the man in the row in front of him and dashed toward Clark.

Mary ran two more yards and started to faint.

"Mrs. Harrison—?" Chloe reached out to help the woman into Clark's vacated chair. "Pete! Lana!" Her classmates were already half out of their seats, not sure what to do next. They immediately moved to help Mary Harrison.

"Kent!" Swaying slightly, Clark turned back to see Whitney giving Ray Harrison a leg up onto the stage. "Kent! Give us a hand!"

Clark grabbed the older man by the forearms and pulled as Whitney pushed. Ray got to his feet and ran to his son, as Clark stooped to help Whitney up onto the stage.

Back at the center aisle, an usher tripped and almost fell against Mary. Pete scrambled past the girls and hauled the shaken volunteer out of the way. He took a water bottle from the man and passed it to Chloe.

At center stage, Ray dropped to his knees and gathered his son up in his arms. Jacobi leaned over them, his lips moving silently, as if he'd lost the power of speech. In his hands, he held the meteorite tipped toward them, its green glow casting over the Harrisons, Whitney, and Clark.

Whitney charged ahead. "C'mon, Kent, don't stop now!"

Clark started to stumble. He could see his veins of his hands writhing and pulsing, turning a sickly greenish black. He glared at Jacobi. "HEY! GET THAT ROCK OUT OF HERE!"

Jacobi jerked upright, as if awakened by Clark's shout. He spun around, rushing to shut the meteorite away in its case.

Clark instantly felt his strength return. He quickly joined Whitney by the Harrisons' side. The quarterback had two fingers pressed to the side of Stuart's throat.

"How is he?"

"Breathing." Whitney shook his head. "But his pulse is weak."

"Oh, my God, he's burnin' up!" Ray looked pale, almost near collapse himself. "I gotta get him to a hospital."

"CLARK!" Lex's shout carried over the growing din of the crowd. Clark looked up and saw Lex threading his way down a side aisle, waving a cell phone overhead. "Ambulance is on its way! I told them to pull around to the rear of the tent!"

"Good work!" Clark looked back over his shoulder at the others. "Did you hear that, Mr. Harrison? Help's on the way."

Clark stared out over the audience. Nearly everyone was in motion, filling the aisles. He could see Lana fanning Mary Harrison in the second-row seats, as Chloe urged the woman to take a sip of water.

Pete stood at the end of that row, guarding the aisle. "Clark, you got things under control up there?"

"I think so. Can you look after Stuart's mom and the girls?"

Pete gave him a thumbs-up. "You're reading my mind, bud. I'll get 'em out of this crowd as soon as I can!"

"Thanks!" Clark returned the thumbs-up, then reached down and pulled Lex up onto the stage. *They should be safe now*. Pete wasn't very tall, but he was nearly as broad-shouldered as Clark, and he had the tenacity of a bulldog.

"My fault . . ." Ray was like a zombie. ". . . this is all my fault."

Lex crouched down beside Ray. "No, it isn't, sir." He pitched his voice low, sounding confident and reassuring. "Try to pull yourself together. You'll want to be able to give your son's medical history to the paramedics as soon as they arrive."

"Right . . . right." Ray closed his eyes and took a deep breath. Clark could almost hear the man's pulse returning to normal. Ray opened his eyes and looked around the stage. "Mary? Where's my wife—?"

"She's still stuck in the audience, Mr. Harrison." Clark put a steadying hand on Ray's shoulder. "But it's okay. She's with friends. They'll meet us outside."

Clark glanced from Ray to Whitney and Lex. "We need to move Stuart outside, to the rear of the tent. The four of us can handle that." *I can myself, if it comes to that.*

"Here, use this." Whitney peeled off his jacket and spread it on the stage.

They eased Stuart onto the open jacket. Then, Clark, Lex, Whitney, and Ray Harrison each grabbed a corner and lifted the unconscious boy in the makeshift stretcher. With Clark at the front, helping support Stuart's head, they made their way down a set of steps at stage right and out the back of the tent.

Behind them, unnoticed in the confusion, James Wolfe sat slouched in front of his monitors. Monitor two showed people crowding into the aisles, leaving the Foundation's more devoted members standing around, looking lost. Monitor one showed a half dozen of their ushers, standing shoulder to shoulder, holding back a few angry men who wanted to rush the stage. And on monitor three, Don Jacobi stood leaning against the podium at stage left, grasping at it for support as his world spun out of control.

*　　*　　*

A light rain was coming down, and the flashing red lights of a Lowell County ambulance lit the night sky, as Pete, Chloe, and Lana finally emerged from the rear of the tent. Between them, the girls were supporting and comforting Mary Harrison.

"Yo, Clark!" Pete ran over to his buddy. "What's the score?"

"The EMTs have checked Stuart out. He's conscious now." Clark lowered his voice as Mrs. Harrison hurried past them to join her husband. "He's conscious but groggy, and he's got a high fever."

"Hey, don't look so down." Pete clapped his buddy on the back. "You did all you could for him."

"Yeah, I guess we did." Clark turned to watch the Harrisons crowd into the back of the ambulance alongside their son and an EMT. *I could probably have carried him to the hospital myself by now, but what if he started convulsing again along the way? I can administer basic CPR, but that's about it.*

They watched as the ambulance pulled out, siren wailing. It roared ahead about fifty feet, then its rear end slid four feet sideways. The vehicle's wheels spun uselessly, digging down into the wet earth, and a sharp burst of profanity came from the cab.

Clark was the first to reach the driver's side. "What's wrong?"

The driver frowned. "Wasn't expecting this much mud. The rain alone shouldn't have been enough to muck things up this bad. Must be an underground spring back here." He eased his foot slowly onto the gas, but the wheels continued to spin. "We're stuck pretty good. Can you guys give me a push?"

"Sure!" Clark gave a whistle, and Whitney, Lex, and Pete came on the run. In seconds, they positioned themselves around the rear of the ambulance. Whitney, used to calling numbers to a team, took charge.

"Okay, on three! One . . . two . . . THREE!"

The driver gave it the gas, and the four young men put their shoulders to the ambulance and pushed. But one of them was all that was really needed.

Unseen by the others, Clark reached under the vehicle, grabbed hold of the frame, and lifted. He sank to his knees in the wet earth, but the ambulance started to rise up out of the mud.

"We're . . . movin'!" Whitney was breathing heavy. "Give it all . . . ya got!"

Clark gave a mighty shove, and the ambulance shot ahead, reaching the compacted gravel of the drive.

Whitney let out a whoop as he and Lex picked themselves up from the muddy ground. "We did it, man!"

"That we did." Lex watched the lights of the ambulance strobe off into the night. "It was easier than I'd expected."

"Speak for yourself." Pete was still on his hands and knees, spitting bits of mud and grass. As Whitney pulled Pete to his feet, Lex looked around. "Where's Clark?"

"Here." Clark slogged up out of the darkness, covered in mud from the waist down. "Ground must've been a little softer where I was standing."

"Wow! You four are a complete mess!" They turned to see Lana and Chloe making their way gingerly across the soggy ground, sharing an umbrella. "You'd better get under cover."

"It's a little too late for that now, Lana." Clark grabbed a corner of his jacket and wrung water from it. "At least this is a warm rain."

"Warm or not, you'd better get yourselves dried off before you all come down with colds." She turned to Whitney. "We ran into Nell on the way out, and she looked pretty upset by all that happened tonight. I think I'd better go ride home with her."

"I understand. C'mon, I'll walk you to her car."

Lana pulled her jacket up over her head. "Peter, thanks so much for all your help in there. Chloe . . . Clark, I'll call you about the next planning meeting. Lex . . . stay safe everyone!" With a wave, she and Whitney headed off around the tent.

"I should be going, as well." Lex wiped a muddy shoe across the grass, without seeing much improvement. "Ah, well, I was meaning to have the car detailed soon anyway. Good night, all."

"The car—!" Pete took a good look at himself and Clark. "Oh, man, we're gonna get mud all over the interior of Pop's car. He'll kill me!"

"No, he won't, Pete. After all, this was an emergency. Your dad's a pretty understanding guy."

"Yeah, but he loves that car. Maybe if I strip down to my drawers . . . ?" Pete looked at Chloe and shook his head. "No, scratch that. No way would he be *that* understanding!"

Clark wrung more water from his jacket. "Look, I'm a lot grimier than you. Why don't I just walk home?"

"That's miles away! It'll take you forever."

"No, it won't. I can set a pretty good pace. Besides, the rain's letting up. I'll be fine, really." Clark started striding away. "Catch you guys later!"

"Clark!" Pete called out, but his friend had already disappeared into the darkness. He scratched his head, chuckling. "That guy is something else."

"Yeah . . . he sure is."

"Hark, the great journalist speaks!" Pete stepped back under the umbrella and his grin faded. "Hey, you okay, Chloe? You've hardly said a word."

"I'm just bummed over what happened. Bummed, disillusioned, and a little weirded out." She spun the umbrella, sending raindrops flying away. "I mean, I thought Dr. Jacobi was the real deal. He was championing all of my theories . . . he said all the right things. And then, it all turned into . . . I don't know what."

"Yeah, I can see how that would weird you out."

Chloe shook her head. "That was just the bummed and disillusioned part. No, I mean what happened to Stuart tonight, with the glowing meteorite and the laser and all . . . !" She gave a shiver. "Pete, I think we might have seen part of my weirdness theory in action."

CHAPTER 10

The glass double doors of the Emergency Entrance whisked open as the EMTs wheeled Stuart into the Medical Center. Dr. Caroline Van Etten came on the run. "Joel . . . Mark! Is that our cancer patient?"

"Check! Male Caucasian, eighteen years old. Convulsed and collapsed at a public event. Convulsions had passed when we arrived." Joel passed her the report. "Conscious, post-ictal. Temperature's one-oh-four. B.P.'s one-twenty-six over eighty-four. Pulse, one hundred and thready. O_2-sat at ninety-eight percent, regular sinus on the monitor. Blood glucose normal. We gave him one hundred milligrams of thiamine on-site."

Van Etten turned to the emergency room's admitting attendant. "Rudy, light a fire under Oncology—we need a consult down here on the double. And call Metropolis General to start arranging for a transfer."

"Right." Rudy was already punching the speed-dial. "Air evac?"

"Only if they can fly low." She frowned. "We might have an intercranial here."

A big man was following along behind the gurney—half-leading, half-carrying a woman along with him. "Dr. Van Etten!" The man looked distraught. "It's my boy—Stuart Harrison!"

Van Etten remembered Ray Harrison from when he'd brought his son to Emergency just two weeks before. The kid looked much worse now. What the devil had gone wrong? She waved to the attendant. "It's okay. They can come along." She scanned the EMTs' field report. "No anti-convulsants?"

"None yet. Like I said, the convulsions had passed."

She looked into Stuart's eyes as they wheeled him into E.R. One. "Stuart, can you hear me?"

"Green . . . green . . ." The words came slowly from behind the breathing mask.

"What was that?" Van Etten could barely hear him.

"I think he's saying 'green.'" The emergency room nurse leaned in to insert a tympanic thermometer in Stuart's ear. She checked it and looked up in alarm. "Temperature's one-oh-five."

"Get some cold packs on him! And set him up for a C.T. scan now!" Van Etten flipped through the report and turned to the Harrisons. "He's not allergic to any medications?"

"No." Mary Harrison shook her head. "None."

"Good." She started leading the Harrisons out of the examining room. "We're going to do a quick scan of your son's head to look for signs of intercranial bleeding or pressure, masses or tumors . . ."

"You'll find a lot of those, Doc." Ray's voice broke, and Mary hugged him tight.

"Of course." Van Etten added a notation on the chart and looked around impatiently. Where was that oncologist? "Anyway, if there're no signs of elevated pressure, we'll do an L.P. That's a . . ."

"Lumbar puncture." The words fell from Mary's mouth as though she said them every day. "You're searching for signs of infection?"

"Right." Van Etten reminded herself that she was speaking to parents of a cancer patient. By now, they probably knew most of the terminology as well as she did. "We need to find the cause of that fever in order to treat it most effectively. It could be meningitis."

"It was that damned rock." Tears were welling up in Ray's eyes. "This is all my fault. I never should've taken him to that show."

"Rock?" Van Etten stared blankly at the Harrisons.

"Stuart was holding a meteor-rock," began Mary, "when it just . . . lit up . . . like a searchlight."

"Yeah." Ray nodded. "One of the boys who helped us afterwards said something about a laser going wild."

Van Etten turned from the Harrisons to the EMTs, who were collecting their field gear. Joel nodded. "They were all at that Foundation tent show. The father took his boy there, hoping to get him healed by some New Age weirdo."

"Yeah." Mark stacked their portable heart monitor on the cart. "We didn't see it, but apparently the quack had him up onstage, doing a laying on of hands with a chunk of space rock, when the lighting went haywire. That's when the kid convulsed."

"Okay." The doctor scribbled a hasty note to herself at the bottom of the chart. "Any deputies on the scene?"

"They were arriving as we left."

Van Etten called out to the attendant. "Rudy, call the Sheriff's Office. Tell 'em we need anything they can get us on a chunk of meteorite that was used at that show. And make sure they know to handle it carefully—it might be harboring bacteria." She steered the Harrisons back to a row of seats next to the emergency admissions desk. "I need to check on that C.T. If you could just wait here, Rudy'll have some paperwork for you to fill out. I'll be back as soon as I can."

Ray and Mary sat down in the admissions area and were soon joined by the attendant.

"Sure you're familiar with this by now, folks." Rudy was sympathetic but brisk. "We need your name, address . . . name of the patient . . . insurance . . ."

"We . . ." Mary couldn't go on.

"We don't have any more insurance. Our policy ran out." There was both shame and anger in Ray's voice. "But you gotta do what you can for our Stu. I'll find the money somehow."

A sharp, even voice called out from behind the Harrisons. "Don't worry about the money. It's covered."

Rudy squinted up at the mud-spattered figure who had just come through the double doors. "And you would be—?"

"Lex Luthor." He was already pulling out his wallet. "Stuart Harrison is to have the best care available, no matter the expense. Is that clear?"

The Harrisons looked up in surprise, and the attendant gaped, as they all recognized the bald young man approaching them. "Y-Yes, sir."

"Good." Lex produced a small, platinum-colored plastic card. "Do you take American Express?"

◆◆◆

From the Saturday edition of the *Smallville Ledger* . . .

Local Teen Critical Following Lecture Incident
By MAY FRANKLIN
Ledger Staff

SMALLVILLE—A Smallville High School student was hospitalized after suffering a seizure at an area event Friday night. Witnesses said that Stuart Harrison of Smallville collapsed onstage at a tent show at the Ascendance Foundation Compound after a lighting projector malfunctioned. Harrison was treated at the scene by Lowell County paramedics and transported to the Smallville Medical Center.

Medical Center spokeswoman Pauline Beckford said that Harrison, 18, was admitted in critical condition. "He was treated by emergency room staff and is now in the care of his family physician," said Beckford.

Witnesses reported that Harrison was in ill health prior to the incident.

The Ascendance Foundation of Smyrna, Delaware, recently leased the former Alton Davis property, 1027 Old Carter Road, for a series of lectures and seminars. The second lecture of their series, dealing with alternate medical procedures, was in progress when Harrison was stricken.

A special unit of the Kansas State Police is assisting Lowell County sheriff's deputies in investigating the incident. Sources told the *Ledger* that the projector malfunction was caused by a "freak short in an electrical system." No official report was released Friday.

Spokespersons for the Foundation were unavailable for comment. The Harrison family could not be reached.

◆◆◆

The Foundation Compound's campground was all but deserted by midmorning Saturday. Many of the campers had vacated the site overnight. Only a few faithful volunteers remained, trying to maintain a semblance of security and dealing with confused new arrivals who hadn't yet heard the news.

Sheriff's deputies remained on the site through midday, questioning the volunteers. A forensics team from the Kansas State Police confiscated the laser projector, the control board, and Dr. Jacobi's meteorite for further study.

All of the lectures and seminars that had been planned for

the weekend were canceled. There was no notice posted on the Foundation's website as to when they might be rescheduled.

Jacobi spent the day in something akin to a state of shock. He answered questions—when he could—like an automaton. At one point during his questioning, a large tray had been knocked over—falling to the floor with a hellacious crash—just a few feet away from Jacobi, and he hadn't even blinked. His condition so alarmed one investigator that she summoned a paramedic and insisted that the doctor be checked thoroughly. By evening, Jacobi was resting in the farmhouse, under sedation.

Wolfe was left to deal with the authorities, the media, and the volunteers on his own. Saturday night, he slipped into town, found a liquor store, and returned with his own brand of sedative.

It wasn't until Sunday morning that Jacobi finally became coherent enough to open up to his partner.

"I was so close, Jimmy. I had that kid in the palm of my hand. The crowd was mine. If only you hadn't switched on that damned laser—!"

"Let it go, will you? How many times do I have to tell you—it was an *accident*. The controls shorted out! The sheriff believed me, why won't you?"

Jacobi didn't answer. He just sat there at the kitchen table, snapping and unsnapping his empty meteorite case.

"Face facts, Don, it's time to cut our losses. We need to pack up and get out of here." Wolfe pulled a flask from his hip pocket, took a deep swig, and passed it to his partner. "I don't think there'll be any criminal charges—we'd have been booked by now. But it's just a matter of time before that kid's father wakes up and slaps us with a civil suit."

"I didn't mean to hurt him." Jacobi stared at his unshaven reflection in the metal flask. "I never hurt anybody before—"

"You've hurt plenty of people, Don. The only difference is that this time you're still around to deal with the consequences."

"Consequences . . ." Jacobi said the word slowly, each syllable lingering on his tongue. "So many consequences."

"That's right. There are. And they're all going to come raining down on our furry little heads, if we don't bug out of here. And soon!"

Jacobi got up and walked over to the kitchen sink. He splashed a couple handfuls of cold water on his face and took a deep breath. Through the window he could see some of the Foundation's more devoted members policing the grounds. "Look at them, Jimmy. It doesn't matter how screwed up things get. There are always a few who will stand by you . . . always a loyal few."

"Yeah, that's very touching, but all the loyalty in the world won't save us from a civil suit. And that kind of litigation could unravel everything." Wolfe grabbed his partner by the shoulder and spun him around. "Will you listen to me? If we leave right now, we can be in Mexico before nightfall. Tomorrow is Monday. With a little luck, we should be able to close out most of our East Coast accounts electronically and transfer the funds to a little bank I know in Veracruz, all before anyone's the wiser."

"What'll that do to the Foundation, to the website—?"

"Forget about the Foundation! That Harrison kid has a better life expectancy!" Wolfe started pacing. "We won't be able to get all of the money. Maybe only seventy-five, eighty percent. But that should be enough to keep us comfortable until this all blows over. Later, maybe we can start over somewhere else—!"

Wolfe's plans were interrupted by the insistent trilling of a cell phone. Numbly, Jacobi crossed the room to pick it up.

"Hello?" Jacobi stiffened. "Oh . . . Mr. Harrison."

It's over. Wolfe could picture a stream of lawyers lining up outside the door. *I should have dragged him away from here last night.*

"What's that? I don't understand . . . !" Jacobi eyes opened wide. "Yes. Yes, I see. Of course, right away."

As Jacobi folded the phone shut, Wolfe picked up his flask and slumped against the wall. "How bad is it?"

"Bad? Nothing's bad." He clutched the phone to his chest. "Nothing's bad at all. Put that rotgut away!" Jacobi put the phone down and crouched down beside a cabinet. He opened the door and removed a bottle of champagne and two glasses. "I'd hidden this away, saving it for a special occasion, and this certainly qualifies."

Wolfe rubbed his eyes and stared at his partner. Jacobi stood tall and confident, his eyes sparkled. "Don, what did Harrison say? What the devil is going on?"

"Calm yourself, Jimmy. There's nothing to worry about." Jacobi popped the cork and smiled. "In fact, I'd say the Foundation just gained a new lease on life!"

◆◆◆

Just a few minutes past two, Dr. Will Manning glanced at his visitor, then peered through the blinds of a consultation room window in the intensive care unit of the Smallville Medical Center. "I've been practicing medicine for nearly thirty years, and I have never had a case quite like this one." In a private room on the other side of the glass, Stuart Harrison was sitting up in bed, happily drinking cranberry juice and using a remote to switch the channels of a wall-mounted television. "The turnaround happened so fast, we never even had to transfer him to Metropolis."

Manning closed the blinds and pulled a chart from a hook on the wall. "When that boy was brought in here two nights ago, he was pale, lethargic, and febrile . . . his temperature peaked at one hundred six degrees." He read over the chart again, as if doubting his own knowledge. "Given all that Stuart had been through these past few years—the surgery, radiation, chemotherapy—I wouldn't have given odds that he'd live to see another dawn, even if he'd been taken directly to Metro General. But then his temperature started to fall. In less than half an hour, it was down to ninety-nine." Manning glanced up at the clock on the wall. "Now, here it is, barely forty-two hours later, and his temperature's ninety-eight-point-eight—almost back to normal. Heart rate is a steady sixty-two beats per minute. Blood pressure one-ten over sixty. Just look at him! His color is the best I've seen in months. And I'd almost swear his scars have started to improve."

The doctor's visitor crossed the room to get a better look through the blinds. Stuart's channel surfing had finally reached the Cartoon Network. He started laughing as Daffy Duck erupted from a sylvan pond to honk Elmer Fudd's nose. Against the stark white of the pillow, Stuart's head seemed somehow rounder, smoother. The pucker of his scars was less visible through his closely cropped hair.

"Yes, I see what you mean. He looks more like a kid with a buzz cut than a cancer patient. And you say the tumors in his brain are actually shrinking?"

"So it seems." Manning bent down to enter his password on a desktop keypad. "After his fever dropped and his other vitals stabilized, I ordered an MRI to see if any further damage had been done." He swiveled the monitor around so his visitor could better see the screen. "Here was the image we got a little over two weeks ago. There on the left-hand side of the screen, you can clearly see the tumors."

The visitor nodded. Several large masses were clearly visible in the cross-sectional image of the skull. Even to a layman, it was obvious that those masses were bad news.

"And here's the MRI we took Friday night."

The image that flowed down the right side of the screen might have come from a different patient. Masses were still present, to be sure, but they were noticeably smaller. The largest was only half the size of its counterpart in the first image.

"Remarkable."

"That doesn't begin to describe it." Manning removed his glasses and tapped them against his palm. "The change was so dramatic, I first thought there must have been a scanning error. So, I ordered additional sets." Another mouse click reduced the first two images in size and added a third, and then a fourth. The tumor masses were smaller and fewer in number in each successive image.

"It's as if the damn things were shrinking before our eyes." Manning rubbed the bridge of his nose and put his glasses back on. "If they keep up at this rate, they'll soon be . . . well, they'll soon be gone!"

"What do you think caused the shrinkage?"

"Well, I doubt that my treatment had anything to do with it, much as I'd love to take credit for this. At Stuart's request, I'd provided little more than palliative care since these recent tumors were found." Manning scratched at an earlobe as he collected his thoughts. "I suppose his fever might have triggered some sort of biochemical change, but I can't even tell you with any certainty what caused the fever."

"Could anything at the lecture have brought it on?"

"You mean the 'great experiment'?" Manning scoffed. "I wasn't there, but from what I was told, it sounds as if it was nothing more than relaxation therapy augmented with sideshow lights and mirrors. The police tested the meteorite and haven't found any signs of contamination. There was nothing more remarkable about it than any other space rock in this county. Stuart's parents, of course, are of a different opinion. His father's calling the whole thing a bloody miracle."

"And what would you call it?"

"It's some sort of spontaneous regression. It's extremely rare, but it does happen. I myself saw such a case when I was an intern. An end-stage liver cancer. After deteriorating for months, liver function plateaued, then began to improve. Five weeks later, the patient was cancer-free." Manning toyed with the end of his stethoscope. "But this regression has been far more rapid. It's wonderful for the boy, of course, but it mystifies me. I've never been a big believer in miracles, but I can't give you any more of an explanation than that."

The visitor considered that. "I guess that'll just have to do for now. You will keep me posted if there's any change?"

"I suppose that I could." Manning glanced back at the glass separating him from his patient. "It's not that I don't appreciate the concern you've expressed for Stuart and his family, but . . . frankly, Mr. Luthor, I'm not sure I should have told you as much as I have."

Lex smiled. "I certainly wouldn't expect you to do anything that would violate your Hippocratic Oath, Doctor. I just want to do all I can to ensure that Stuart has the best medical care available." He offered Manning his hand. "You'll help me with that, won't you?"

◆◆◆

Monday afternoon, Chloe got her usual pass to leave the study hall and headed for the *Torch* office. Once there, she booted up the old reliable desktop computer and checked her e-mail. Waiting for her was a string of messages, all from the same address . . .

Subj: **Good News on Stuart Harrison!**

Date: 4/22/02 10:07:43 AM Central Daylight
Time

From: doliver@cosmicladder.com (Douglas
Oliver)

To: chloes@smallvilletorch.edu

We have received word from Stuart
Harrison's family that his condition is
continuing to improve. His temperature was
a normal 98.6 degrees as of eight o'clock
this morning, and his latest MRI shows just
one tiny tumor remaining.

The doctors at the Smallville Medical
Center are encouraged by Stuart's progress,
but have been unwilling so far to discuss
the possibility of his release.

More to come!

Subj: **Monday Morning Update on Stuart
Harrison**

Date: 4/22/02 11:09:24 AM Central Daylight
Time

From: doliver@cosmicladder.com (Douglas
Oliver)

To: chloes@smallvilletorch.edu

We have finally received an explanation as
to why doctors at the Smallville Medical
Center have yet to consider Stuart's
release.

Medical Center policy requires that
pediatric cancer patients must maintain a
normal temperature for at least 48 hours
before they can be released. (Because
Stuart's recent tumors metastasized from a
cancer that originated when he was younger,
he is still considered a pediatric
patient.)

More information will follow as it
becomes available.

Chloe scrolled down the list. "Oh . . . my . . . God." There had been three additional messages from cosmicladder.com when she signed on. Now there were four.

She quickly clicked through the messages. They were being posted about once an hour. *These guys could give the National Weather Service a run for their money.* Chloe opened a new file and archived the letters. Then she went on the Web and resumed a search that she'd started over the weekend.

Chloe was so intent on her screen that she never even heard the next bell ring.

◆◆◆

Tuesday afternoon, Clark rushed home from school and raced through his chores. As soon as he finished, he retreated to his room, booted up his computer, and went online. Clark called up his favorite search engine and typed in "Stuart Harrison."

Rumors about Stuart's condition, fueled by Douglas Oliver's e-mails, had been flying all over school for the past two days, each one wilder than the last. If even half of them were to be believed, the senior's chances for survival had dramatically improved since Friday night.

Aside from a recent entry at www.cosmicladder.com— *Yeah, like I'd trust that!*—the newest article that came up in response to Clark's search was a three-day-old item archived on the *Ledger* website. *Should have known, they always run a few days behind publication.* He tried a different approach, changing the scope of his search, looking for articles on medical miracles. Clark breezed through a score of websites. His eyes darted across the screen, reading the pages as quickly as they appeared, but he couldn't find anything that seemed to relate to Stuart's case.

Frustrated, Clark retreated after dinner to his private space in the barn loft for some quiet time. He punched the POWER button on his battered old boom box and played with the tuner. Reception was spotty, punctuated by the static of a distant storm. Clark finally settled for the signal from a distant AM station and plopped down on the swayback couch. His impact with the cushions started a chain reaction in the springs that sent a scarred old basketball tumbling off the couch. Clark scooped up the ball and bounced it a few times against the plank floor. He tossed it up against the rafters across from him, catching it on the rebound, and tossing it back again. Clark continued the game of toss and bounce for nearly ten minutes, sinking into a kind of Zen state. After a while, the rhythm of toss, bounce, and catch began to fall in time with the beat of the music on the radio.

The ball had just fallen back into Clark's hands when the opening notes of "Sweet Georgia Brown" began to whistle from the speakers. He broke into a broad grin. Clark tossed the ball high and wide. As it left his hands, he was already up off the couch and across the loft. There, the ball all but fell into his hands.

"Okay, Kent, want to try a little one-on-one?" Clark tossed the ball and dashed back to his original spot. He moved so quickly that—to him—the ball seemed to freeze in midair.

Clark caught the ball he'd thrown to himself, flipped it into the air, and spun it on the tip of his left index finger. "One-on-one sounds fine to me. But let's make this a little more challenging. I'll be shirts, you be skins!"

Clark threw the ball, peeling off his shirt as he bolted

across the loft. The shirt hit the couch just as the shirtless Clark caught the ball. Back went the ball, and back went Clark, this time scooping up the shirt and pulling it on in the process. He caught the ball in the last possible instant. "Hah! You've got to be faster than that!"

Back and forth he dashed, playing against himself. So quickly did he move that there appeared to be two Clarks playing ball—one with a shirt, one without.

"Clark!" His mother's voice called up from the yard below. "You have a visitor!"

"Wha—?" Clark stopped dead in his tracks. The ball ricocheted off the side of his head, struck a high rafter, and dropped down the stairs.

"Hey!" Chloe ducked to the side, grabbing hold of the railing as the ball thunked past her.

"Sorry." Clark reached over and shut off the radio. "Guess I . . . messed up that free throw."

"What were you *doing* up here?" Chloe looked around, puzzled. Dust was settling all along the old plank flooring. "From downstairs it sounded like horses tap-dancing!"

"Just shooting a few hoops."

"Really?" Chloe looked around the big open loft. "Where's the hoop?"

Clark pointed to a section of rafter about twelve feet overhead. "I imagine it to be right about there. Picturing a hoop in a constant position helps combine mental and physical exercise at the same time. It's sort of . . . virtual basketball."

"All right." Chloe considered that as she looked him up and down. "So why are you half-naked? Not that I'm offended." she added hastily.

"I . . . uh . . ." Clark glanced around. His shirt lay on a bale of straw ten feet away. "I was starting to work up a sweat and didn't want to get all pitted out."

Chloe reached the shirt first and picked it up. "You must

have ditched this just in time. Still smells springtime fresh!" She held it out to him, enjoying the way the muscles of his arms and chest moved when he took it from her.

"Thanks. Just give me a sec." Clark half turned away to pull the shirt back on, affording Chloe a welcome glimpse of his back.

"No hurry." There was an almost teasing quality to her voice.

Hearing that, Clark quickly yanked his shirt back down into place. "So . . . what brings you over here this time of evening? Starting an exposé on clandestine sports activity?"

"Hardly." She sat down on the straw bale. "I was looking for someone who would listen. I need to vent a little . . . hope you don't mind."

"I'm all ears. I've hardly seen you the past couple of days. What's up? Does this have anything to do with Stuart?"

"More with Jacobi. Actually, the word on Stuart keeps getting better and better. The last I heard, not only is his temperature holding at normal, but the last of the cancer has vanished. Oh, and he's eating everything in sight. Rumor has it he may even go home soon."

"Really? Wow! If it's true, that's great!"

"Tell me about it. If I could get through the school year without having to write another obit, that would be fine by me."

"That's about the best news we could get." Clark knelt down beside her. "So why the long face?"

"Because I think that Donald Jacobi is a con artist, and I'm furious that I ever let myself get taken in by him. I can't believe I was so naive."

"Hey, you can't be a crusading journalist twenty-four/seven. You'd burn out."

"Fair enough. But you'd think I could've maintained *some* objective distance. But when I met Dr. Jacobi, it was as if everything I'd ever learned, read, or heard about reporting flew right out the window. His theories and mine?" She held her first two fingers together tight. "Just like that. Clark, he even knew my name!

"Here was this scientist who acknowledged my work—all the stuff that had gotten me on the principal's bad side. Jacobi was going to get to the bottom of the meteorite weirdness and tell the world about it. He was going to make people *listen*." Chloe's voice grew very small. "I thought it was going to be so great.

"He told me what I wanted to hear, and I lapped it up like a hungry kitten." She looked deep into Clark's eyes, her face a mix of anger and frustration. "Even on Friday night, when he breezed through all those case histories without mentioning me, I continued to believe in him. Okay, some of his presentation was a little over the top, but I kept telling myself he had to do that to get people's attention." Chloe frowned at the memory. "I should have *known* better, especially after seeing all that New Agey cosmic ca-ca on his website. It wasn't until the members of his 'flock' started rising and the ushers began passing the plate that the penny finally dropped for me!

"Clark, it was nothing more than a big phony revival meeting. He just tarted it up with flashing lights to make the whole thing *look* like science! I think he was exploiting the meteorites to make money. In another town, he'd probably use something else. I think the *only* purpose of the Ascendance Foundation is to make money. I just can't *prove* it yet."

She shook her head. "I started off-balance, and then other things *kept* me off-balance. I wanted to start investigating as soon as Stuart collapsed, but I had to help his mother. Don't get me wrong, I was happy to help—"

"I'm glad to hear that."

"—but what I really wanted to do was run backstage and start asking the tough questions. I caught a glimpse of James Wolfe as we were exiting the tent. He looked shell-shocked, but he was starting to look angry, too. All I could think of was the Man Behind the Curtain from *The Wizard of Oz*."

"Chloe!"

"I know, I know. That doesn't prove anything. But it was one more reason to *look* for proof." Chloe pushed herself up off the bale and started pacing. "I've spent the past few days trying to dig up background on Jacobi, his buddy Wolfe, and their Foundation. I tracked down every paper that Jacobi has written—not that there were many—and, at best, they're reviews of other people's work."

She kicked the bale. "He hasn't done *any* original research on DNA. He hasn't done any research on the eradication of disease. He hasn't done any research on the extension of life. He hasn't done any original research on *anything*! I don't think that man has ever set *foot* in a laboratory even once his entire *life*!"

"Chloe, chill! It's going to be okay. You saw through him."

"But did anybody else? After Stuart collapsed on stage, I thought that Jacobi was finished, at least in this town. But now the faithful are returning."

"What do you mean?"

"Remember how I told you that Jacobi had put me on the Foundation's e-mail list? Well, in the past day and a half, they've been posting progress reports on the Foundation as well as on Stuart's condition. They reported a slow stream of cars back to their campground, so I went out this afternoon to check on it myself—and it's true. Evidently, some of the out-of-towners who bailed on them Friday night got the word and have come back to ask for forgiveness. By this weekend, Jacobi will probably have *all* of them back. And they'll be convinced he can work miracles."

Clark leaned against a rafter. "Well, it's tempting to believe in miracles. What do you believe? Does Jacobi have anything to do with Stuart getting better?"

"Jacobi? No. His meteorite? Yes. Something definitely happened when that rock got zapped."

"Chloe, Stuart had seizures before."

"None that were followed by a complete recovery from cancer! Clark, most of the strange things that happen around here turn out to have some connection to those green glow-in-the-dark meteorite crystals. I can't believe that this is just a coincidence. *Jacobi* is a fake, but the weirdness effect is *real*. That's why I say he's just *exploiting* the meteorites." Chloe started playing with the ends of her hair. It was a nervous habit that Clark had noticed before. She fell into it only when she was especially upset.

"Hey, don't take it so hard. It's not as if this is your fault."

"No?" Chloe gave a sardonic laugh. "Would Jacobi have come here in the first place if he hadn't read my website?"

"Who knows?" Clark threw up his hands. "He already had a space rock that came from Lowell County, so he must have known something about the area. He probably would have shown up around here sooner or later."

"Well, yeah . . ."

"And if Jacobi hadn't shown up, then maybe Stu Harrison wouldn't be getting better right now. Look, let's assume that Stuart's recovery *is* an example of the weirdness effect. Without Jacobi, what are the odds that Stu would have encountered a meteorite crystal *and* a malfunctioning laser?"

Chloe brightened a bit. "Probably zero. I hadn't thought of that. Clark, that is an excellent point." She scowled. "But that still doesn't let Jacobi off the hook. This whole Foundation business still smells. I *hate* it that they're using the local weirdness to soak people for a lot of money. *I feel exploited.*"

"I hear that. But if Jacobi and his Foundation are really as slimy as you think, chances are you're not the only one who's noticed. Sooner or later, they're going to slip up."

"I hope so."

"C'mon, cheer up. You know they will." Chloe started to smile, and Clark put a hand on her shoulder. "And when they do, I'm sure you'll have an exposé ready!"

Chloe gazed dreamily up into his face. "You really think so?"

"Uh . . . sure." Suddenly aware of his hand, Clark eased it off and away from her shoulder. "We've been friends since—what?—middle school?"

"Right, middle school." Chloe glanced away momentarily.

"Chloe, in all that time, I've never once known you to give up on anything."

"No, I guess I never have." She playfully punched Clark's triceps, and they exchanged grins. "And if I'm going to have that exposé ready, I'd better start digging deeper."

"Just don't dig yourself in *too* deep."

"What, me worry?" Chloe's grin twisted a little at one end. "If I find myself getting in a hole, I know you'll be around to throw me a rope." She paused at the top of the stairs. "Thanks, Clark. Thanks for listening."

"Anytime."

He stood at the top of the stair, watching her go. Clark liked Chloe, he really did, but he felt she sometimes took this reporter business a little too seriously. She was always prying into things like some small-town Woodward or Bernstein. *Chloe probably won't be satisfied until she lands a job with a major newspaper.* Clark shook his head. He admired her drive, and he enjoyed occasionally helping her chase down stories, but he couldn't understand why she would want to make a career of it.

Clark turned and crossed the barn's upper level to the open loft door. For several minutes, he just stared out at the stars. *Astrophysics, now* that *would be an awesome career.* The night sky had always intrigued Clark, and learning that he had come from somewhere out there had only increased the fascination. He was swiveling his telescope around, to check out a star in Ursa Minor, when he caught a glimpse of movement out of the corner of his eye. Looking down, he saw Martha waving at him from a window, and he waved back. *Thanks for the fast heads-up on Chloe, Mom! I'd have had a hard time explaining how I could play basketball with myself.* Behind him, a creaking step sounded in the stillness of the loft.

Clark turned around, smiling. "You forget something—?"

He froze with his mouth half-open.

The figure on the stairs wasn't Chloe.

It was Lana.

CHAPTER 11

Lana looked up at him in surprise. "I don't think I've ever left anything here. Have I?"

"Uh, no . . . not you . . . uh . . ."

"Were you expecting someone else?"

"Yes. No! I mean . . ." Clark thought fast. "My mom had called up from below a few minutes ago. I thought that maybe she had come looking for something. But it wasn't her . . . it's you!"

"Ah!" Lana nodded her acceptance. Still, she seemed uncertain. "I haven't come at a bad time, have I?"

"Not at all." Clark realized that he was staring at her and broke it off, afraid that he was making her uncomfortable. "What brings you out tonight? Something on your mind?"

"Definitely." Lana exhaled the word, the relief in her voice overcoming the uncertainty. "I was out walking, and I saw your light on up here, and I thought . . . !"

"Sure. Here, have a seat." Clark spread an old horse blanket over the worn cushions of the couch. "Take a load off and tell me what's wrong."

She settled back and started over. "It's sort of complicated. Everything has been so crazy since last Friday."

"For just about everybody."

Lana nodded. "Nell is in such a state! She was all gaga over that Dr. Jacobi until Friday night's performance. That really shook her up. But now that Stuart's condition is improving, she's getting all schoolgirly again. It's much worse this time. She spent all day yesterday volunteering at the Foundation Compound. And this afternoon, I caught her sending Jacobi flowers and a little note." A shiver ran across her shoulders.

"Are you getting cold, Lana? I think there's another blanket here somewhere."

"Hmm? Oh, no. It's just that for a second there, I imagined Jacobi becoming my new 'uncle.'" She managed to repress a second shiver. "Nell is spending so much time at the Compound. And she's given Jacobi so much money! Money that should be going back into her flower shop, or into the Talon. It's all so weird. It's as if our roles have suddenly reversed. I'm really getting worried about Nell, but if I try to say anything, she insists that I just don't understand. She gets very defensive about Jacobi. It's almost as if he's put a spell on her."

Lana fell silent, staring out the loft door at the night sky. Clark remembered what Chloe had said about the returning faithful, and felt uneasy. Lana's worries about Nell put more of a human face on the problem. *I'm beginning to understand why Chloe got so worked up.*

"Lana, for what it's worth, not everyone is entranced by Donald Jacobi." He briefly summarized his conversation with Chloe (not mentioning how recently it had occurred or where). "It's like I told Chloe—if she's seen through him, other people will, too."

"I hope so. Maybe I should talk with Chloe myself, share what I know."

"Maybe. I just wish I could do more to help you."

"Well, if you think of some magical way to bring Nell to her senses, let me be the first to know. Seriously, Clark, you've already been a big help. At least you didn't tell me to just ignore Nell."

"Who would tell you that?"

"Oh . . . Whitney." She shook her head. "He thinks I'm getting upset over nothing. He keeps telling me that I should

just block Nell out and go on with my own life. That's easy
for him to say. But he didn't block things out when his father's health got so bad—he *obsessed* over it. What Whitney
blocked out were his friends. At first, he wouldn't talk about
it at all . . . not even to me!"

"I remember. He gave all of us the silent treatment." *Until
I called him on it.*

Whitney had been uncommonly withdrawn, not wanting
to discuss his father's health problems with anyone. The
quarterback had indeed shut it all in, and shut everyone else
out. He'd so alienated Lana that she'd started paying more
attention to Clark. *But then, I found out about his dad's heart
condition. I couldn't take advantage of that. I kept thinking
how I'd feel if* my *dad became seriously ill.*

Clark would have rather discussed anything other than
Whitney Fordman, but it was obvious how much this had
upset Lana. And he couldn't stand to see her that way.

"Whitney's still pretty worried about his father, Lana. You
can't expect him to think straight about other people's problems with their parents. They must all seem pretty minor to
him, at least, compared with what he's facing. When Whitney tells you to just ignore Nell's . . . interest in Dr. Jacobi,
maybe it's because he can see his mom being widowed
soon . . . and marrying again. I can't imagine he likes to
think about that too much."

"I suppose you're right." Lana canted her head at Clark.
"In fact, I'm sure you are. How did you get to be so perceptive, anyway?"

"I don't think I'm all *that* perceptive."

"*I* do. How do you do it? What's your secret?"

I've had lots of practice studying "normal" people. I only
look *normal. I'm not even human, I'm just passing.* He
wasn't ready to tell her that. "Maybe it has to do with my
being an only child."

"I'm an only child, too, but I feel so clueless sometimes."

"Doesn't everybody?" Clark scratched his head. "Being perceptive? I don't know, maybe it has to do with the way my folks brought me up. We've always been close. In a way, I feel almost as much a part of their generation as I do of ours. It gives you a different view of things."

"I have to admit, you do have two of the coolest parents."

"Yeah, I really lucked out." He smiled. "I've learned a lot just being around them, working alongside them."

"Oh? Like what?"

"I'm not sure where to start." Clark rested one foot on the bale of straw. "They've shown me how to anticipate things . . . and how to cooperate. You have to when you're living and working on a farm." He plucked a few straws loose and rubbed them between his fingers. "This stuff didn't bale itself, you know."

"No, I suppose not." There was a grave tone to Lana's voice, but a sly smile on her lips. "Then it's more of a farm perspective?"

"I never thought of it that way, but—yeah. You have to stay aware of what's happening around you. You have to know when to rotate your crops and replenish the soil—just wishing the minerals back won't cut it. You really learn a lot about cause and effect."

Outside a cow mooed plaintively, and Clark had to laugh. "There's another example. Even if you've chosen good bloodlines, you still have to watch after that newborn calf like a hawk if you want to raise a real gold-medal winner. And even then there's no guarantee."

"The farm as an allegory for life . . . !" Lana leaned forward, resting her forearms across her knees. "It seems so obvious, once you mention it."

"Yeah, it does—doesn't it?" Clark looked intrigued by his own train of thought. "You have to work hard, but that's not enough by itself. You have to work smart, too. And sometimes, despite all your planning and all your hard work, things still go wrong. It doesn't rain. Or it rains too much. Or you get exactly the right amount—but instead of rain, it falls as hail or snow and wipes out the crops you just planted."

"That sounds so frustrating. It must feel like the whole universe is out to get you."

"Oh, sure. But you can't let yourself dwell on that, because it isn't. Out to get you, I mean. If there's one thing I've learned from Mom and Dad, it's that the universe doesn't really care, one way or the other. It's just the way things turn out sometimes." Clark pushed back from the bale. "It might be your responsibility to help out afterwards, but it's nobody's fault that it happened."

"No. Because sometimes, things simply go wrong." Lana nodded slowly, more seriously now. "Sometimes people get very ill for no good reason. Even good people, like Stuart Harrison." She slid forward to the edge of the couch, clasping her hands together, almost as if in prayer. "And sometimes . . . sometimes people are just in the wrong place at the wrong time. Like my mom and dad were."

"Lana . . ."

"It's okay." She glanced down at the floor briefly to compose herself. "You know, I've often fantasized about what a glamorous life I would have had, if they hadn't died. That we would have lived in a fabulous town house in Metropolis, or traveled the world." There was a sparkle in her eyes, as she turned to face Clark. "But then I stop and think . . . no. They owned acres and acres of fine, fertile land in the middle of Kansas. I would have grown up a farmer's daughter . . . and that would have been just fine." Lana rose from the couch and walked toward Clark. "When I hear you talk about farm life, it gives me just the tiniest hint of what my life might really have been like."

"I'm sorry if I—!"

"No." She put a finger to his lips. "Don't be. It's a nice fantasy. I like imagining myself living on a farm."

"I've never had to imagine that. It's been all around me for as long as I can remember. My fantasy was always to go out into the world in search of adventure. But maybe you're on to something. Maybe everything we need is right here . . ."

Lana stood very close to Clark now, gazing up into his eyes. The loft grew quiet. He slowly leaned forward.

And the silence was suddenly split by a melodious warbling from Lana's pocket.

"Ohhh—!" Lana angrily pulled a tiny cell phone from her pocket and flipped it open. "Hello? Yes, Nell, I'm fine." She rolled her eyes heavenward. "I was just taking a walk to clear my head. Uh-huh. No, I'll be home soon. All right. Bye."

"Technology!" There was exasperation in Lana's voice as she folded the phone away. "Sorry, I thought I'd turned it off."

"That's . . . all right," Clark lied.

"I should probably be going."

A million words flew through Clark's brain. He tried desperately to find the ones that would persuade Lana to stay there with him, even if for just a few minutes longer.

But what he said was, "Sure."

Clark followed after her to the top of the stairs. "I'm sorry I wasn't much help in solving your problems."

"I didn't really expect to find a solution . . . just a sympathetic ear." Lana smiled softly, and his heart melted. "I always feel better, talking these things out loud. Thanks, Clark. You're a good friend."

"Any time, Lana."

Clark leaned over the rail, watching her descend the stairs, much like a drowning man watches a ship disappear over the horizon. He resisted the temptation to stare through the loft floor after her. He turned and mentally cursed himself in every way he could think of, for not being more helpful, more charming . . . for failing to make her forget all about Whitney Fordman. If he could just do that . . .

In a heartbeat, Clark could see it all: He and Lana could get married and help the folks with the farm. Eventually, they could buy part of the acreage and expand onto adjoining property. Maybe buy some of Nell's land. Their future together unfolded before his eyes, and it looked just perfect to him.

Caught up in his thoughts, he missed the sound of footsteps behind him.

"Ahem."

Clark spun around, to find Martha standing at the top of the stairs. "Mom? What . . . ?"

"I just thought I'd see if I could interest you in joining your father and me for some popcorn. Or are you expecting more young women tonight?"

"Uh, no." Clark looked around. "No, I doubt it."

Martha raised an eyebrow. "Something wrong, Clark?"

"I was just . . . daydreaming. You've heard of people having a mental flashback?"

"Yes . . . ?"

"I think I may have just had a flash-*forward*."

Late Wednesday afternoon, a white van bearing a WMET News logo pulled into the main drive of the Smallville Medical Center. It progressed no more than thirty feet before it was met by a Lowell County deputy sheriff.

The van's driver rolled down his window as the deputy approached, clipboard in hand. "There a problem, Officer?"

"No problem." The deputy added the van's license number to the list on his clipboard. "Just trying to make sure the emergency lanes stay clear. You're from Metropolis, right?"

"Right. Ed Dixon, WMET."

From the passenger's seat, a smartly dressed woman leaned across, favoring the deputy with her best on-air smile. "Hello, I'm Kelly McDonald. We're running a little behind. We're here to cover—!"

"I know why you're here." The deputy finished annotating his list and used his pen to point out a side road. "Bear left there and keep going till you reach a stand of trees. The north lot is just beyond it. You'll see the staging area when you get there."

Ed followed the deputy's instructions and soon came upon the wooded area. Just past the trees, he braked the van to a stop, his eyes blinking in amazement. "Looks like we've got ourselves a little competition, Kelly."

A line of vehicles stretched out before them, each bearing the logo of a radio or television station from a different city. Kelly read them off as they drove past the occupied spaces. "Dallas . . . Amarillo . . . Wichita . . . Denver . . . Chicago? They must've driven all day. Look, Ed—CNN is here!"

Ed shook his head as he eased the van into an empty slot. "I'll bet there haven't been this many reporters in these parts since '89."

"Tell me about it." Kelly flipped open a mirror and checked her teeth for errant bits of food. "This may be a bigger story than we thought. Come on, we'd better hurry."

Ed shouldered his camcorder, tossed Kelly a microphone,

and the two of them rushed to join a throng of newspeople clustered in front of the little hospital's main entrance.

"Hey, Kelly!" A lean, sinewy form fell in alongside her. "Here to interview the Miracle Boy?"

Any lingering remnant of Kelly's on-air smile dissolved. "Hello, Nixon. I never expected to see you out in the hinterland. I would have thought this story was too wholesome for the *Inquisitor*."

"You wound me, Kelly."

"Don't make me wish for things I can't have, Roger."

Roger Nixon gave a sharp, barking laugh. "This story is right up my alley. Terminal kid goes to a tent meeting, gets cured—that's page one for sure! Yeah, you'd be surprised at some of the stories I've dug up around here."

"Heads up!" Ed swung his camcorder around. "Here they come."

Glass double doors slid open with a soft pneumatic whisper, and a small group emerged from the hospital. Flanked by his parents, Stuart Harrison strode up the concrete walk toward the gauntlet of microphones and camera lenses.

"Stuart!"

"Over here, son!"

"How's it feel to have a new lease on life?"

"What are your plans—?"

"To what do you attribute—?"

"QUIET!" Ray Harrison thrust out a big, beefy hand. His unexpected bellow momentarily silenced the reporters. "That's better! Now, if you'll all just hold your horses, my son has something he'd like to say. Stu . . . ?"

"Hi, folks." Stuart took a step forward, raising his hand in a shy, casual wave. "I wasn't sure I wanted a big send-off like this, but . . . well, when you get the kind of lucky break I did, I guess it's important that everybody hear about it. So that, maybe, other people might have a chance to share in that luck. But, first off, I'd like to thank Dr. Manning and everybody at the hospital. They've always been super to me . . . even if they did want me to spend a couple more days here."

Stuart grinned at his mother. She smiled back at him through teary eyes.

Kelly McDonald jumped into the lull. "So you're going home early?"

"Doesn't seem too early to me!" Stuart's honest retort raised a few hearty laughs from the reporters. "I feel healthy, and all the tests say that I'm healthy. Once my temperature dropped to normal, they couldn't give me any reason why I should stay. No good reason, anyway."

"Then, it's true that your tumors are no longer considered life-threatening?"

"They're *gone!*" Stuart patted the top of his head. "It's just like they were never there. And I owe it all to this man back here. Dr. Jacobi—?"

As Stuart called his name, Jacobi stepped forward. He had been standing just behind the Harrisons, all but unnoticed by the reporters until now. Stuart shook Jacobi's hand.

"Doc, I owe you the world's biggest apology. Last Friday night, I think I was angrier than I've ever been. Dad just about dragged Mom and me to your lecture. I didn't want to go. I thought you were a big phony, and I still felt that way when I went up onstage. I figured that, even if it was the last thing I'd ever do, I'd show you up." Stuart's eyes started to tear up. "But I was wrong. You cured me! I'm here to tell the world that you saved my life! Thank you . . . thank you!"

Camera shutters clicked like hyperactive crickets as Stuart hugged Jacobi to him and Ray Harrison embraced his wife, both of them weeping freely, joyously. Many of the reporters and camera operators began to blink back tears.

"No, Stuart. I didn't save your life. I merely supplied the

means, the opportunity." Jacobi continued to look at Stuart, but projected his voice so that the waiting microphones picked up every word. "But I didn't know if it would work. That's why I called it an experiment."

He gazed out into the sea of cameras. "Any reputable scientist will tell you that most experiments end in failure. My initial tests with a meteorite fragment—from this very area—had indicated that it produced subtle energies which could provide significant health benefits."

Jacobi put his arm around Stuart's shoulders and turned him so they both faced the cameras. "This brave young man's condition was so grave, so serious, that I decided to take a chance. Admittedly, it was a spur-of-the-moment decision. At best, I hoped that I might alleviate some of the terrible stress on his system, give his body a chance to fight back against his disease."

The lens of a CNN camera moved in close, and Jacobi addressed it directly. "What we got was a breakthrough greater than any I have ever experienced in any laboratory. It was a wonderful, magnificent accident—a true 'Eureka Moment'!"

Jacobi turned back to Stuart. "My boy, you thanked me— but I'm the one who should be thanking you. I've been working for years to find a way to unlock the energies bound up in that meteorite. Friday night, we found it together! We didn't just destroy your tumors, we've found the next rung of the great cosmic ladder that will lift humanity to a higher level. Now I at last know how to proceed with the work of the Foundation. We stand on the threshold of a new golden age, all thanks to you!"

Stuart smiled. "It's like you said, Doc, we never know what we can accomplish until we try."

CHAPTER 12

Dawn was especially clear Thursday morning over Metropolis. A gentle west wind had blown away the usual morning haze, and the sunlight glistened off the giant globe atop the Daily Planet Building, turning it into a golden beacon. In the offices below, night watchmen punched out, turning their keys and their monitor stations over to the morning crew. Garbage trucks rumbled through the streets at a tortoiselike pace, scooping up the refuse of the previous day, trying to complete their rounds before the worst of the rush hour traffic arrived.

As the city awoke, a long black limousine sped down Bessolo Boulevard. It braked briefly for a red light at Clinton Street before turning right. Three blocks down, a step van tossed off bundles of the *Daily Planet*'s early edition in front of Shayne's News-of-the-World. And, as he had for over half a century, Old Pop Shayne grabbed the papers and hauled them over to his newsstand. He was just snipping the wire from the first bundle when the limo glided to a halt at the curb and flashed its lights.

"Awright, awready! I'm comin'."

Pop fished a fresh, wrinkle-free copy of the morning's *Planet* from the middle of the bundle, as per his customer's preferences, and shuffled over to the curb. The tinted glass rolled down with a barely audible whir, and a well-manicured hand thrust out a crisp new twenty-dollar bill. Pop exchanged the newspaper for the twenty and began to rummage through the pouch pockets of the old canvas apron at his waist. The hand waited patiently, as Shayne counted out his change.

"Five . . . and ten makes twenty. Here ya go—!"

The hand withdrew, the window slid shut, and the limo pulled away from the curb. Pop watched it go for a bit, then spat in its general direction.

"And a good mornin' to you, too, Mr. Luthor!"

A man wearing a hard hat looked up from the stand's display of sports magazines and shook his head. "Rich guy like that, you'd think he could at least leave you a tip."

"Lionel Luthor? He *does* tip. Always pays me double to get an unwrinkled paper. But that ain't the point." Pop started moving the rest of the *Planet*s onto the shelf. "He could still spare the time to say 'Good morning'."

"Well, sure. Why not?" The Hard-Hat scooped up a paper and handed Shayne a dollar. "That don't cost anything."

Pop took one last glance in the direction of the departed limo. "You wouldn't think so, would ya?"

In the back of the limousine, Lionel Luthor flipped through the paper, barely glancing at the front page, searching for one particular story.

"So . . . it made the national news once again." There was bile in his voice as he folded the pages back to display a three-column wire service photo of Stuart Harrison and Donald Jacobi. "Nearly half a page in the *Planet*. And I can just imagine how the *Inquisitor* is handling it." Lionel skimmed over the text. "It probably would have rated even more space here if Congress wasn't in full dudgeon over the new finance bill. Do you see that final paragraph, Damian?"

"Yes, Mr. L." Damian Marco perched uncomfortably on a jump seat, facing his boss.

"Read it." Lionel smacked the paper against his aide's chest. "Aloud."

Damian cleared his throat. He hated to read aloud. He'd hated it ever since stumbling through recitation in Sister

Mary Katherine's second-grade class, and he knew that he wasn't going to like it any more today. "Jacobi also announced that the Ascendance Foundation would embark immediately on a major fund-raising drive. 'We intend to purchase land in Lowell County for the construction of an Institute for Advanced Meteorite Research. We will be collecting—'"

"That's far enough, Damian." Lionel sat back and steepled his fingers. "Do you know what land he plans to buy?"

Damian knew the answer all too well. "The Davis property, Mr. L."

"Yes, the Davis property! Jacobi and Wolfe already have a lease with an option to buy. They're going to buy the property their Foundation has already occupied. The property I wanted. That I *still* want."

"Mr. L, I've been working night and day to dig up dirt on Jacobi, but he's like Teflon. And his partner's practically a cipher. I can't find anything that would—!"

Lionel grabbed the knot of Damian's tie, twisted it, and pulled him closer. "Everyone has a past, Damian. You can't tell me that these sideshow charlatans don't have some dirt in theirs." He shoved the man back against the left rear door of the limo. "Get out."

"Sir?"

The limo came to a stop. "Jacobi and his Foundation are an intolerable problem. I don't want to see you again until that problem is solved." Lionel pressed a button on the console at his side. The left rear door powered open, and Damian tumbled out onto the pavement. As he scrambled to his feet, he could see Lionel staring out at him.

"Do not fail me again."

The door swung shut, and the limo moved on, leaving Damian alone and shaking in the middle of the street.

From Thursday's regional edition of the *Metropolis Inquisitor* . . .

MIRACLE BOY GOES HOME
Cops Return 'Miracle Meteor' to Doc
By Roger Nixon

SMALLVILLE—Stuart Harrison's first cancer surgery came when he was just in middle school. The doctors carved away a chunk of his scalp and crossed their fingers. But early last year, Harrison was back under the knife again.

This time, the surgeons had to open up his skull and remove an ugly malignancy that was growing in his brain. They seeded the inside of his head with radioactive isotopes before closing it up, and put him through a round of chemotherapy. But it wasn't enough. The tumors came back. The best oncologists in the state of Kansas had met their match.

But last week, in a tent set up in the middle of corn country, Stu Harrison's life was saved by a chunk of rock that had fallen from the sky when he was just a boy.

"It's a miracle," said his mother, Mary, who lives with her son and husband in a split-level home on the outskirts of Smallville. "The tumors are just gone. His doctors can't explain it, but I don't care. I have my boy back."

The cancer specialists may be at a loss, but Stuart's father, Ray, isn't. He told the *Inquisitor* that he took his family to that tent Friday night, to a lecture given by the geneticist Dr. Donald Jacobi, in hope of finding help for his son.

"I'd read up on Dr. Jacobi's work, and heard him speak a couple of nights before. I would've taken Stu to his Thursday night seminar if I'd had the cash," Ray admitted. "Jacobi's coming to Smallville was a sign. He was the best chance we had."

Jacobi, who works on behalf of the Ascendance Foundation, downplays his own role in Harrison's miracle recovery. "I was guiding Stuart through a series of imaging exercises, using a small meteorite as a focal device, when a laser in our video projection system malfunctioned," he said. "The coherent light beam activated elements within the meteorite, causing a release of energy. And that, in turn, triggered a reaction within Stuart's tissues. It was the happiest of happy accidents, even though it all appeared quite frightening at the time."

Local authorities immediately impounded Jacobi's meteorite and rushed Stuart Harrison to the Smallville Medical Center in a feverish state. But as his fever broke, it was clear that his condition had dramatically improved.

Yesterday, less than six days after he was admitted, Stuart walked out of the hospital cancer-free.

What are his plans now? "I'm actually looking forward to going back to school. I've missed out on a lot of studies, but if I buckle down, I can still graduate with my class." And after graduation? "I'd like to help Doc Jacobi and the Foundation with their work."

If Stuart does eventually assist the doctor, he won't have far to go. Upon Harrison's release from the hospital, Jacobi announced that the Ascendance Foundation plans to open an Institute for Advanced Meteorite Research outside Smallville later this year. "The State Police have completed their investigation of the accident and have returned my meteorite sample," said Jacobi. "While the Foundation will continue to study that sample, we look forward to expanding our research. We will be collecting many more samples of the meteorites of Lowell County, in hopes of finding new ways to eradicate disease and improve the quality of life."

◆◆◆

Martha Kent had just come inside from changing a fan belt on the truck when the phone started ringing. Hurriedly wiping her hands with a paper towel, she snapped up the handset on the third ring.

"Hello?"

There came the sound of papers rattling at the other end of the line. "Mrs., uh . . . Kent?"

"Yes?" Martha stretched the word out an extra syllable. The hesitation in her caller's voice had her suspicious.

"My name is Andy March. How are you today?"

"Fine. If this is about—!"

"I'm a member of the Ascendance Foundation. As you may know, we're trying to increase our store of meteorite fragments for the—!"

"Stop right there!" Martha could feel what her grandmother would have called her Irish rising. She took a quick breath and went on. "I'm sorry, but I can't help you. We don't have any meteors here."

"Probably none that you're aware of, I'm sure. But I understand that your land covers quite a few acres. There could be fragments buried all over."

"I doubt that. This is a working farm, and our plows would have dug them up long ago."

"Well, some might have escaped your notice, you know. I'd like to come out and go over your—!"

"No, Mr. March." There was flint in Martha's voice. "Our property is clearly posted—no trespassing is, or will be, allowed. Please make a note of that. And I'd appreciate it if you'd add this number to your no-call list. This is the third call from your group that I've answered today, and I don't care to get any more."

"Uh—!"

Martha clicked off the phone and just stopped herself from slamming it down. Her mother had always been a stickler on phone etiquette, and Martha usually felt a slight twinge of guilt whenever she hung up on someone. But not this time. She took another deep breath and counted to ten before she trusted herself to place the handset back in its cradle. Martha turned and stalked out the back door, pausing only long enough to pull a pair of old boots on over her shoes.

Jonathan Kent was out behind the barn, hitching a manure spreader to the tractor, when he spied his wife headed his way. "Martha . . . ?" He knew something was up from the force of her step. As she drew nearer, he could see that the red of her face was halfway to matching that of her hair. "What is it? What's wrong?"

"It's those Foundation idiots! They keep calling and calling, wanting to hunt for meteorites on our farm! And we're not alone. They've been calling every farm in the area, as far as I can tell! The Tuckers, the Roudebushes—"

Jonathan didn't say a word. His wife didn't show her temper often, and never without good cause. He'd learned long ago that, on these rare occasions, it was best to let her get it out of her system.

"—the Mosbaughs, the Wilsons. Oh, the Wilsons!" Martha's eyes flashed. "Most of our neighbors have had the good sense to turn them down, but not the Wilsons! They offered to let the meteorite hunters on their land for ten dollars a person and twenty-five for each rock they find. I swear, if I live to be a hundred, I will never talk to that Freida Wilson again!"

Well then, at least some good will come of this. Jonathan stood in awe, recognizing in his wife's tirade the same fierceness that a mother bear would display in defense of her cub.

"I can't believe the greed of some people—the sheer, unthinking greed! They don't care who they hurt. Just *one* of those damned rocks can make Clark sick. Too many might kill him!"

"They don't know that, Martha." Jonathan drew her into his arms and held her tight. "We didn't know until just a few months ago. And we don't dare tell anybody."

"It's all so frustrating. Isn't there anything we can do to stop this?"

"Not that I can think of. The EPA declared the meteorites harmless years ago, so no one's been afraid of them. And now, Jacobi's beating the drum to convince people that they're good for you. I don't know how we'll ever convince people otherwise. Not without drawing a lot of unwanted attention to Clark."

Martha sank into her husband's embrace. "I wish we could gather up all of those rocks and send them back where they came from."

"Me too, hon. Me too. Still, if Jacobi's stooges can find most of the meteorites and consolidate them all in one place, it might make them easier for Clark to avoid." Jonathan held out his palms as his wife gave him a frown that would curdle milk. "Just looking for the silver lining."

"Well, they'd just better keep their meteor-rocks far away from our son." Martha folded her arms. "And I swear, if they call me one more time, I'm going to reach through that phone and yank out their tonsils!"

Jonathan just nodded gravely. *Whatever you say, Momma Bear. Whatever you say.*

◆◆◆

"'The Institute for Advanced Meteorite Research'! Well, that's just marvelous!" Dr. Hamilton crumpled the newspaper clipping into a ball and tossed it the general direction of an overflowing wastebasket.

Lex retrieved the wad of paper as it tumbled from the refuse pile. "I thought you'd want to keep on top of what the competition is doing."

"Competition?" Hamilton grimaced as he repeated the word. It seemed to leave a bad taste in his mouth. "I suppose that's what it is, now. Unfortunately, splashy fringe types like Jacobi often make it harder for unconventional topics to get serious study and funding. Few scientists have wealthy patrons these days, and I can't do all the work myself."

"You sound as though you're convinced there's a lot more to investigate here." Lex smoothed the crumpled paper over a corner of a lab table. "Do you think it's possible that the meteorites could have major beneficial effects?"

"Possible? Yes. But almost certainly not at the grandiose levels that Jacobi claims. The problem is, that's what people respond to. It's an age-old scenario: Snake-oil salesman comes to town, cures sick boy, gets his name in all the papers, then sits back to bask in the glory and rake in the cash."

"Funny, I never took you for a man who was all that interested in glory." Lex cocked an eyebrow at Hamilton. "And the first time I offered you money, you showed me the door."

"'Glory'?" Hamilton waved a hand dismissively. "I had a

small taste of fame once upon a time. Nice, but not very filling. And, of course, it didn't last. It rarely does." He plucked
a pair of safety glasses from a rack above a cluttered lab
table. "In the last half of the twentieth century, Jonas Salk
probably saved more lives than any other man then alive.
Today, his is just the name on a vaccine that too many people take for granted, if they think of it at all. No, the world
can keep its fame."

"And money?"

"Ah, yes. Money. That other great intoxicant." Hamilton
set the safety glasses on the bridge of his nose. "I can't
imagine what it must have been like for you, Luthor, growing up the son of a billionaire. All that money . . . I wonder
how well you would fare without it?"

"No doubt a question my father has pondered many
times."

Hamilton glared at him through the safety glasses, but
Lex wore a perfect poker face. The scientist shrugged and
went on. "I myself grew to adulthood with relatively simple
tastes. During my career in academia, I enjoyed several
flush years, but I never lived above my means. As a result,
when all the grant money evaporated, I was able to afford
this modest facility." He gestured to the barn around them.
"Hardly state-of-the-art, but it allowed me to continue my
work after a fashion. No, Luthor, money is merely another
tool to me—a means, not an end."

"An admirable philosophy, Doctor. Tell me, why did you
finally change your mind about the . . . quality of the tool I
offered you?"

"Don't play coy, Luthor. You know damn well why! Your
spies dug up dirt on my past indiscretions. You could have
made life in this small town very difficult for me. Instead,
you offered funding and autonomy, and I needed both to
begin the next step in my research."

Something in the scientist's tone caught Lex's attention. "You've found something?"

"Perhaps. Consider: The meteorites have been linked to unexpected—sometimes bizarre—changes in several individuals. As even 'Doctor' Jacobi pointed out, most people have not been affected at all. This suggests something subtle. Each change was unique, which clearly suggests that other factors, different for each person, were involved." *Maybe even effluent from the LuthorCorp fertilizer plant.*

"But it also suggests that some odd new factor, something not previously part of the human equation, is at work. And I think I might have discovered that factor."

Lex frowned. "You've found out how the meteorites affect human beings?"

"No, no. Working out the exact mechanism is a long ways off. But I think I know why the occasional odd effect is so *very* odd. Look at this." Hamilton tapped the keys of his computer, and a long list of elements appeared on his monitor screen, each name accompanied by a set of graphics.

"Very colorful, Doctor, but it just looks like several rows of broken rainbows to me. What does it mean?"

"This is a spectrographic analysis of one of the meteorites I've been studying." Hamilton mouse-clicked on the top two listed items, highlighting and enlarging that section of the display. "These first two show the presence of the usual suspects—iron and nickel, quite common in meteorites." He scrolled down the screen. "Here are some traces of copper, zinc, carbon. Now, these lines down here are interesting." He indicated a graph just below the listing for carbon. "They indicate unusually high levels of krypton."

"Krypton?"

"An inert gas. It's used commercially in fluorescent lamps, flash tubes, and some thermopane windows."

"I know what it is, Doctor. Why is it there in such quantity?"

"There must have been large concentrations of the gas where the meteors were formed. At any rate, these are all indications of known elements, commonly found on Earth. Ah, but *this* one." Hamilton scrolled to the bottom of the listing. "This is something else altogether." Another click enlarged the final listing, the spectrograph of "Unknown."

"It's still just lines to me. Now they're bigger lines. What does it mean?"

Hamilton looked at Lex pensively. "It could indicate contamination, or perhaps a mixture that didn't completely separate out. But if I'm very, very lucky, it could mean that I have discovered a new element."

"A new *element*?" Lex glanced from the computer screen to a huge poster of the periodic table that was tacked up to a partition wall. "As in 'hydrogen, helium, and lithium'?"

"Precisely. We may have to set a new place at the Table."

Lex groaned.

"Seriously, I'll want to repeat the experiment—and I'll need to run additional tests before I can be certain—but if it is a new element as I suspect, I would peg its atomic number at one-twenty-six."

"One—?" Lex's eyes widened. "One-*hundred*-twenty-six? I thought that naturally occurring elements went up to only about ninety."

"Ninety-two, actually. That's uranium. We've created over a dozen heavier elements in the lab, all of them radioactive, and most of them highly unstable. But this . . . this goes far beyond them. If it truly exists, this particular one would be classified as a super-actinide. Radioactive, of course, but with a relatively long half-life." Hamilton tapped the screen and seemed almost about to smile. "It's long been theorized that certain superheavy transuranic elements could exist. Elements where the atoms had a so-called magic number of protons in the nucleus." Now, Hamilton did smile. "One-twenty-six is one of those magic numbers."

"I'll take your word for that, Doctor. But if you're right, why hasn't this been discovered before? I've read the reports issued by the Environmental Protection Agency and the National Science Foundation, and neither mentioned any significant radiation."

"I believe the exact wording was 'no significant increase over background radiation.' And that's absolutely correct, actually, but it's of no particular consequence here. Finding evidence of an entirely new element is another matter altogether from measuring overall radiation. Why didn't anyone else discover this? I honestly don't know."

Hamilton looked contemplative. "Some very accomplished scientists took part in the initial studies. It's possible that their samples contained isotopes of this element that were more unstable. If that was the case, those isotopes might have broken down into other elements before they could be detected."

Lex thought about that. "So you're saying that they might simply have been unlucky?"

"It happens. Bad luck is annoyingly common in the sciences. When 'Doctor' Jacobi told the media that most experiments end in failure, he was—for once—speaking the plain, unvarnished truth. If I have indeed found a new element, it has come only after years of study. And, of course, the new equipment was a huge help." Hamilton gestured toward the burnished metal case of an apparatus mounted on a nearby metal test stand.

"It's ironic. The Smallville meteor shower prompted a flood of new research dollars, but only a trickle of that money has gone toward the actual study of recovered fragments. Most of the funding has been routed to finding ways to prevent future impacts." He held up one hand. "Don't get me wrong. Impact prevention studies are long overdue. Even now, we remain vulnerable to meteor and asteroid strikes . . . as vulnerable as the dinosaurs were. All my work—all of *everyone's* work—could be wiped out in a single strike."

"Let's hope it doesn't come to that." Lex looked back at the screen. "At any rate, I'm glad that I was able to add to the 'trickle.' What's next?"

"As I said, repeating my experiments and running additional tests. I must be certain of my results. Some years ago, a research team thought that they had found a new superheavy element in a meteor, but their original results couldn't be duplicated." Hamilton stroked his chin. "And I should try to refine a purer form of the element from the raw ore. But to do that, I'm going to require more meteorites. And that is where I now face unwanted competition." He paused to light a Bunsen burner. "Jacobi has his addle-brained followers scouring the countryside for any rock that even looks like it might have fallen from the sky."

"Yes." Lex looked again at the newspaper clipping. "This does come at a bad time."

"That is what galls me the most. It took me years to get to this point, and now . . . !" Hamilton scowled. "Jacobi is a fraud. He doesn't have a clue as to what he's really playing with, but that doesn't make him any less of a threat. If he continues to pursue this 'Institute' of his, he could set my work back years!"

"Don't worry. I have people looking into Jacobi's operation, and I suspect that I'm not the only one. You just continue with your research, and let me handle this." Lex handed the clipping back to Hamilton, and turned to go. At the door, he looked back. "By the way, Doctor, you're right about Jacobi. He has no idea what he's playing with."

Hamilton watched in silence as Lex exited the laboratory. He weighed the tattered newspaper clipping in his hand.

And then, he fed it to his Bunsen burner.

CHAPTER 13

On the inside, it appeared to be just another Friday at Smallville High School. Attendance was taken and quizzes given. Surreptitious notes were passed in the study halls. The principal's office distributed the usual number of tardy slips to all of the usual latecomers. The cafeteria even featured a choice of fish cakes or macaroni with meat sauce for lunch.

The students and teachers of SHS tried their best to go about their normal routine. But there was no way that this Friday could ever be normal. This was the day that Stuart Harrison returned to classes.

Clark had missed the bus that morning and arrived on foot, only to find over a dozen reporters huddled together at the edge of the school grounds, sipping tepid coffee from Styrofoam cups. As he drew near, microphones were thrust at him, and voices shouted out.

"Stuart—?"

"Just a few words—!"

"Stuart, over here!

"Hey!" Clark shoved a camera lens away from him. "Get that thing out of my face!"

"I don't think it's him!"

"Yeah, hair's too dark."

"Kid, do you *know* Stuart Harrison?"

"What's he like?"

"He goes to my school. Hey, back off." Clark shouldered aside an especially aggressive reporter and kept going. He didn't stop until he was safely inside the school's main doors. As he turned around to stare back out through a window, Chloe hailed him.

"You make it through the gauntlet all right?"

"Chloe, what is going on? Who are those people?"

She joined him at the window. "Bunch of news agency stringers. I hear they started showing up just after dawn. They were banished to the edge of campus by order of Principal Kwan." Chloe sadly shook her head. "They've been there ever since, watching for any sign of the Miracle Boy. Poor souls."

"Poor souls? They're like vultures!"

Chloe ignored the slur on her fellow reporters. "They're wasting their time. Kwan arranged to have Stuart smuggled in via a bread truck. He's been here for half an hour already."

"Good for him." Clark turned away from the window. "It was bad enough just being mistaken for Stuart."

Chloe shrugged. "Like it or not, Stuart is news."

"That's no reason to put him through hell." *If this is the way they respond to a "miracle cure," how would they react if they ever discovered* my *secret?* Clark frowned. "And you want to be one of them?"

"No." Chloe wrinkled her nose, as if she'd just smelled something disgusting. "Those are the galley slaves of the Fourth Estate, the lowest of the lowly. I never want to be like them. You don't have to be a creep to be a reporter, Clark."

"Well, I hope not."

"But you do have to be crafty." She smiled. "I've been working on my exposé, and I'm thinking we should make a return trip to the Compound."

"The Compound, huh?" *Couldn't you have planned this before they started collecting meteorites?* "And who do you mean by 'we'?"

"You and me, and Pete. What do you say?"

"I'd say you don't believe that Jacobi has morphed into a

true humanitarian. I mean, about establishing his new Institute."

"Let's say I'm skeptical. Maybe he has changed, but I went to last night's lecture and it was run just like before, your donations greatly appreciated."

Clark was surprised. He'd mentioned the Institute just to stall for time. He hadn't expected to hear this. "You spent money on another lecture?"

"No way! I simply went back to the Compound and said I'd like to do a follow-up feature on their new plans. And, presto, another free ticket.

"Like I said, the format was the same, even if Jacobi's line of patter was on the nobler side. Now, maybe he really has had a change of heart—I'm willing to grant that it's possible—but I refuse to take it on faith. So . . . are you up for a little investigative skulking?"

"I think that would be a big mistake, Chloe."

"What? Why?"

Because the Foundation is stockpiling rocks that make me sick as a dog. "Uh, because the people working for the Foundation probably aren't going to tell you anything useful. They're mainly volunteers, right?"

"Right. They're almost like Dead-heads—they've put their day jobs on hold to be faithful little Foundation staffers."

"Uh-huh. And how successful do you think you'll be, if you show up and start grilling the faithful in full ambush-journalist mode?"

"You have a point." Chloe bit her lip contemplatively. "I don't want to tip Jacobi off too soon."

"Exactly!" Clark breathed a sigh of relief. "You need to dig up more background on the Foundation—maybe keep your eyes and ears open for signs of discontent among the workers and follow up on that when they're off the Compound."

"Very good, Clark!" She smiled at him. "Sure I can't convince you to work for me on the *Torch*? You already have the instincts of a reporter."

"I do?" Clark winced.

"It's not a personal failing." Chloe started to chuckle. "I meant that as a compliment." As she headed for her first class, she turned back and gave him a wink. "I look forward to seeing your by-line on a story."

Clark shook his head. "That'll be the day!"

Between classes, Stuart moved through the halls like a young god. It was as if his long illness had never happened. Stuart walked with a strong, surefooted stride. His skin had taken on a warm, healthy glow. His hair was already longer and thicker.

Many classmates stepped back to make way as Stuart passed among them. Some called out a greeting or encouragement. He acknowledged each and every one with a broad grin.

"Stu! Good to have you back!"

"It's good to be back!"

"Lookin' good, man!"

"Thanks. Feeling good, too!"

As Stuart crossed into the school's north corridor, he spotted a student bending over a water fountain. "Clark? Clark Kent!"

It took a beat for Clark to recognize the tall fellow who called out to him. "Stuart?" It was hard to believe that this was the same young man whom he'd helped carry from the tent just a week earlier. "Wow, you look great!"

"Yeah." Stuart chuckled. "I've been getting that a lot." He reached out and grasped Clark's hand. "Listen, my father told me what you and the other guys did for us. I want to thank you for that, and for giving the ambulance a push. I really appreciate it."

"That's okay. I'm glad I was there to help." Clark was a little surprised that the popular upperclassman knew him by name. "You'd have done the same for me."

"Well, I hope that's never necessary. But, yeah, if you ever need a hand—!"

"STU-U-U-U!!" Whitney came tearing down the corridor in full roar. He slid to a halt beside them and threw a couple of air punches to just in front of his old friend's belly. "I knew you were too mean and ornery to die!"

"Ford-Man!" Stuart laughed and grabbed Whitney in a bear hug. He lifted the surprised quarterback a full foot off the floor, gave him a hearty shake, then let him drop.

"Dude!" Whitney took half a step back. His eyes were nearly as wide as his smile. "It's true! You're your old self!"

"Stronger than dirt but only half as dusty!"

"Man, it's too bad the season's over. We could've used you on the line!"

"Aw, you got along fine without me. 'Sides, I'm a little too busy these days for sports. I have a lot of class time to make up. Principal says, if I can maintain my GPA, I've got a good shot at landing the Carter Scholarship."

"The Carter—?" Whitney's smile started to falter. "No kidding? That pays full tuition to any college in the country."

"Hey, would I kid you? Yeah, if I can win the Carter, I'm set. Anyway, between getting back up to speed on studies, and helping Doc Jacobi out with some Foundation work, I'm going to be a busy boy for a while."

"Yeah, I guess so. I've been pretty busy myself lately. Since my dad's been laid up, I've been filling in a lot at the store."

"Whit, I didn't know." Stuart's smile faded. "Is it serious? Why didn't you say something?"

"Aw, you had enough to worry about."

"Not anymore." Stuart snapped his fingers. "Hey, you should bring your dad out to see Doc Jacobi. A few meteorite sessions might be just what he needs."

"I don't know, Stu. This isn't cancer. It's his heart." Whitney was uncomfortable talking about this, even with an old friend. He glanced over at Clark, his eyes asking for help in changing the subject.

"Stuart?" The three young men turned to find that Lana had joined them. "Is it true what I've heard? You're working for the Foundation?"

"Lana, hi! Yes, I am. It's the least I can do. After all, Doc Jacobi gave me back my life."

"How can you be so sure of that?"

"Lana!" Whitney was flabbergasted by her challenge.

"It's okay, Whit. This is nothing new. The Doc told me that he's faced plenty of skeptics in the past." Stuart gave his full attention to Lana. "Heck, I was a skeptic myself. But, well, you were there, right? You saw what happened."

"Stuart, I'm really, really glad that you're well. But last Friday night, I saw a flash of light, and then I saw you collapse onstage. That's all."

"Lana, you gotta understand." Stuart leaned forward and took her hand. For a moment, Clark thought he was about to kiss it. But he just held it, very gently. "I was dying. I had maybe two months left to live at the most—that was the best the oncologists could promise. Then I took part in Doc Jacobi's experiment, and look at me now!

"I'm not dying anymore, Lana. The tumors are gone, and so are the scars from all my previous surgeries. I've been completely healed!" Stuart straightened up and threw out his chest. "I'm gaining back the weight I'd lost over the past couple of months. I'm me again. The other doctors couldn't explain it, but I'm sure it was Doc Jacobi's meteorite that cured me."

"Stuart . . ." Lana hesitated. "It's great that you're feeling so good again, but you can't know for certain—!"

"Who knows what's 'for certain' in this crazy world, Lana?" Stuart looked at her as though she was the only other person on Earth. "Not even Doc Jacobi knows exactly *how* the meteorite cure worked, but it did. It must have. If it hadn't, I wouldn't be here, alive and well. That's why the Doc's work is so important. If we can study enough of those space rocks, and figure out their secret, maybe we could cure everybody. Maybe we could even change the world!"

"That's . . . a beautiful thought, Stuart." Lana could see how earnest he was. "I wish I could believe that some good could come out of that meteor storm."

"It killed your parents. I know." Stuart again took her hand. "And I can only imagine how much hurt that caused you, Lana. But a lot of weird things have happened this past year, and I'm telling you, those meteorites can be used for good. I'm living proof of that.

"I have so much to be thankful for." Stuart looked around him, his gaze taking in Clark and Whitney, as well as Lana. His smile broadened. "You've all been so good to me and my folks. This morning, Principal Kwan told me about the benefit concert you were planning. I don't know how to thank you."

"No thanks necessary, Stu." Whitney gave his friend a playful punch to the shoulder.

Lana frowned at Whitney. "Actually, it was Clark's idea."

Clark waved off the credit. "Sort of. But Lana did all the real work."

"Then, I just hope you didn't go to too much trouble on my account, Lana, 'cause it's not really necessary now."

"Oh—? How so?"

"Lex Luthor picked up the tab for my recent hospital stay, and Doc Jacobi's making arrangements to cover any outstanding bills from before."

"He is? Really?" Lana seemed surprised. *Well, at least that would be a* good *use for all the money Jacobi's been taking in.*

"Really. I'm telling you, he's a great guy. I'd like to talk to you more about the Foundation's work"—Stuart checked his watch—"but I've got to get to my next class."

"We all do." Lana laughed nervously. "And me with an algebra quiz this period."

"Mr. Staples's class? I'm headed that way. Let me walk you there."

"Okay. Sure." Lana gave a little half wave to Clark and Whitney and fell in beside Stuart, other students parting to let them pass.

Whitney opened his mouth as if he meant to say something, but nothing came out. He just stared, dumbstruck, as Lana and Stuart disappeared around the corner. It took him half a minute to find his voice. "What just happened there?"

Clark looked confused by the question. "They left for class."

"No, before that." Whitney gestured impatiently. "When Stu was telling Lana about all that meteor stuff. The way she looked at him. It was like I wasn't even here."

"As if neither of us were here, Whitney."

"Well, yeah! So what just happened?" Whitney's face was a portrait of utter disbelief. All his life, he had been a winner. He always ran with the in crowd, dated the prettiest girls. Excelling at sports, he was an average student who nevertheless maintained good grades by charming the easy teachers and studying hard for the tough ones. Over the years, Whitney had become adept at eliminating the compe-

tition, whatever or *who*ever it was. But until now, Stuart
Harrison had never been part of the opposition.

Fordman and Harrison had been friends—and often teammates—for as long as either of them could remember. Stu
was a stand-up guy, and Whitney would have done anything
for him. But now, the quarterback realized that Stuart might
be a serious rival for Lana's affection.

Whitney looked completely baffled. *What the hell do I do
now?*

Clark took half a step back and studied Fordman. There
was no way Whitney could fight his old friend, even if he
wanted to. It wasn't just that Stuart had made a miracle recovery from a life-threatening disease. Stu had been well
liked even before he'd fallen ill. He was, Clark realized, the
one person in town who might be even more popular than
Smallville High's star quarterback.

"Welcome to my world," muttered Clark.

"What?"

"Nothing, Whitney." Clark sighed. "I don't know what to
tell you. Sorry."

"Yeah . . . well . . . see ya." Whitney turned and lumbered
off to his next class. Clark had never seen him move with
less confidence. Unlike Stuart, Whitney had little chance of
landing a scholarship at this point. With his father ill and the
Fordman family business on shaky ground, his future had
never looked rockier. And now, there was a possibility that
Whitney might lose Lana. To his best friend, no less.

To his surprise, Clark found himself feeling sorry for the
golden boy.

◆◆◆

By Saturday morning, James Wolfe knew for certain that
the situation had gotten completely out of his control.

On the surface, things were better than Wolfe could ever have imagined. The publicity following Stuart Harrison's miracle cure brought money rolling into their coffers. Jacobi's lectures had resumed in the middle of the week to great acclaim. Every seat in the big tent had been filled. There had been standing room only. Donations filled the ushers' buckets nightly, and paid subscriptions to the Foundation website had tripled.

From a window in the second floor of the old Davis farmhouse, Wolfe could see their campground area. Every space was full and would, he knew, remain that way through the weekend.

Outside, there was constant activity in what everyone was starting to call the Ascendance Compound. Several members of the Foundation continued to scour the countryside, digging up meteorite fragments and depositing them in the barn adjacent to the farmhouse. And there always seemed to be one camera crew or another on the grounds, following Jacobi around as he pontificated on the promise and importance of his latest breakthrough.

The media presence made Wolfe edgy, and he holed up in his room whenever the cameras came around, which meant that he had spent much of the past three days skulking about the second floor, going stir crazy. He'd seen more of Jacobi on television than he had in person. Wolfe finally resorted to sending messages to his partner through their security staff, just to arrange a meeting to discuss the weekend's lectures.

Wolfe was pacing the floor of the downstairs parlor, when Jacobi finally arrived.

"There you are. It's about time!" Wolfe crossed the room and made sure the door was locked. "What kept you? Having tea with the *60 Minutes* crew?"

Jacobi laughed and saluted his partner with a long cardboard tube he carried. "Just attending to a little business,

Jimmy. And, of course, I had to greet some of the newly en-
lightened faithful on the way in."

"Of course." Wolfe gave a sarcastic snort. "Look, Don,
we're going into our biggest weekend ever. We have to plan
out the program very carefully."

"That's no problem. We'll start with the usual opening.
I'll spend the first ten to fifteen minutes working the audience, then we'll run the edited tape of the miracle cure, and
end by introducing Stuart." Jacobi pulled a large roll of papers from the tube and began to unroll them on the parlor
table. "We'll let him tell his story—the boy's getting good,
a real natural—then I'll take over again and talk about the
upcoming clinical trials. If no one in the audience has stood
up to make a donation by then, you signal one of our plants.
We can wing the rest of it."

"I suppose. But I still want to go over a few cues." Wolfe
stopped, his attention drawn to drawings on the papers Jacobi had unfurled. "What the devil is that supposed to be?"

"Architectural renderings of the Institute for Advanced
Meteorite Research!" Jacobi stepped back to survey the perspective drawings. "These are just the preliminaries, but
aren't they beautiful?"

Wolfe was aghast. "You spent good money hiring an architect?"

"Not 'an' architect, the best firm in the region. I thought
it would be good public relations to stick with local talent,
people with a feel for the area, rather than bring in someone
from out of state."

"But why go to all this trouble for—? Oh, no." Wolfe's
jaw dropped, and the color began to drain from his face.
"Don't tell me you're serious about going through with this
pipe dream."

"It's not a pipe dream, Jimmy. I've outlined the plan to
every reporter I've met with this week. We talked about it—"

"*You* talked about it! And I thought it was *just* talk—just sucker bait for the rubes. I never for one moment believed that you actually wanted to *build* in this cow town."

"We already have an option to buy this land, Jimmy. You insisted on that in the lease."

"That was just to build our credibility with the local bank!" Wolfe ran both hands through his hair, as if trying to keep his scalp from splitting open. "Do you have any idea what a project like that would cost us?"

Jacobi nodded thoughtfully. "We'll need to establish a substantial building fund, but I have every confidence that we can do that. I've started checking into government grants."

"Have you lost your *mind*?" Red-faced now, Wolfe grabbed his partner roughly by the lapels. "We've been very lucky here, luckier than we have any right to be. A week ago, I thought that we were cooked!"

Jacobi broke free of Wolfe's grasp and shoved him back. "A week ago, I saved a young man's *life*. I *cured* him, Jimmy!"

"That was a *fluke*! You fell into a manure pile and pulled out a pony. Don't press your luck—there are still too many things that could trip us up."

"If I cured one, I should be able to cure others. What's gotten into you, Jimmy?" Jacobi sounded almost disappointed in his partner. "We can't stop now."

Wolfe took a deep breath and tried to massage away the pounding at his temples. "Don, we *have* to stop now. This is the sweetest deal we've ever pulled, but *it can't last*. Yes, we can probably milk it for another week or two, but then we'll need to move on."

"We're not moving, Jimmy. The Foundation is going to put down roots here." Jacobi's voice was firm. "I am going to build my Institute. I will collect all the meteorites I can, and test them until I understand how to make them work. I will lead the world into a new golden age."

"Oh, my God." Wolfe turned pale again and sat down heavily on a sofa, practically falling onto it. He stared up at Jacobi in total horror. This was something Wolfe had never expected. This changed everything. "You've bought into the con."

"It's not a con, Jimmy. Not anymore. It will take a lot of hard work on our part, but we can do this—I know we can! And I am going to need all your help, all of your skill, to pull it off. Help me, Jimmy!" Jacobi held out his hand.

"No. No way, no how!" Wolfe evaded the offered hand, scrambling up off the sofa and backing away from his partner. He knew genuine evangelical fervor when he saw it, and he saw it all over Jacobi's face. "I can't work a con if my partner's a believer! It'll all fall apart for sure. I am out of here!" He strode to the door and unlocked it.

"Where do you think you'll go, Jimmy? Cleveland?"

Wolfe froze with his hand on the doorknob. Some things hadn't changed. Some things were still the same.

"No, not Cleveland." The edge was back in Jacobi's voice, cold and cutting. Wolfe knew that tone all too well. "It wouldn't be safe for you to go to Cleveland—would it, Jimmy?" That edge meant that Jacobi had decided on a course, and not even an earthquake could budge him. He would do whatever it took to carry out his plan. "No, there are still too many people back there who would just love to know where to find you."

Sweat beaded up on Wolfe's forehead, and he slowly turned around. "You wouldn't . . ."

"I wouldn't *want* to." Jacobi crossed the room. "I'd rather have you right here, alive and healthy, helping me take the Foundation to ever greater heights. We're a team, Jimmy—it wouldn't do to break up our winning combination now. Not when we're on the verge of launching such a great project. We have an opportunity to make a real difference in the world, a real contribution, and we must not waste another moment."

"Don, I'm old and I'm tired . . ."

"Nonsense! There's nobody better qualified than you to run this operation. I don't want to have to train some new kid." Now it was Jacobi who grabbed Wolfe, but gently, with one hand on his shoulder. "Do this for me, Jimmy. Help me get the Institute up and running. Afterwards, if you still want to leave—no problem. You can pack up and go wherever you like. I won't say a word."

Yeah, like I haven't heard that tune before. Wolfe hung his head.

"Tell me that you'll stay, Jimmy."

What choice do I have? Wolfe pushed the door shut behind him. He could hear the lock click shut. "I'll stay."

"That's my man!" Jacobi clapped him on the back. "Now, I believe there were some cues you wanted to discuss for tonight's performance?"

Wolfe nodded and slowly walked away from the door.

◆◆◆

Sunday after lunch, Clark finished a few lingering chores, and set off on a brisk cross-country hike. Walking always helped clear his head, and it was a good day to get out. Besides, he was almost leery of kicking back in his loft, afraid that someone new might drop by to vent. He hadn't minded listening to Chloe, and he'd provide a shoulder for Lana to lean on anytime, but when Whitney Fordman started looking for answers—! Well, Clark had to draw the line somewhere. *Everyone unloads on good ol' Kent. Who am I supposed to unload on?* There were his parents, but he leaned on them too much as it was. Pete was pretty good at talking him through a mood, but he'd been preoccupied all week. Clark looked down the road and smiled. The answer was right in front of him.

He strolled up to the gate of the Luthor Castle and thumbed the button.

"Good afternoon, Mr. Kent."

Clark waved toward the lens of a hidden camera. He knew that the metallic voice belonged to one of Lex's security people, but he was never sure which one. Lately, he'd taken to thinking of the unseen guard as "Raspy."

There was a soft buzz, and the massive barred gate began to swing open. Clark quickly slipped through and headed up the gracefully curving drive. Ahead of him stretched the imposing castle that Lionel Luthor had shipped from Scotland, stone by stone, and rebuilt here years before. It had sat empty until just the past year, when Lionel had sent Lex to oversee operations at the Smallville plant.

A castle on the plains. Clark smiled at the thought. He knew that Lex had originally been less than thrilled to be posted to Lowell County. He'd thought of it as a dead end, a sort of exile. But that had changed after Clark saved his life. *He seems settled here now. Maybe life in Smallville is doing him some good. He's certainly done a lot of good for Smallville already.*

The big oak door of the mansion swung open with his first knock, and a dark-suited butler bade him enter.

"Afternoon, Louis. Is Lex around?"

The butler gave a slow, formal nod. "The master is running laps. You can no doubt intercept him by the main stair."

The main stair? Clark followed the hall deep into the heart of the mansion. Sure enough, as he reached the great staircase, Lex appeared on the landing. He was clad in white shirt and shorts, and a sheen of perspiration coated his scalp.

"Lex!"

"Clark . . ." Lex descended the stairs with a measured, deliberate gait, and stopped at the bottom to catch his breath.

Clark ran his hand along the dark wood of the balustrade. "Is it really a good idea to run stair laps here?"

"Why not? I want to stay in shape, and this is a great cardio workout." Lex picked up a towel that had been draped over the banister and mopped his brow.

"No, I mean, is it good for the stairs? The wood is so nice."

"It was built to be walked on, Clark. Or run up, in my case. This staircase is at least a hundred years old." Lex draped the towel over his shoulders. "If it can survive being torn down, shipped across the Atlantic, and reassembled, I doubt that my lap work is going to do it much harm. Come on . . ."

Lex led Clark into a large adjacent room. He retrieved two bottles of springwater from the refrigerator of a corner wet bar, and tossed one to Clark. "So what brings you here?"

"I was just out taking a walk. Thought I'd drop in and say hello." Clark stopped with the bottle halfway to his lips. "I should have called first, shouldn't I? I'm sorry."

"Mmph!" Lex took a sip from his bottle. "It's all right. My door is always open to you, Clark. You know that." He gestured to the big mahogany pool table by the fireplace. "Join me in a game of stripes and solids?"

"Sure." Clark started racking the balls, while Lex pulled a couple of cues from a cabinet mounted along one wall. "I was talking to Stuart Harrison the other day. He said that you paid the bill for his stay in the hospital."

"That's right." Lex handed Clark a cue.

"That was a nice thing to do."

"Nice." Lex chuckled. "You know, there are any number of people who would be surprised to hear that word applied to me." He began chalking up. "Given the circumstances, I just wanted to make sure Stuart got the best of care. Besides, I have to admit, I was curious to see if there was any known medical explanation for what had happened at that tent meeting. Mind if I break?"

Clark leaned on his cue. "Hey, it's your table."

Lex sent the cue ball smacking into a good, clean break, scattering the other balls across the felt. The twelve ball teetered for a moment at the edge of a corner pocket, and then fell in. "Looks like I'm stripes." He moved around the table to line up his next shot. "I would have offered the Harrisons help with the rest of their outstanding medical bills, but I knew that you and Lana had been planning a benefit to that purpose, and I didn't want to get in your way. I hear that the good Doctor Jacobi has since rendered that benefit unnecessary."

"According to Stuart, yeah." Clark looked out over the table. "I suppose that's a good thing. At least we know that some of the money the Foundation's collected is going to a good cause."

"I take it that you doubt Jacobi's abilities to heal the sick and infirm." Lex scored a solid hit on the fifteen ball, but just missed sending it into a pocket. "Your shot."

Clark began chalking his cue. "I don't know what all to believe about Jacobi, but I don't trust him. I've talked to a few people who actually subscribed to the Ascendance Foundation website." He fitted the cue through his left hand and sent the one ball sailing into a side pocket. "One of them even showed me a few pages of the 'members only' section, and I didn't see anything there worth paying $14.95 a month."

"Neither did I."

"Don't tell me that you signed up!"

"Just for a one-month trial subscription. Aside from some vague promises about the power of the meteorites, most of it was predictable New Age nonsense about auras and vibrations and 'recharging your DNA.'" Lex grinned. "I wasn't aware that DNA could be jump-started like an old car battery."

"Tell me about it." Clark moved to the end and sighted up the table. "Chloe's been doing some digging, and as far as she can tell, Stuart was the first one with a really serious disease that Jacobi managed to 'cure' with his meteorite. All the other people that he's supposedly helped, have suffered from inflammations like bursitis or tendinitis, or from very mild cases of multiple sclerosis." He sent the cue ball ricocheting into the two ball, knocking it into the pocket in the far corner. "Things that either come and go, or clear up on their own."

"Yes, that's more or less what I've been able to determine, as well. Up until this point, Jacobi has been very careful not to promise anything from his meteorite 'research' that could easily be disproven. On the other hand, you and I both know that the meteorites of Lowell County have been the cause of some rather outré effects."

"I know. Stuart's cure was the first really good thing to be connected to the meteorites." Clark remembered what Lana had told him about Nell. "It just burns me that the Foundation is using this to soak money from a lot of decent people." With an angry lunge of his cue, he sent the three ball careening into the four ball, sinking both.

Lex looked up at Clark. "Is this a hustle?"

"Chloe thinks so."

"No, I meant—!" Lex shook his head. "Never mind. Go on."

"The impression I get is that, for the past few years, Jacobi had just used his meteorite as a glow-in-the-dark prop, like for crystal power or something. He more or less admitted that Stuart's cure was an accident." Clark sent the cue ball whizzing across the table toward a small cluster of balls. It knocked the ten ball into the five, which then started rolling slowly down the table. "I don't think that Jacobi knew that there was anything special about the local meteorites until he found Chloe's website." At the far end of the table, the five ball bumped past the fourteen and dropped into a corner pocket with a soft thunk.

"Nice shot. The question is"—Lex tapped the end of his pool cue—"is Jacobi a total fraud, or does he believe the claptrap he's been spreading? It's been my experience that many of these self-styled therapists and teachers are quite sincere. And Jacobi has been carrying a meteorite around with him for some years now."

Clark's stick glanced off the cue ball. He got a horrible, sinking feeling deep in his gut. "You don't suppose that he's been affected, do you? Like Rickman and Tippet?"

Bob Rickman and Kyle Tippet had been partners, just a couple of ordinary, run-of-the-mill salesmen, until they had been trapped in their car during the meteor storm. After they were freed, they discovered that they'd both gained uncanny powers of persuasion. They could literally compel anyone to do their bidding. Kyle didn't like what had happened to him and became a recluse, avoiding contact with people. But Bob liked it very much and used his power to become an industrial magnate.

Rickman had seemed unstoppable until he returned to Smallville and tried to acquire the Kents' land. Clark was able to resist his power, but no one else was. For a while, it looked as though the Kents might lose their farm. Rickman's threat had finally been ended with help from Tippet. When it was all over, Bob Rickman was dead and Kyle Tippet had vanished.

"No, Clark, I doubt very much that Jacobi has gained any special powers from his meteorite. He's just naturally charismatic. That in itself can be dangerous enough." Lex applied a bit more chalk to his cue stick and contemplated the table. "But remember what he said about not having had a cold for over three years? There may be something to that besides hot air." He considered one shot, rejected that, and moved into a new position across the table from Clark. "Did you know that mildly elevated white blood cell counts are common among the citizenry of Smallville?"

"Really?"

"Especially in those who'd lived here prior to '89. And particularly in those who were young children at the time of the meteor storm. A little gem of information I picked up from my personal physician." Lex banked the cue ball off the side of the table, sending it clicking sharply against the fifteen ball—but too hard. The ball hit just shy of the pocket and bounced back. "Ah, so close!"

Lex pointed his stick across the table at his friend. "Think about it, Clark. Aside from Stuart Harrison, how many locals of our generation have suffered life-threatening illnesses?"

"Well, there was . . . no, he and his folks had just moved here from Iowa." Clark thought for a moment. "Nobody."

"Precisely. Remember the malleable young lady who impersonated me . . . and you?"

"Tina Greer. Yeah, she'd had a bone disease that cleared up after the meteor storm. Just like your asthma!"

"Yes." Lex shifted his cue stick from hand to hand. "Jacobi may be on to something after all. Perhaps we should all keep a chunk of meteorite on hand."

Yeah, that would be all I need. Clark's expression soured. "I think I'd rather keep my distance for now. Those green rocks have had too many bad side effects."

"Granted, that has been a problem. But just imagine what

might be accomplished if we could eliminate all the ill effects and amplify the beneficial ones."

"Now you're starting to sound like Jacobi. Isn't that what he has planned with his Institute?"

"That's what he's announced. But to pull it off, he'll need to attract scientists with much better credentials than his own. Whether he can do that remains to be seen. Oh, it's your shot, by the way." Lex surveyed the table. "I'm afraid I've left things in a mess for you."

"No kidding." Clark walked around the table, stopping every few feet to check out angles. "This will be tricky." The striped balls blocked any easy shots. He scooped up the chalk and began slowly rubbing it onto the tip of his pool cue. "The problem is, there really is something to the whole meteorite thing. Let's suppose, just for the sake of argument, that Jacobi isn't a fake. If he believes completely in everything else he says, that still makes him pretty flaky."

Lex nodded. "I would tend to agree."

Clark bent over the table. He sighted down his cue for a second, then straightened up. "What if he sets up this Institute and attracts more 'scientists' like himself? A lab full of flakes might just wind up unleashing more crazy weirdness around here."

Lex frowned. "That is a distinct possibility."

"Yeah, that's what I'm afraid of." Clark shook his head and leaned back down over the table. With one smooth thrust of the cue, he sent the white ball barreling forward, smacking into two of the striped balls. They, in turn, collided with the others in a chain reaction that sent the six and seven balls spinning into opposite corners, dropping them both into the pockets.

"I don't believe this." Lex stared down at the table. Six striped balls sat scattered across the felt. The eight ball was nestled near a side pocket, with the cue ball at rest just ten inches away. "Clark, are you sure that you haven't been experimenting with meteorites?"

"Believe me, Lex, I try to stay as far away from them as I can!"

"Then, how . . . ?" Lex waved his cue over the table.

"This?" Clark modestly tipped his head. "It's just simple geometry."

"Never my best subject. Though there's obviously something to be said for its mastery." Lex rubbed his chin and gave his friend a wry look. "Well? Don't just stand there grinning! Go ahead and knock in the eight ball!"

Game over, Clark leaned back against the wall. "Best two out of three?"

"You're on."

CHAPTER 14

It was midafternoon by the time Clark left Lex's mansion. Nightfall was still hours away, but he knew that the large wooded area between the Luthor estate and Hickory Lane would provide all the cover he needed to race home. Clark stepped into the shadow of the trees and—once he was out of sight of any passing cars—cut loose. He sprinted through the glen, covering miles in a matter of seconds. Clark ran so fast that he was no more than a passing blur to the fauna of the woods. To his own eyes, the birds seemed frozen in place, suspended in midair.

As he burst from the woods, Clark slowed to a more human pace and jogged on down Hickory Lane to the Kent farm. He left the road and turned down the drive. That was when he spotted the Ross family sedan parked midway between the house and the barn.

"Hey, Clark!" Pete came out the back door, licking his fingers.

"Hey, Pete!" Clark jogged to a halt and stood there, pretending to catch his breath. "Good pie?"

"Yeah, your mom's is the best in the county." He stopped. "How did you know?"

"You still have a little on your chin."

Pete ran a finger over his chin and licked it blissfully. "Make that the best in the nation."

"What brings you over here? Besides the pie, I mean."

Pete swept an arm toward the car. *"Le Coupe de Ross!"*

"No, seriously."

"I am being serious. Cast your mind back to two Friday nights ago. Remember our slip-slidin', mud-divin' ambulance rescue? Remember how you said my father wouldn't kill me on account of how understanding he was?"

"Uh-huh. And I was right." Clark poked Pete's shoulder with his index finger. "I must have been. You're way too solid to be a ghost."

"You were partially right. After I brought his car back with a muddy interior, Pop was not happy. Then I explained how and why it got muddy, and he said he was proud of me." Pete popped the trunk of the car and bent down to rummage around inside. "So, no, he didn't kill me." He pulled a large cardboard box from the truck and handed it to Clark. "He decided to work me to death instead." Pete slammed the trunk lid shut. "Pop made me wash the car and shampoo the entire interior. And that was just last weekend."

"And this weekend?" Clark shook the box gently.

"I had to wash it—*again*. And now, he wants me to wax it! That's crazy, right? Who waxes cars anymore? I mean, it's not as if it's a classic or something." Pete shook his head. "He says this'll be good for me. Teach me responsibility. Build character. All the usual parent-speak."

"Let me guess." Clark lifted a rag and a jar of Turtle Wax from the box. "You were wondering if I'd give you a hand."

Pete looked at him sheepishly. "Would you?"

"Yeah, I'd probably better." Clark tossed him the jar. "You're already enough of a character as it is."

"That's my man!" Pete pulled another rag from the box. "Which side you want, driver's or passenger's?"

Jonathan strolled from the living room into the kitchen, trying (unsuccessfully) to stifle a yawn. "I was having this wonderful dream about pie." He gazed at the still mostly full pan on the table and broke into a grin. "But I see that it wasn't a dream at all. Strawberry rhubarb?"

"Uh-huh." Martha gave him a peck on the cheek. "And

you would've gotten the first piece, if you hadn't fallen asleep watching your movie."

"Well, someone certainly made a dent in the baked goods." Jonathan kissed her full on the lips. "Mmm . . . wasn't you. I take it our wandering boy has returned from his hike?"

"Yes, but he hasn't gotten to the pie yet. Peter Ross beat you both to it this time."

"You mean I'm facing competition from *two* teenage boys?" Jonathan opened a drawer and reached for a fork. "I'd better get to work while there's still some left!"

"At ease, Private." She plucked the fork from his hand. "Backup pies one and two are in the oven right now." A timer on the counter gave a ding. "And it sounds like they're done. While they're cooling, why don't you go see how the boys are doing out back?"

"Might as well." Jonathan sat down to pull on his shoes. "What are 'Tom and Huck' up to this afternoon?"

"I believe 'Tom' came over to get 'Huck' to help him whitewash a fence." Martha opened the oven door and started transferring the pies to a cooling rack.

"Ah, that old trick." Jonathan finished cinching his laces. "Just what sort of 'fence' are we talking about?"

"I'm not sure of the make, but I think it has an automatic transmission."

"Gotcha."

Jonathan took one last lingering sniff of the cooling pies and headed out the back door. As he rounded the corner of the house, he saw the boys buffing Dale Ross's car to a brilliant shine. Pete seemed to be razzing Clark about something.

"Must be nice, knowing someone with his own pool table. Probably lets you waltz right in and play whenever you feel like it, huh?"

"It's no big deal, Pete. I'm sorry I even brought it up."

"If you really want to be sorry, just mention your new buddy around my father. Ever seen a black man turn red?" Pete wiped a bit of wax from the base of the car's radio antenna. "Believe me, that is something you do not want to witness up close!"

"What, just because of that business deal—?"

"Business deal?" Pete blew a raspberry. "A screw job is more like it. Lex's old man bought controlling interest in the creamed corn plant that Dad and my uncle Bill worked so hard to establish. Then, he sold off all the assets and set up a fertilizer plant on the site. A *fertilizer* plant. I tell you, Pop has no use for anyone named Luthor."

"I can relate, Pete. My dad feels pretty much the same way."

Jonathan decided he'd been eavesdropping long enough. "I feel the same way about what?" He knew darned well what the answer was, but he wanted to hear it directly.

"Oh, uh—hi, Mr. K." Pete started gathering up the buffing rags. "We were just talking about fathers in general. My father . . . you . . ."

Jonathan cocked his head. ". . . Lex's father?"

"Dad, we weren't comparing you to—!"

Jonathan held up a hand. "I overheard a little of what you two were talking about. And I do sympathize with your father, Pete. Most people who've dealt with Lionel Luthor have fared even worse. Every land deal he's been involved with around here has been crooked."

"Every one?"

"Every one I know of, Son. Remember how I told you about the Bells, the Guys? How they lost their land?"

"Your dad's right, Clark. The Luthors always play with marked cards."

"That's exactly right, Pete. And something else—maybe

the thing I like least about the Luthors is the way they try to buy everything."

"Come on, Dad, that isn't true."

"Oh, no?" Jonathan pointedly looked at Clark. "Remember that new truck Lex tried to give you?"

"Truck?" Pete gaped at Clark. "When did he give you a truck?"

"After Clark pulled him out of the river."

Pete was stunned. "You never told me about any truck."

"There didn't seem to be much point." Clark started scuffing at the grass with the toe of his shoe. "Dad made me return it."

Pete whipped his head around to stare at Jonathan. "You made him give it *back*?"

"That's right." Jonathan crossed his arms. "I didn't like where the money to buy it had come from."

"You can't blame Lex for that, Dad. And he's put his money to work making things better for people. He's helped the Harrisons, the school—!"

"Oh, I'll concede that Lex seems to have done some good around here. He's not Lionel Luthor—not yet. I know, I know." Jonathan waved off his son's objections. "I shouldn't blame Lex for what his father's done. And I try not to. It's not his fault, the way he was brought up—but he's still a Luthor. I wouldn't expect anyone to grow up as part of that family and be even halfway honest. It's a classic case of—!"

" 'Nurture over nature'!" Pete blurted it out almost before he realized it. "Sorry, Mr. K. I didn't mean to interrupt. Ms. Wesley—our bio teacher—was talking about that just last week."

"Sounds like she knows what she's talking about. I remember an old saying my father used to quote: 'Just as the twig is bent, the tree's inclined.'"

"Dad, that 'old saying' was from Alexander Pope, and he was writing about education."

"Well, Pope knew the score, too." Jonathan nodded thoughtfully. "But there are all kinds of education, Clark. And the kind that rubs off on children from being around their family is one of the most basic. Lex may have been raised in the lap of luxury, but did his father ever bounce him on his knee? I don't know, but I'd guess not. That boy is one of the coldest people I've ever met."

Clark threw up his hands. "Well, now you're not being fair at all. How much time have you really spent around Lex? You hardly know him. So he's a little laid-back."

" 'Laid-back'? He has ice water in his veins!"

"Dad!"

"Remember the day you pulled Lex from the river? How he acted afterwards? He was the one who'd been driving like a maniac, who'd nearly gotten himself killed—but from the way he strutted around, you'd have thought he was in charge of the rescue. I'll never forget that smug look on his face when he introduced himself. I half expected him to hand me his business card next."

"Yeah." Pete snickered. "Probably from a waterproof platinum case."

Jonathan snorted. "No doubt."

"All right, that's enough! That's just a gross exaggeration. And *you* weren't even there, Pete." Clark was getting annoyed. "We were all pretty shaken up that day. And Lex doesn't always keep his cool."

"Oh, yeah?" Pete was a little annoyed himself. "Name one time that he lost it."

Clark remembered the night Lex found him staked out in that field as the Scarecrow. He would never forget the horror in Lex's voice.

But Pete didn't know what had happened that night. Neither did Clark's parents.

And he knew that if he told them about it now, they

wouldn't be all that interested in Lex's role. They'd focus on what had happened to him, on who had done it. And they'd want to know why he hadn't told them about it before.

Even if he got them to listen, his father would probably still dismiss Lex's reactions. Clark could hear him now, calling it "the exception that proves the rule."

"It's *happened*, all right? Plenty of times."

"Whoa!" Pete was surprised by how steamed Clark was becoming. "It's okay, man. I believe you."

"I'm tired of people writing Lex off, before the fact."

"Take it easy, Clark!" Jonathan wasn't happy, being challenged this way in front of Pete. "I was just saying—!"

"I *know* what you're saying, Dad. I hear it all the time. You've *never* given Lex half a chance."

"Well . . . uh . . . I gotta be going." Pete gathered up his supplies and eased back toward the car. He'd witnessed enough arguments between his older brothers and his own father. He didn't want to be in the middle if these two went at it. "See you around, Clark. Mr. K."

"Yeah." Jonathan gave him a nod in place of a wave. "Give your dad my best, Pete."

There was an awkward silence between the Kents as Pete pulled away.

Jonathan took a deep breath and broke it.

"Clark, I know you think of Lex as a friend, but—!"

"Dad, I'm just tired of hearing you talk about him as if he were already a lost cause. You're letting your opinions of Lex's father color how you look at him, and you always have."

"All right," Jonathan admitted, "I suppose I have. I wish I didn't feel that way, but there it is." He leaned back against a fence post and rubbed his eyebrows, just above the bridge of his nose. "The name Luthor has been part of too many raw deals in this county. The Ross corn plant swindle is just one example."

"Dad, *listen* to yourself. You're talking about Lionel Luthor again. Lex had nothing to do with any of that."

"Yes, and he might prove me wrong. But I'm not banking on it. Lex is his father's son, Clark. He has a lot of family history to overcome."

"And you're not going to go out of your way to cut him any slack, is that it?"

Jonathan's face was turning red. "He's grown up accustomed to power. And the bottom line is—power corrupts."

"It doesn't have to. Or do you think *I'm* in danger of becoming corrupt?"

"I never said that. I'd never suggest such a thing."

"Then don't go around speaking in absolutes." Clark's face was reddening now as well. "You're pretty fond of quoting Pope. Well, here's another one for you: 'The fate of all extremes is such, / Men may be read, as well as books, too much. / To observations which ourselves we make, / We grow more partial for th' observer's sake.' Think about *that*, Dad."

"Son . . . ?" Jonathan blinked and found himself alone in the yard. A trail of settling dust was the only indication of the direction Clark had taken. Jonathan shook his head and followed the trail to the house, muttering to himself. "What're they teaching kids these days? I didn't read any Pope until my senior year. When did *he* get so smart?"

"Jonathan . . . ?" Martha looked up as he entered.

"Where's Clark?"

"I don't know. He stormed through here like a tornado, said not to hold dinner for him, and left. What is going on?"

"We . . . had a bit of a discussion."

"Jonathan, what did you say to him?"

"I merely suggested that Lex Luthor might not be the most trustworthy member of society."

Martha sighed. *Here we go again.* She knew Jonathan's opinion of their son's newest friend all too well. She understood his misgivings—she had a few about Lex herself—but she also worried over how unbending her husband could be. "You know, you could be wrong about Lex."

"I could be. But I don't think so." Jonathan paced halfway around the kitchen, then turned and paced back. "You mark my words, Martha, time will prove me right about that kid."

"Okay, let's assume you're right. You haven't convinced Clark, have you?" She put both hands on her hips. "You keep up this way, and you'll just wind up alienating our son. That won't do either of you any good."

Jonathan stopped pacing and ran a hand through his hair. "You're right . . . as usual. I just don't want to see him get hurt."

"Neither do I, but we can't pick his friends for him. Clark's a big boy now. We have to trust him to do the right thing."

"I know. It's just that . . . I keep remembering all the stupid things I did when I was his age. I'd like to spare him some of that."

Martha smiled and hugged him. "I remember some of those things. They weren't all so stupid. And Clark has an advantage you didn't have."

"And what would that be?"

"A more open and understanding father."

Jonathan grimaced. "I don't know that Clark would agree right this moment. I'm not even sure I would."

"Well, there's always room for improvement." She planted a little kiss on his cheek. "But you're not afraid to admit when you're wrong. Maybe you should just be a little more willing to admit it to Clark . . . and a little more accepting of his friends."

He kissed her back. "I'll try."

"That's all I ever ask." She smiled up at him. "So . . . looks like it's just going to be the two of us for dinner. When would you like to eat?"

"I don't know. I'm not very hungry right now."

"Neither am I. But then, I've been nibbling at pie fixings all afternoon. We should have some vegetables to tide us over . . ." Martha stared at the counter. "That's odd."

"What's odd, hon?"

"The pies I set out to cool. One of them is missing."

◆◆◆

Clark trudged along a back-country road at no more than a human pace, trying to walk off his dark mood. He knew that if he stayed at home, he would just get angrier, and maybe say something to his father that he'd really regret later.

Clark was angry on Lex's behalf, but he was also genuinely troubled over what Pete and Jonathan had said. He had never known his father to lie to him. And Pete was always straight with him. They both tended to exaggerate, but usually for the sake of a joke, not about the serious stuff. And they were both serious about Lex.

And they had never both been wrong about something at the same time.

But they had to be wrong about this. *I know Lex better than they do. He's nothing like his father.* At least, nothing like the man his father was supposed to be. Clark realized that he knew Lionel Luthor mainly by reputation, and by a few veiled references Lex had dropped. Maybe it was time he learned more.

Clark returned to the gated castle on Beresford Lane and buzzed for admittance.

Lex looked up as his friend entered the main hall. "Clark? I didn't expect to see you back here so soon." He noticed that Clark was carrying a small package and seemed somewhat agitated. "What, you want another game already? Didn't you beat me enough for one day?"

"No, it's not that. It's . . ." Clark hesitated. "Well, I needed to get away from the house. I don't want to wear out my welcome, but I was wondering if I could just hang out here for a while . . . ?"

"Of course. You can tell me all about it over dinner. I'll have Monique set an extra place."

"Thanks. I brought dessert." Clark started opening the package. "This is to make up for earlier. Mom always said we should never go visiting empty-handed."

"Clark, that really wasn't necessary—" Lex peered into the package. "Is this by any chance homemade?"

"Strawberry rhubarb. My mom's specialty."

Lex took the package and put an arm around his friend. "In that case, I think we should have dessert first."

◆◆◆

When the Talon opened in 1940, it was hailed as the finest theater of its kind. People flocked there from all over the county to see first-run motion pictures, especially during the dog days of summer—in addition to movies, it was one of the first establishments in Smallville to feature airconditioning.

In 1977, during a showing of *Close Encounters of the Third Kind*, Laura Potter struck up a conversation with Lewis Lang, who was working at the Talon's concession stand during a break from college. That conversation led to a summer romance, and eventually to marriage.

They were hardly the only couple who found love there. The Talon was a popular dating spot for generations of young men and women.

But by the end of the twentieth century, the old town theater had fallen on hard times. Competition from cable television, video rentals, and suburban multiplexes had done in the Talon. Lex Luthor finally purchased the property with the intent of putting a parking garage on the site . . . until the daughter of Laura and Lewis Lang came to him with a plan for renovating the building.

Now, the lobby of the Talon dispensed coffee and pastries, in all their many forms. Shelves of the latest bestsellers reached up to the mezzanine. The stage sat ready for next weekend's performance by a folk-rock trio out of Wichita.

This particular evening, at a table just a few yards from the coffee bar, Whitney Fordman sat nursing a cup of Jamaica Blue Mountain and feigning interest in a copy of *Sports Illustrated*. Every few minutes, he'd look up at the clock on the wall and double-check the time against his own watch. Finally, he turned to the young lady behind the counter and spoke up.

"When is it that you close tonight?"

Lana looked up from the register's monitor terminal and sighed. "Seven-thirty, Whitney. That's our usual closing time for Sunday nights. And it hasn't changed in the fifteen minutes or so since the first time you asked me."

"I'm sorry, Lana. I'm not trying to be a pain. I'm just . . . a little jumpy, I guess."

"Maybe you should switch to decaf."

"It's not the coffee. It's me . . . and you. I wanted to talk with you earlier this afternoon, but when I dropped by your place no one was home."

"I'm not surprised." Lana's nose crinkled a bit as she frowned. "Nell probably left early for the Compound. There's yet another lecture tonight."

"At first, I thought maybe you were out somewhere. With someone. Maybe Stuart."

"Stuart Harrison? He's probably at the Compound, too. I think Jacobi's grooming him to be the Boy Wonder of the Cosmic Ladder or something."

"Anyway, I finally thought to look for you here."

"Well, you found me." Lana put a hand on top of the register. "This is my natural habitat when we're shorthanded. By the way, you still owe us for the coffee and the magazine. That's six-fifty with tax."

"Oh. Right." Whitney fished the cash from his wallet. "Babe, I just wanted to—!"

"When I'm working, it's 'Lana,' not 'Babe,' okay? And I *am* working here. Between ringing people up, I'm running our new inventory program. I'm a little busy right now." She handed him his change. "You've been helping staff *your* family's business—I'd think you would understand."

"I know. I do." He took a deep breath. Family businesses were the last thing he wanted to think about at that moment. What he wanted was for just one thing in his life to be the way it used to be. "I'm sorry to bug you. I can see that you're busy." Whitney turned to go, then stopped and turned back. "I'm just bummed that we hardly see each other outside of school anymore! Either I've been busy at the store, or you've been busy here. It all sucks!"

"Yes, but what can we do? We have responsibilities. I can't just arbitrarily close the Talon on the spur of the moment." She looked up as a young couple entered. "People expect us to follow posted hours."

"Look, I'm free right now. How about if I give you a hand here? Help with closing or whatever you need. Then I'll drive you home. That way, we can spend a little time together. What do you say?"

Lana studied him. "All right. You can bus those tables over there. And when you're done with that, I have a big stack of boxes in the back that need to be broken down."

"I'm on it, ba . . . uh . . . boss!" Whitney shot her a salute and sprang into action.

Lana had to smile a little. For someone who was often in-credibly obtuse, Whitney could still be very sweet.

◆◆◆

"All right, Kent—out with it." Lex stared across the table at Clark. "You and your family have kept this secret long enough."

"Secret?" Clark stared back at him, momentarily confused.

"Don't play innocent with me."

Clark saw an intense look in his friend's eyes, and began to feel some concern. It had bothered Lex that he couldn't remember more about his rescue from the river. He had hired a team of mechanics to inspect the wreckage of the Porsche, but they hadn't been able to tell him how the roof had gotten peeled back. Once, Lex had bluntly challenged Clark over it. Lately, though, he seemed to have gotten over that obsession. *Is he starting to suspect again . . . ?*

"I have to know, Clark." Lex scraped his fork through the last of the crumbs on his plate. "If your mother can bake pies like this, how is it that you Kents don't each weigh around four hundred pounds? What, do you all have some extra fat-burning gene?"

"Ah!" Relieved, Clark leaned back and stretched his arms

wide. "It just comes from clean living and hard work, Lex. You don't see many fat farmers."

"I knew there had to be a catch." Lex grinned, but he also noted the definition in Clark's arms. "Perhaps I should get rid of my free weights and just help you bale hay. Some hard, honest work might do me good." He laughed sardonically. "Even better, it would annoy the hell out of my father."

"Lex . . ." Clark leaned forward. "About your father . . ."

"Yes? What about him?"

"Seems to me I've been hearing about Lionel Luthor most of my life . . ."

"And very little of it good, I would guess."

"He conducted a lot of land and business deals in this area, and none of them worked out very well for the people around here. The Bells, the Guys, the Rosses—none of them have been happy with the way things turned out." Clark set down his fork. "But your father—he didn't set out to screw them, did he? I can't believe that anyone could be so . . . so . . ."

"Calculating?" Lex looked totally unperturbed. "You don't know my father. I wouldn't be at all surprised if it's true. In fact, much of it, I'm sure is true. And the rest . . . ? Let's just say that I think it's very likely. Lionel Luthor is one of the coldest S.O.B.s you're ever likely to encounter— in this country, at least—and proud of it."

"How does that make you feel?" Clark bit his tongue, instantly regretting the question. It reminded him of those reporters who badgered the relatives of murder victims—or murderers. ("So, Mr. Jones, how did you feel when the police discovered the bodies your son had hidden in the deep freeze?")

"Feel? Nothing really." Lex voice was calm, even, and totally detached. He might as well have been discussing a cloudy day. "I learned a long time ago that where my father is concerned, feelings are irrelevant. No, worse than irrelevant. Feelings are dangerous around my father. They just get in the way." One corner of Lex's mouth arched into a frosty little smile. "So now I just . . . *study* my father. To learn what not to do."

But you've already learned how to be cold. You can cut yourself off from your feelings as easily as you'd flip a switch. Lex had obviously learned this in self-defense—but that didn't make it any less creepy. More, if anything. *What else has he learned from his father? And what must Lionel's father have been like—?* Clark veered away from those thoughts—they were too close to Jonathan's arguments against the Luthors.

"It must be a pain, when people automatically assume that you're just like your father."

"The 'Chip-off-the-Old-Block' Syndrome? I get that a lot. Actually, it can be useful for doing business. There are a number of people who will go to great lengths to avoid crossing me." Lex chuckled darkly. "It's funny, in a way. Especially when I think of all the times when my father has insisted that I'm not tough enough." He shrugged. "It doesn't really bother me, Clark. By now, I've heard it all."

Clark suddenly recalled their conversation of a few weeks ago. He remembered Lex telling about the cruel taunts he had endured over his baldness. "Kids, too," taunted him, Lex had said. Clark thought about the one time he had seen Lionel Luthor up close. Lex's father had long, expertly styled hair. Had Lionel himself ever . . . ?

"There's no need to look so appalled, Clark. If I wanted out, I could just take my trust fund and join the Peace Corps. But that wouldn't make me enough of a disappointment to my father. The fact is, I enjoy the little war of wills I have going with him. I'm taking him on at his own game now.

And someday, I'm going to win. On my own terms, of course."

That wasn't as reassuring as Clark would have liked, but he seized on the last bit. "On *your* terms. That's what I'm talking about. Everyone assumes that you're *just* like your father. Even *my* father does! It drives me crazy."

"I appreciate that, Clark, but there's no need for you to be so concerned. I'm not."

"But when Dad goes on a rant—!"

"Your father is cautious for a reason. You obviously mean a lot to him. He's a good man, Clark, even if he does wish that I lived on a different continent. I have a lot of respect for him."

"You do?"

"Oh, yes."

"I don't understand. Why . . . ?"

"Look around you, Clark. Take a good look at this place. What do you think I wonder whenever I meet someone? Anyone?"

Clark gazed at the rich wood wainscoting and the thick oak beams, looked over the many paintings and tapestries that adorned the walls and thought about how this castle had come to be built here. Lionel had spared no expense on a house that he himself never even planned to live in. Clark tried to imagine the amount of money tied up in these walls. He thought about some of the exotic folk who passed through the castle. Most of them were predatory business types, and that included Lex's girlfriends. Sometimes, *especially* Lex's girlfriends.

"You wonder what they're after. What they want from you."

"Exactly. You don't have to sound so sad about it—it's just human nature." Lex gestured at the remains of their dessert. "Everyone wants a piece of the pie. Everyone—

except for you and your folks! None of you has shown *any* interest in my money. Or my influence. Or anything else. You proved *that* beyond a shadow of a doubt. Your father wouldn't even let you keep that truck I gave you. It was bizarre! I had to learn more about you Kents."

Clark began to laugh. "You mean, if my dad had let me keep that truck . . . ?"

"You might never have seen me again." Lex pretended to make a notation in an imaginary ledger: " 'Debt paid. Now back to business.' But no, your father had to be stubborn and make you return my gift. So now you're stuck with me!"

Clark was still laughing as he shook his head. "No, I still say you paid me back the night you cut me down from that pole." *More than you know.*

"Don't change the subject. We were talking about that truck. You wanted to keep it, didn't you?"

"Oh, yeah. It was pretty sweet."

"Still, you respected your father's point of view, and gave the truck back." Lex shook his head, clearly bemused. "I'm not used to dealing with people who have principles, much less those who actually live up to them. I tell you the truth, Clark—to me, you were like beings from another planet."

"Lex, my folks are not unique." He thought about that for a moment. "Well, okay, maybe they are. But there must be plenty of other good people out there."

"Not in my experience. Your parents are a national treasure, to be nurtured and protected. Look where I live, Clark." Lex gestured to the walls around them. "I'm used to it by now, but even I admit it looks like it should be the set of an old Hammer film. Your home is a haven in comparison—literally a haven. Remember when that shape-shifter impersonated me to rob the savings and loan? Where did I go afterward?"

"Our place. But I thought that was because I'd seen 'you'

running from the bank, and you wanted to ask me about the impostor."

"I did. But I could have just called." Lex rubbed a hand across his chin and looked directly at his friend. "The proof of my innocence was not yet common knowledge at the time. The truth is, I felt safe going to meet you there. And to his credit, your father listened and didn't throw me out. Even he knew I wasn't a crook. At least, not that kind."

"A 'national treasure,' huh?" Clark grinned. "I can't wait to tell Dad, just to see the expression on his face."

"Don't bother. Considering the source, he'd probably never believe it." Lex got up from the table. "You have a good family, Clark. Go home to them."

CHAPTER 15

On the north side of Smallville sat an establishment called Denehey's PitStop. Outside were ten gas pumps, four of them dispensing diesel fuel, and a three-bay garage fully equipped with hydraulic lifts. Inside the large central building, just to the right of the cashier, you could find aisle after aisle of sale items—everything from video-game cartridges and American flag decals to pork rinds and antelope jerky. In the far corner, just past the self-service coffee machines and the display of cellophane-wrapped pastries (sell-thru date: anywhere from three months to three years), was a short row of fiberglass booths where a traveler might pause for a few moments while ingesting a prepackaged microwaved sandwich.

Monday morning, shortly after ten, James Wolfe sat alone at the end booth, using a small plastic tube to stir the nondairy creamer into a sixteen-ounce "Big Slurp" coffee, as he read his copy of the *Daily Planet*. Page 1B showed one of the architectural drawings (in color, no less) of the proposed Institute for Advanced Meteorite Research, along with an article about how the Ascendance Foundation was cutting back on its lecture series to concentrate on the new building projects. *Yeah, yesterday's lecture was the last one for the foreseeable future. Don is actually shutting down a proven moneymaker before its time.*

Wolfe took a tentative sip of the coffee, made a face, and tore open two packets of sugar. *He's serious about this. He fully intends to settle down here. I give it two months, tops, before he and the Potter woman are married.* He didn't see how things could possibly get any worse.

"Mr. Wolfe?"

"Eh?" Wolfe looked up from stirring the bitter coffee, to find a stranger standing alongside the booth. There was nothing flashy about the man. He was dressed simply, in dull colors, from his loafers to his cap. The mirrored sunglasses that hid his eyes were the only thing at all distinctive about him.

"You're one of the gentlemen from the Foundation, aren't you?"

"Yes. Yes, I am." Wolfe automatically slipped into his best meet-and-greet smile. "May I help you?"

"Maybe we can help each other. I understand that you've had some problems in the past."

"Problems? I don't understand—"

"Back east. In Cleveland, I believe."

Wolfe could see his smile freeze in place in the reflection of the stranger's glasses. "I'm afraid you must have me mistaken for someone else. I've never been to Cleveland."

"Oh, I think you have, Mr. Wolfe." He leaned in closer. "Or should I say, Mr. Wilbury?"

Wolfe eyes darted around, looking to see if anyone was within earshot. "What do you want?"

"I just want to talk. But this isn't a very good spot. You never know who might come in." A tight smile flickered over the stranger's face. "My car's parked outside, just around the corner. Right next to yours, in fact. Why don't you meet me there in a minute or two, and we'll have us a little conversation?"

Wolfe pretended to read his paper, but his eyes never left the man. The stranger strolled over to the cashier, where he bought a copy of the *Inquisitor* and a Zagnut bar, before shouldering the glass door open and exiting. Wolfe forced himself to choke down about half of the coffee before he rose and walked outside as nonchalantly as he could manage. Around the corner of the building, he found the stranger waiting in a car right next to his, just as promised. He looked around twice before opening the passenger's side door and getting in.

"Nice car you have there, Mr. 'Wolfe.' Foundation buy that for you?"

"It was a gift. A recent donation from one of our members."

"Must be nice."

"Look, what do you want? Who are you?"

"Who I am doesn't really matter. It's who you are. You've used a lot of different names in the past." The stranger thumbed through a file folder. "Winslow, Winslade, Wilbury. That last one was the name you were using when you pulled that con job in Cleveland, the one where everything went so badly. One of those wrong-place-at-the-wrong-time things, wasn't it? Something about the guy you were fleecing being on the outs with the mob. There was gunplay, a dead body or two. And you wound up in the middle, spilling your guts to save your sorry ass. I've got to hand it to the Feds, though, they really came through for you. Witness Protection Program gave you a new identity; plastic surgery gave you a new face. And after a while, you fell in with Jacobi and started the Foundation racket. Very slick."

"How did you get your hands on that file?"

"Collecting information is my job, Jimmy. People hire me to find out things. Now, take your buddy Jacobi—he's practically a public figure. Cagey fella, but I was able to find out all about him right down to his college grades." The stranger made a clicking sound with his tongue and shook his head. "Not very good, were they? You were the tougher one to pin down. I kept getting dead ends. And that made me suspicious." He tapped the side of his head with the file folder.

"The Feds did a good job on you, Jimmy. But they couldn't change your fingerprints, could they?"

"You're not working for the mob, or I'd already be dead. What do you want? Money?"

"Money? No, your pockets aren't deep enough, Jimmy. See, your Foundation has set up shop in a most unfortunate location. Certain parties don't want you there. They would like you all to go somewhere else, preferably far away."

"We can't do that. My partner has already made plans—"

"Then you'll just have to make him change those plans."

"You don't know Don Jacobi. When he sets his mind to something—"

"Who are you more afraid of, your partner or the mob?" The stranger waved the file folder at him. "It would be a real shame if this information got to the wrong people. Now, if you close down this show and get out of town, no one will ever have to know. But if you don't . . . ? Well, having your story plastered all over the papers will be the least of your worries, now won't it?"

"You . . ." Wolfe pulled a handkerchief from his pocket and daubed at his brow. "You can't do this to me. Please—!"

"It's not my decision to make now. It's yours. You have until the weekend." The stranger's lip curled into a sneer. "I suggest you get busy."

Wolfe backed out of the stranger's car and swung the door shut. He leaned back against his own car, heart pounding, as he watched the vehicle pull away. Wolfe fumbled in his pocket for his keys, and when he finally managed to pull them free, he dropped them. He scooped them up off the pavement, his hand trembling slightly as he slipped the key into the door lock. Wolfe slid behind the wheel and licked his lips. He checked his wristwatch and sighed. He desperately wanted a drink, but the liquor store wouldn't open for another hour and a half.

Wolfe would have been even more nervous if he'd noticed that one of the truck stop's mechanics had been watching him from the shadows of the garage area.

As Wolfe's car pulled away, the mechanic stepped to the back of the garage and fed coins to an old pay phone. He punched in a special number that he'd committed to memory and cupped his hand around the receiver, as much to muffle any garage noise as to ensure his privacy.

The phone was answered on the third ring.

"Yes?"

"It's Arnie down at the PitStop, Mr. Luthor. You wanted I should call if I ever saw anything suspicious."

At the other end of the line, Lex Luthor listened intently. "I see. And you got the license number of the other car? Good work, Arnie—give it to me. Uh-huh. And Wolfe's just left? Yes, Arnie, this is very interesting. If you see or hear any more, be sure to let me know. I'll be in touch."

Lex hung up and sat back in his chair. From the sequence of numbers Arnie had given him, he knew that the plates had been issued to a car from the Metropolis area. Lex knew that didn't prove anything—after all, millions of plates were issued in Metropolis every year. But he couldn't shake the feeling that the man who had met with Wolfe was somehow connected to Lionel Luthor. Lex doubted that his father was directly calling the shots (the old man sought plausible deniability in all things), but it was quite possible that some underling, or series of underlings, was involved. The question was, who?

He retrieved the phone and hit a number near the bottom of his speed-dialer. One ring got him a pickup.

"City Room. Nixon."

"Hello, Roger. Can you talk?"

"Yeah, just give me a sec . . ." The sound of a door closing carried over the phone, and background noises all but disappeared. "All clear, Lex. If this is about Jacobi, I haven't uncovered much more on him than I gave you last time."

"Every little bit helps, Roger, but this first item ought to be a little simpler. I have a license plate I want you to run down for me."

Nixon copied down the number. "You're right, that's definitely a Metro area plate. Shouldn't take too long to trace— half an hour at the most."

"Good. Now getting back to the Foundation, what *have* you been able to find?"

"Not much on Jacobi, though I'm supposed to be getting a copy of his college transcripts later today. And Wolfe— man, that guy is another matter!"

"In what way?"

"Wolfe's like a ghost. I can't find anything on him at all. It's as if the man didn't exist before he started working with Jacobi."

"That's impossible, Roger. Everyone leaves a paper trail of some sort."

"Hey, I'm just telling you what I found—or didn't, in this case."

Lex mulled that over. "Keep digging, Roger. I get the feeling that Mr. Wolfe's past might provide us with the missing piece of this puzzle."

◆◆◆

Wolfe sat in his car outside the Smallville Savings & Loan, wondering what he should do next, what he *could* do next. If he didn't close down the Compound and get out of town by week's end, he was as good as dead. The stranger had made that very clear. But Wolfe couldn't shut things down without Jacobi's cooperation, and that wasn't about to happen. He was tempted to pack a bag and head for the border, but that wouldn't do him much good.

If he tried to run, there'd be a dozen hit men on his tail by the end of the week. The stranger wouldn't need to expose him; Jacobi would do that himself, probably while acting aggrieved and betrayed. Wolfe could hear him now. He suspected that Jacobi could play the victim as easily as he played the scientist and humanitarian.

Jacobi's professional persona—the attitudes he struck, the language and postures he employed—was so practiced now that it wasn't even acting anymore. "Doctor Jacobi" was more like a separate, fully realized personality that he could assume at will. And now that Jacobi was buying into the con, the professional persona was becoming his primary personality. Or was it that a sincere version of the professional personality was emerging?

Which one is the real you, Don? Even I'm not sure anymore.

He knew that his partner had been a preacher's kid, like he was. But Wolfe had rebelled early on, had not only run with a bad crowd, but become its ringleader. That had earned him a juvenile record—sealed, as little as that now mattered—under his old name. Jacobi, on the other hand, had never gotten into any formal trouble with the law as far as Wolfe knew. *He was probably a little smart-ass . . . probably knew just how far to push.* Wolfe remembered the early discussions they'd had about faith. Jacobi sneered at the whole idea of religion, but he'd seen firsthand how much some people needed it. They'd both learned how that need could be exploited for gain with very little risk.

Until now.

I'm in a hell of a fix. Wolfe didn't know who the stranger was—or how far he could trust him—but he knew what to expect from Jacobi. His partner would never be persuaded to just fold the tents and steal away. Especially not now.

If there really was such a thing as a leap of faith, Jacobi had experienced it. *Just like a bolt out of the blue.* Wolfe had seen the look in his partner's eyes. *And he was stubborn enough to begin with.* He remembered how he'd tried to pursuade Jacobi to postpone the Smallville trip until after Atlanta and the Southern tour. *Fat lot of good that did me.* And that had been when Jacobi was still running a con. Now that the con man had become a true believer himself, trying to persuade him of something—anything—he didn't want to do . . . well, that was just reaching for a new level of futility.

For that matter, did he even trust Jacobi enough to risk telling him the truth?

Well, how much had he been able to trust him before? Certainly, Jacobi had kept his secret for years now. Then again, why wouldn't he? The money had been good. They'd had a good thing going, a winning team. Wolfe was the organizer, the fixer, and Jacobi was the front man, the schmoozer. Wolfe had handled the dirty work, taking care of all the details, while his partner handled the big picture. *Yeah, and part of that big picture is keeping me in my place.*

Wolfe looked out the window at the drugstore down the street. Were drugstores in Kansas licensed to sell liquor? He couldn't remember. Wolfe licked his lips again. He could really use a drink. *No.* He shook his head. *That's what got me into this mess in the first place.*

If only he hadn't gotten drunk that night in Baltimore. A quart of Scotch had loosened his tongue, and he told Jacobi all about Cleveland, his new identity, everything. Ever since then, his partner held that knowledge over him. *Partner . . . yeah, right. We were never equal partners, certainly not after that night.*

After Baltimore, they hadn't been friends, either. Not really. Wolfe wondered if they ever had been.

Wolfe gripped the steering wheel hard. This was getting him nowhere. He had to think. There must be some way out of this. Maybe he *should* level with Jacobi.

What would happen if he laid all the cards out on the table? What if he told Jacobi that someone—obviously, a very powerful someone—wanted them out of town and was willing to put Wolfe's very life in jeopardy to make it happen? What then? Would such a bald, honest statement shock enough sense into Jacobi that he'd let them move on?

Maybe. But he didn't think so.

Jacobi might decide that he could overcome whoever it was who wanted them to leave town. Wolfe was certain that would just get them *both* killed. But could he convince Jacobi of that? He had his doubts.

Wolfe chewed his lip. *I'm dead if I do, and dead if I don't.* If he couldn't run, and he couldn't talk sense into Jacobi, what could he do? There had to be a third alternative. But what?

Somewhere down the block, a clock started to chime the hour.

Wolfe checked his watch as the twelfth chime sounded. He got out of the car and stood beside it for a minute. Then he pulled himself together, stepped up onto the sidewalk in front of the savings and loan, and looked again toward the drugstore.

◆◆◆

"Clark, wait up!" Pete slammed his locker shut and ran to catch up to his friend. "You okay, man? I didn't see you this morning."

"Yeah, I know. Missed the bus." Clark gave him a crooked grin. "So, who won this morning's bet—you or Chloe?"

"All wagers are on hold until she pays me back for parking." Pete fell into step alongside Clark as they headed into the school cafeteria. "Seriously, are you okay? I feel bad about bugging out on you yesterday. I didn't mean to cause a blowup between you and your dad."

"Oh, that." Clark shrugged. "Forget about it, Pete. Dad and I . . . vent a little once in a while. It's over."

"You're sure?"

"Yeah."

"Then we're still buds?"

"Are you kidding me?" Clark thrust out his hand.

Pete grinned, gave him a high five, then spun around and gave him a low five. "To the end, my friend, to the end!"

◆◆◆

Jacobi had the plans for his Institute spread out all over the farmhouse's dining room table. He'd added two extra leaves to the table, extending it to a full twelve feet, and now he had all of the proposed layouts side by side. Jacobi could check the arrangement of room and walls on different floors just by glancing from one set of prints to another. He smiled. Everything was shaping up nicely.

A door opened in the back of the house, and Jacobi looked up to spy Wolfe entering with a small cardboard box.

"Ah, Jimmy, there you are. Have the weekend receipts been deposited?"

"Everything's been taken care of, Don."

"I was starting to worry. What kept you?"

"Oh, the usual Monday madness." Wolfe shifted the box, turning it so that he could hold it against him with one arm. "Traffic, errands, people wanting me to stop and talk. And we have to stay on good terms with the public. Assure them that we're going to be good neighbors, and all."

"Yes. Yes, we must." Jacobi rose from the table. "I'm so

glad to hear you say that. I want to be a very good neighbor to the people of Smallville. They should be among the first to reap the benefits of the Institute—after the members of the Foundation, of course."

"Of course."

"They've all been so good to us, Jimmy. So supportive. Within a year, perhaps two, we should be able to give them riches beyond their wildest imaginings."

"Riches?"

"Health, Jimmy—perfect health!" Jacobi reached down, running a hand over the plans, smoothing out a wrinkle in the paper. "We will heal their infirmities, extend their lives, ensure that their children grow up strong and vital . . . and their children's children. I can see us creating a heaven on Earth."

Wolfe didn't say a word. The messianic quality was in his partner's voice now, as well as his eyes. He had heard something like it years before, when old Reverend Mike would fire up a crowd. But it was all part of the act with the Reverend. Wolfe saw the gleam in Jacobi's eyes and knew that this was no act. Not any longer.

"You know, Jimmy, when I was a boy, it was a dream of mine to become a physician. But I just didn't have it in me. Not the skill, and certainly not the grades." Jacobi chuckled, then grew solemn. "Now, I finally have a means to really help people, to end their suffering. My God, what a gift. Think of it, Jimmy. Just *think* of it!"

All Wolfe could think of were the Bible study classes his father used to teach. The old man's favorite story was that of Saul of Tarsus, of how Saul underwent a major conversion on his way to Damascus and became the apostle Paul. *Old Saint Paul wound up getting martyred for his trouble, and so did a lot of his followers.* It could be dangerous to hang out with true believers.

"Jimmy?"

"Yeah, what an image. I, uh, kind of got lost in it myself."

"That happens so easily, doesn't it? I have to remind myself to keep one foot in the real world. Speaking of which, did you run down that list of contractors I wanted?"

"Hmm? Oh, yeah." Wolfe reached into the pocket of his jacket and pulled out a folded piece of paper. "Our man Eaton at the S and L recommended three who would be able to handle the job—all of them in the area."

"Good, good." Jacobi took the list and started poring over it with all the fervor of an archaeologist inspecting the Dead Sea Scrolls.

Wolfe scratched his chin. "You know, Don, before we put this job out to bid, I think we should have a little celebration."

"A celebration?"

"Yes, show off all the plans to our little resident colony of Foundation members. After all, there are about a dozen people in our little inner circle here who left their jobs to run our security, our day-to-day operations. They're a part of this, too, after all."

"That's a *wonderful* idea, Jimmy." Jacobi beamed. "You've finally caught the spirit of this, haven't you?"

"Well, I try." Wolfe gave him a broad smile in return.

And he made it look sincere.

CHAPTER 16

Tuesday afternoon after school, Clark entered the Talon to find Lex slouched back in a corner seat, cupping a latte in one hand and his cell phone in the other. Lex's expression was unsettled.

"Bad news?"

"Eh? Oh, no, Clark. Just unsatisfying." Lex slipped the phone into an inner pocket of his jacket and gestured for Clark to sit down. "If you're looking for Lana, I'm afraid she isn't here yet."

Clark did his best to hide his disappointment and took a seat. "What's up?"

"I've been trying to run down some information on our friends at the Foundation." Lex frowned. "I haven't been having much luck, but it appears that other parties might have."

"Other parties?"

"Yesterday, Jacobi's partner Wolfe was observed having a lengthy discussion with an unidentified individual on the outskirts of town. I've yet to get a name for that individual, but he was driving a car that had been rented in Metropolis, using a credit card issued to a small firm called Bradley & Morgan. You'd never guess it from their name, but I happen to know that they specialize in private investigations."

Clark's eyebrows inched toward his hairline. "You're saying that Wolfe was meeting with a private eye? What's up with that?"

"I don't know. But given the Metropolis connection, I suspect that LuthorCorp is somehow involved."

"LuthorCorp?" Clark lowered his voice and leaned closer. "You've heard something?"

Lex shook his head. "It's just a gut feeling at this point. So far, I've been unable to find any indications that my father is directly involved." He took a sip of his latte. "Which means, of course, that he is."

"Wait a minute—there's no evidence that your father has anything to do with this, so . . . ? Lex, that doesn't make any sense."

"It would if you knew my father like I do." Lex looked over his cup at Clark. "Did your dad ever insist that you join—oh, say—the Future Farmers of America?"

"What?"

"That's what I thought."

"Lex, I haven't given you an answer."

"Oh, yes, you have. Jonathan doesn't try to run your life. Lionel, on the other hand, tries to run everyone's life. I've lost count of the organizations, the schools he's forced me into. I loathed about eighty percent of them. The others I merely pretended to hate." Lex grinned and set down his cup. "All part of the game. At any rate, I'm sure that my father is incensed by all the publicity Jacobi's Foundation has garnered. One of the meteorite mutations did occur right at the fertilizer plant, after all. On his watch. He's still furious that the story became public at all."

"Huh." Clark slouched back and got a faraway look in his eyes.

"You look particularly contemplative. Was it something I said?"

"Sort of. Your father's name came up in connection with the meteorite weirdness a couple of weeks ago."

"Oh?"

"Yeah. Chloe is of the opinion that Lionel has been using

his influence to keep a lid on some of the weirder news out of Smallville." Clark looked up. "Could he do that?"

"He's done worse, and for much less reason than he might have here. Trust me, Clark, where my father is concerned, *anything* is possible."

◆◆◆

Stuart Harrison arrived at the Foundation Compound shortly after school, to find the last few of the permanent campers drifting into the barn.

"Stuart, there you are!" Jacobi came up behind him. "I'm so glad you're here. Just in time for the big celebration."

"Celebration?"

"Come on in and see."

In the barn, meteorites had been arranged in a great circle, casting a soft green light over the interior. A dozen workers were milling around just beyond the circle, where a table had been set up beside the Foundation's RV. The staffers stood there, munching cheese and crackers and fresh fruit, and sipping from large plastic cups, while Wolfe dispensed punch from a large bowl.

"Donald! And Stuart. Well—here you go." Wolfe shoved cups into their hands. "Everyone needs a little something to toast the next great step."

As he took a cup, Stuart noticed that Wolfe was wearing clear plastic gloves, like the ones the cafeteria workers wore at his school. Wolfe saw Stuart's puzzled look and laughed. "The local Health Department's cracking down. Their newest regulations say I have to wear these if I serve more than six nonrelated people."

"Even for a private party? That sounds pretty strict." Stuart swirled the dark purple liquid around in his cup.

Wolfe laughed again. "Bureaucracy! What can you do?"

He pointed to the cup. "Don't worry, it's nonalcoholic. Not too sweet, is it?"

Stuart took a tentative sip. "No. Tastes pretty good."

"All right, then." Wolfe clanged the ladle against the side of the punch bowl. "If I could have your attention please! Dr. Jacobi has a very important announcement. Don . . . ?" Wolfe motioned his partner toward a small riser alongside the table.

Jacobi stepped up to great cheers from the little gathering. He raised his cup in acknowledgment. "Members of the Foundation . . . my friends . . . I thank you. Before we get started, I think we all owe a show of thanks to the man who arranged this little gathering . . . the man whose great skills are indispensable to us. So let's all drink a toast to our own James Wolfe! Jimmy, hop up here and take a bow."

Wolfe stepped onto the riser and modestly waved a cup of his own.

Jacobi took a sip of punch and gestured to the meteorites that ringed the group. "Around us, we can see part of the bounty of our past week's work. And this is only the beginning. Thanks to your support and that of thousands of contributors, we will soon be breaking ground for the Institute of Advanced Meteorite Research!"

Wolfe lifted his cup high into the air. "Here's to the Institute!"

"To the Institute!" The members echoed Wolfe's salute and drained their cups.

Jacobi smacked his lips as he lowered his cup. "By now, you have heard me speak about our cosmic legacy many times. Most of you bore witness to the healing of our new young member Stuart Harrison!"

Another cheer went up. And those standing close beside the Harrison boy reached over to shake his hand or just to touch him. Stuart felt a little uncomfortable. *The way they act, you would think I was the Second Coming*. He smiled politely and lifted his cup in Jacobi's direction.

"Thanks to Stuart, and thanks to you, this Foundation is about to embark on a great new adventure. For years, I have spoken of DNA as a great cosmic ladder. Well, that ladder is about to get an extension, isn't it?" The crowd laughed weakly at the doctor's little joke. Jacobi blinked, feeling a bit light-headed, but continued on. "I have every confidence that these meteorites, these gifts from outer space, will do so much more than just enable us to cure disease. They'll make us all better. Stronger! Smarter! They'll give us the push we need to advance up that evolutionary ladder . . . to the next great cosmic level . . . making us true citizens of the galaxy . . . bringing us . . . one step closer . . . to the angels . . ."

Jacobi looked out at the crowd. They were strangely quiet. Many were swaying from side to side. Their features seemed to be twisting, distorting. No, Jacobi realized that his vision was blurring. He peered down into his cup stupidly. And then his left knee gave out, and he slid sideways down onto the riser.

Stuart tried to take a step forward to help Jacobi, but his feet felt bolted to the floor. All around him, people started toppling over. Stuart looked up to see Wolfe still standing on the riser. It was only then that Stuart really noticed Wolfe's cup; it was still nearly full, and the liquid in it seemed lighter in color.

Before Stuart's eyes, the scene grayed out. Then everything went black.

Wolfe dumped his cup into the punch bowl and stepped down from the riser. "Sorry about this, boys and girls, but I just couldn't think of any other way out." He crossed the floor, stepping around the fallen bodies, and secured the two front barn doors, bolting them shut from the inside. His pri-

vacy ensured, Wolfe returned to the circle. He grabbed hold
of the nearest unconscious form by the shoulders and
dragged it inside the meteorite circle.

Wolfe was drenched with sweat by the time he stepped
back to look at his handiwork. Twelve foundation members
lay unconscious, radiating out toward the center of the circle. A foot or so from each person's head was a meteorite. In
the middle of the circle, Stuart Harrison was laid out with
his arms outstretched in a cruciform position.

"I really wish you hadn't shown up tonight, Stuart. I
didn't want to make you part of this, but it was too late in
the game to change plans." Wolfe shrugged. *Oh, well. This
should make it look even more like a cult ritual.* He checked
his watch. *Fifteen minutes. Not bad, but I have to pick up the
pace.*

He rounded the end of the riser where Jacobi still lay
sprawled. "Donny, Donny, Donny. This is all your fault, you
know. If you hadn't kept buying me drinks that night back
in Baltimore, you never would have found out about Cleveland." He pulled a cardboard box out from under the table
and removed an empty bottle that had once held an over-the-
counter sleep aid. Wolfe placed it in Jacobi's hand and gently squeezed the fingers shut around it. He repeated the
process with the ladle from the punch bowl. "Let's get a
good set of prints here, just in case." Wolfe replaced the
ladle and carefully slipped the bottle into Jacobi's jacket
pocket. "You never know what might be recovered."

Wolfe crossed over to the RV and opened the door, backing away as steps automatically slid out from the vehicle. He
returned to Jacobi, yanking his partner up into a seated position and grabbing him roughly around the waist. Wolfe
gave a mighty heave and straightened up, throwing Jacobi
over his back. Shouldering the man's dead weight, he lumbered back to the RV. Wolfe took one step up, and almost

lost his balance. He grabbed hold of the doorframe, steadied himself, and then carried his burden inside. Wolfe staggered up the aisle to the front of the RV and fell forward, dumping the unconscious Jacobi across the center console. He crouched there on the floor for a second, gasping for breath.

"Either you've put on a few pounds, or I'm in worse shape than I thought." Straddling the console, Wolfe shoved Jacobi into the driver's seat, pushing his legs into position under the steering wheel.

"There, now!" Wolfe ran a hand over his face. His hands, inside the plastic gloves, were as sweaty as his brow, but that couldn't be helped. Wolfe wasn't about to chance leaving any fresh prints behind. He checked his watch again.

Twenty minutes. Okay. My safeguards are already planted and ready to be armed. Just one last little step in here. Wolfe went to the back of the RV and retrieved a metal case. He set it on the front passenger's seat, snapped open the lid, and pulled out Jacobi's original meteorite. He placed the glowing rock on his partner's lap and pushed him forward over it.

"There we go. Can't have you becoming one with the angels without your piece of the rock." Wolfe perched on the console, watching Jacobi's chest slowly rise and fall. "I wish it didn't have to end this way, Don, I truly do. But you backed me into a corner, and the safest way out was right over you. I know we had some good times together, but I have a destiny of my own to fulfill." He hit a button on the dashboard, and the windows of the RV's cab rolled down with a soft electric whir. "When the cops finally check your computer, they'll find quite a history. All sorts of documents related to suicide rituals and cults . . . Heaven's Gate, Order of the Solar Temple. They're all in there, along with a copy of an e-mail from me, questioning your stability—and your reply, banishing me from the Compound. Of course, by the time that's found, James Wolfe will be long gone, just like he never existed." He gazed out the window at the Foundation members spread out on the floor. "A shame about those poor fools. At least they'll achieve their 'cosmic destiny' peacefully in their sleep. I could have slipped poison into that punch, instead of a sedative, but I just couldn't bring myself to kill them." He turned back to Jacobi. "You're going to be the one responsible for that, Don."

Wolfe grasped Jacobi's hand around the key and inserted it into the ignition. The RV's engine roared to life, and began pumping out carbon monoxide.

◆◆◆

Clark was walking home along Route 5, when he came to the Old Carter Road. He'd been giving a wide berth to the Foundation's property ever since Jacobi's volunteers started collecting meteorites, but after talking with Lex, he was starting to have second thoughts.

Chloe would say, "You're finally *starting to have second thoughts."* Clark suddenly realized that he was probably the only one in town who was close friends with both Chloe Sullivan and Lex Luthor. If both of them smelled smoke, there probably was a fire.

And if Lionel Luthor really is taking a greater interest in the Foundation, then maybe I should, too. We all *should.* Of course, if Jacobi was a fraud, it might be just as well if Lionel shut him down. Except . . . except that Stuart Harrison really had been cured. Clark doubted that Jacobi actually had anything to do with that—but maybe the meteorite did. Right now, no one knew for certain. But if Lionel Luthor buried the Foundation, maybe no one would ever know.

Clark remembered what Chloe had been saying for the past week, about both the miracle cure and the Foundation.

Her hunches have always been pretty good—sometimes better than she realizes. He stared off down the road. If he scoped out the Compound without taking Chloe along, she'd never let him hear the end of it. *But I don't want to risk having her see what the space rocks can do to me.*

He thought of how upset Lana had been over all the time her aunt had been spending at the Compound, the money she'd been turning over to Jacobi. *If I could prove that the Foundation is crooked . . . !* Clark smiled. Back when Lana was still a cheerleader, he used to daydream that he was the captain of the Smallville High football team, the star player who won all the games, and won her heart. Getting the goods on Jacobi wouldn't turn him into a star, but it just might make Lana sit up and take notice.

And if I did find something concrete, I could always tell Chloe that I felt the tug of my "reporter's instincts." That was close enough to the truth. If he smiled innocently and used the same phrase she had used to describe him, she wouldn't stay mad for long.

The question was, what could he hope to find?

He wasn't even sure what to look for. And there still was the matter of the meteorites. Clark recalled how sick he'd felt the night of the lecture—*like death warmed over. And that was from just one of the space rocks. Who knows how many the Foundation has collected by now?*

Clark kicked a rock by the side of the road, sending it flying out into the middle of a field. It all seemed hopeless. It seemed pointless, as well. Was the Foundation really his problem? No, it wasn't. He stomped on down the road. *I have enough unanswered questions in my life as it is!* He was several paces farther along Route 5 before he stopped abruptly, almost tripping over his own feet. "*Just block it out.*" That was Whitney Fordman's answer to this whole mess.

It certainly wasn't Lex Luthor's. What had Lex said before the lecture? "Everything that happens in and around Smallville is my concern."

Clark frowned. *It's my concern, too. If you can't help people in your own hometown, what good are you?*

He weighed his options. *There's plenty of cover around the perimeter of the Compound, and it'll be dark soon. If I get in a tight spot, I can just back out fast.*

"Right." Clark squared his shoulders and turned back down the Old Carter Road. *It's time I checked things out for myself.*

When he was about a hundred yards from the Compound, Clark spotted a car pulling out of the main drive. The driver looked his way just a second before turning and cruising off in the other direction, away from Smallville. In the deepening twilight, the man never even noticed Clark standing off along the shoulder of the road. But Clark saw him. From Chloe's description, he knew it had to be Wolfe.

Clark approached the Compound warily, keeping an eye out for the Foundation's volunteer security force. He had a dozen excuses ready, should he be challenged. But no challenge came. The grounds appeared empty. *That's odd. There's no lecture scheduled for tonight, but you'd think there'd be some signs of life. I know Stuart said he'd be coming out here after school. Everyone must be inside.*

⸱ ⸱ ⸱ There was a deathly stillness to the grounds, as Clark made his way up the drive. *Maybe I should just march up to the door and ask to speak with Stuart.* Instead, Clark cautiously stepped into the shadow of the farmhouse. Its curtains were mostly drawn, and no lights shone through the windows. The only light on the grounds came from a series of newly installed mercury vapor security lamps set on poles around the Compound. *This is definitely lurching into* Twilight Zone *territory.* Clark stared intently at the farmhouse, and its walls became transparent to his eyes. He saw a maze of pipes and wiring, the translucent silhouettes of timbers and furniture, but no sign of human habitation. *Where is everybody?*

As he crossed back over the drive, Clark heard a low mechanical hum coming from the barn, and stopped to listen. *Sounds like an engine of some kind. Maybe a generator?* He concentrated again. The walls of the barn seemed to melt away under his stare, and he nearly jumped back from what he saw. There, stretched out in the middle of the barn floor, were more than a dozen human skeletons. A number of big rocks appeared to be spaced at regular intervals around the skeletons. The centers of those rocks glowed with a light that made Clark's eyes water. Just past this circle sat a massive vehicle, something like a bus. And Clark realized that its engine was running.

He blinked twice, and the X-ray vision faded.

"*HEY!*" Clark ran forward, shouting. "Can anybody in there hear me?" He pounded on the metal-reinforced barn doors. It was only then that he noticed the bits of old rags, sticking out here and there along the bottom of the doors, and the faint odor of car exhaust seeping out through the cracks. "Oh, my God!"

Clark took a step back and launched himself shoulder first at the big barn doors. A long four-by-four timber, hung across the doors, splintered under his attack. The doors swung wide, and a fog of exhaust rolled out through the open doors, thick with the noxious smell of petroleum. Clark knew it was also thick with colorless, odorless carbon monoxide. *Am I too late?* He backed up again, filling his lungs with clean air, and ran into the barn.

Clark got to within a few feet of the meteorite circle before his legs buckled under him. He fell to his hands and knees, a wave of nausea threatening to empty his stomach.

Clark looked ahead through the pale green glow, and thought he saw a sign of movement. He shook his head hard. Was he just imagining it? No! He looked again and saw a chest rising and falling. The man on the floor ahead of him was still breathing.

Clark kept his mouth clamped shut, holding in his breath and choking back the nausea. He forced himself forward and reached for the nearest meteorite. It burned in his grasp. The pain radiated from his hands, running up his arms and into his chest. Clark could feel every nerve along the way, as if each one were being scraped raw. With a desperate effort, he flung the rock away from him.

The meteorite flew like a bullet through the side of the barn. Light from an exterior mercury vapor lamp shone through the hole in the wall. The added light fell near the circle's center, illuminating the outstretched form of Stuart Harrison. *STUART!* Clark lurched to his feet, and his heel caught on something. He tripped and almost fell, but managed to steady himself. *What did I hit?* Clark reached down and his hand brushed across a piece of the timber he had split while forcing his way in.

He grabbed hold of the timber and stood it on end. It was nearly five and a half feet long, from end to splintered end. *Not quite a ten-foot-pole, but it'll have to do!* Using the timber as a crude crutch, Clark staggered forward. As he approached the meteorite circle, he set his feet wide and swung the timber. It connected with a meteorite and sent it tumbling away across the barn floor. Clark smiled grimly through gritted teeth and launched himself around the circle, batting away meteorites as he went. As the glowing rocks shot off into the far corners of the barn, he could feel his strength returning. But his chest was burning. As weakened as he'd been, he knew the air in his lungs wouldn't last him much longer. *Got to shut off that engine!*

Clark tossed the timber aside and half ran through the open door of the RV. There, at the front of the cab, he saw Donald Jacobi slumped over the steering wheel. Jacobi's face was lit with a soft green light. Clark spun around, grabbed the doorframe to steady himself, and violently threw up. The RV shook along with him.

Choking and gasping for breath, Clark steeled himself and turned back into the cab. He could feel himself weakening with each torturous step. His legs failed again and he fell forward, clipping his chin on the vehicle's center console. He crawled up over that padded hump, feeling the vibration of the engine below. *Got to keep going. Can't stop now!* Grasping the steering wheel, Clark pulled himself across the console. The meteorite was now just inches away from his head. Veins popped out on his forehead, green-black, his blood boiling through them.

Kneeling over the console, Clark yanked the meteorite from Jacobi's lap, but his momentum threw him off-balance. He tumbled backward into the passenger seat, slamming his head against a hard metal case. The meteorite fell heavily across Clark's chest. His lungs burned as if on fire.

Clark struggled to right himself, and the case fell forward onto the floor, lodging under the dashboard. Clark turned his head, seeing the case in the glow of the meteorite, cursing himself for having overlooked it. Had he noticed it before, he might have been able the scoop up the meteorite and save himself. It was too late for that now.

The meteorite weighed just a few pounds, but to Clark it felt like half a ton. In desperation, he gripped the sides of the rock and heaved. Slowly, it began to rise . . . one inch, then two. The muscles in his arms felt as though they might tear loose from the bones. His pulse pounded in his ears.

And then, roaring like a wounded bear, Clark flung the meteorite up and off of him. The rock sailed up over Jacobi's head, through the open driver's side window, and out into the barn beyond.

Clark clawed his way back over the console. He felt a little stronger, but his vision was blurring and his lungs still ached. He needed air, fast. Clark grabbed hold of the shift lever, throwing it into drive, then shoved Jacobi aside and slammed his foot down onto the gas pedal. The RV rocketed forward, slamming into the back wall of the barn. The windshield safety glass shattered around them as the vehicle broke through, out onto the Compound grounds.

Clark shut down the engine and pulled hard on the emergency brake, bringing the RV to a skidding halt. Clark sat there, sucking in the cool, clean air. As soon as his head was clear, he quickly checked Jacobi for a pulse.

"Okay, you're going to live." Clark stood up, letting Jacobi slump back in his seat. *I'm not sure you deserve to, but that's for a judge to worry about.* He pulled the keys from the ignition and stepped down from the RV, again filling his lungs with fresh air. Clark was starting to feel like his old self again. He tossed the keys under the RV and started back toward the barn. *Now that it's open at both ends, this breeze ought to clear the air in there pretty quickly. And the meteorites should be dispersed enough to let me see how much first aid the others need. It's going to be okay.*

That's when the barn caught fire.

CHAPTER 17

Several miles away, Wolfe glanced at the clock on the dashboard. The road was clear, but he'd forced himself to keep his speed a few miles under the limit. Now he reflexively started to give it a little more gas. Almost immediately, Wolfe eased off on the accelerator and cut back to his original speed. He didn't want to get pulled over, and there was no longer any need to hurry. His little "safeguards"—two small firebombs he'd planted up in the rafters of the barn— ought to be going off right about now. He had used a remote control switch to arm their timers just before he'd pulled out of the Compound's drive.

Clark, of course, knew nothing of that. He just heard the gentle "whump" of the bombs going off and looked on in horror as fire shot through the upper reaches of the barn. Clark dashed into the building, flinging two unconscious people across his shoulders and speeding out of the burning building with them. He set them down as gently as he could and raced back into the barn for two more. But by his third trip into the barn, Clark found himself slowing a bit. With his fourth, he was breathing heavily.

Midway though the fifth rescue run, Clark found himself straining under his load. *It's the meteorites*, he realized. *There are so many of them in there, I get a little more exposure each time. But I can't stop now!*

Flaming debris was starting to rain down from the rafters as he headed in a sixth time, and he struggled to keep the limp victims from sliding off his shoulders. *C'mon, Kent, you can do it! Just one more trip!*

His feet felt like blocks of lead as he lurched across the

concrete slabs of the barn floor. Fire roared all around him. The last body lay sprawled just a few yards away, but as Clark stumbled toward the prone form, it was all he could do to stay upright.

Come on! Just . . . one more . . . !

Clark grabbed the man, but couldn't raise him. It was as if he weighed fifty tons. *What . . . what's wrong?* He pulled at the man's jacket, trying desperately to budge him. And as he pulled, the jacket's side pocket ripped open and a fist-sized chunk of glowing green rock rolled out. Clark tried to kick it away, but his strength was fading fast. The rock rolled just a few feet. Clark again grabbed the man, this time by an arm, and slowly began to drag him from the growing inferno. Inch by painful inch, he pulled that last man. With each succeeding step away from the green rock, it became a little easier. Ten feet from the open doors, Clark finally felt strong enough to pick up his burden. As he stooped to pick up the man, there came an awful cracking sound from overhead.

A burning beam fell straight toward them.

CHAPTER 18

Halfway across the county, James Wolfe flipped on his high beams as he headed south down a back-country road. He turned on the radio just in time to hear that the Dave Clark Five were feeling glad all over. Opening his window a crack, Wolfe sucked in a lungful of the sweet country air, held it for a beat, then expelled it in a slow even breath.

"Hoo-wee! Lordy, I wasn't sure I could really go through with it, but I did. Can't believe I'm finally free."

Wolfe glanced over at the satchel on the seat next to him and gave it an affectionate pat. It held the past weekend's cash receipts and all the money that he'd been able to skim from the Institute building fund in the past twenty-four hours. *Not that it hasn't been fun, Don. But after all you put me through this past month, I'm gonna have a helluva lot more fun out on my own!* He knew it wouldn't be easy to get all that cash out of the country. Border crossings had grown a lot stricter in recent years. He would have to salt the money away in a series of small accounts, then transfer it a little at a time. That would keep from raising any alarms. But he would have plenty of time to worry about that to-morrow.

Right now, he didn't have a care in the world.

◆◆◆

Clark thrust his hands up into the air, catching the huge wooden beam as it fell. The momentum of the falling beam forced him down on one knee, but he would yield no further. Flames licked around Clark's hands as he forced himself to his feet. For an instant, he held the beam high over his head. He lowered the weight a fraction and gathered his strength, and then he hurled the beam across the burning structure. It smashed through a wall, as Clark scooped the last man up and raced out of the barn.

Out on the soft cool grass, far away from the raging pyre that had once been the Davis family barn, Clark dashed from body to body, checking for vital signs. All were alive and breathing on their own, but he couldn't rouse any of them. It wasn't until Clark bent over Stuart Harrison that he started to get a response.

"Stuart? Can you hear me?"

"Uhh? Yeah . . ." Stuart stared, his eyes unfocused.

"Stay with me, Stuart! What happened?"

"Drugged . . ."

"Somebody drugged you? Who? Was it Jacobi?"

"No . . . not Doc . . . drugged him . . . too . . ."

"Then who did it? Who drugged you?"

"Wolfe . . ."

"Wolfe? Jacobi's partner?" Clark remembered the glimpse he'd caught of the man in the car, leaving the Compound. "You're sure?"

"He handed out . . . the punch." Stuart looked puzzled, as if he were trying to recall something that had happened a long time ago. "I didn' . . . drink as much . . . as th' others. Saw Wolfe . . . still standing . . . " He fell back asleep.

Clark rose to his feet, his shadow stretching out across the grounds as the fire blazed on behind him. *Wolfe, huh?* He knew that the Old Carter Road continued west for another twenty miles before it teed into the Cimarron Pike. Clark checked his watch. *Just about no traffic out that way. By now, he could be halfway to Oklahoma.*

Sirens wailed in the distance, and Clark turned to see a long row of flashing red lights approaching from the east.

He looked back down at the unconscious figures. *Not much more I can do for you here. But if I hit the road now—!*

Clark raced west across the Compound, blurring away into the night.

◆◆◆

When the radio signal began breaking up, Wolfe reached over and tuned down the dial. He breezed past two country stations and a gospel choir, lingering briefly over a distant ball game before giving up and switching to the FM band. There he found Michael Nesmith singing about flying down to Rio.

"Rio! Rio by the Sea-o!" Wolfe let out a long nervous laugh. *Yeah, that sounds good, fella, but I think I'll look for a spot that's a little less traveled . . . someplace where nobody will notice me.* It had been a while since he'd seen the ocean. He could get a boat in Corpus Christi and head down the Gulf Coast or out into the Caribbean. *Yeah, maybe find myself a little island where . . .* "Huh?"

Not a hundred feet ahead, a figure seemed to appear from out of nowhere.

Clark stepped out into the middle of the right lane, holding up one hand. "STOP!" His shout was loud enough to be heard even over the blare of the car's radio.

"Damn-fool way to thumb for a ride!" Wolfe cut the wheel sharply, veering into the left lane. "Good way to get yourself killed!" He angrily hit the gas and blew past at close to seventy miles per hour. "Crazy young punk—!" He looked back over his shoulder.

The road behind Wolfe was already empty. It wasn't that the boy could not be seen in the darkness. It was more like he had disappeared.

Wolfe shook his head. *Just a trick of the night.* At the

speed he was now traveling, he'd caught no more than a glimpse of the figure. But it seemed to Wolfe that he'd seen that kid before. *Where was it . . . ?*

Clark stepped out of the darkness again.

This time, he stood directly in the middle of the road, barely fifty feet ahead of the speeding car. Wolfe flashed his lights, but Clark didn't move. Again, he thrust his hand up.

"I said STOP! The game is OVER!"

Wolfe hit the brakes and the sedan began to fishtail, tires squealing. As he held tight to the wheel, fighting to keep control, his left front fender hit the boy, sending him flying backward off the road and into a field. The right front wheel skidded off the road, ramming into a concrete culvert abutment. The car came to an abrupt halt, its air bags inflating and shoving Wolfe back hard against the seat.

The con man clutched his chest, gasping to regain the breath that had been knocked out of him. He tore at the rapidly deflating air bag, as he tried to clear his head. "Damn kid . . . must have had a twin." Wolfe threw the car in reverse and gave it a little gas. It inched back from the abutment. He put it in drive and tested the wheel—everything was still working. He could still get away. And he really had to move now, before someone came along and found that kid's body.

But then, "that kid" emerged from the field. Alive and well. Stalking right toward the car.

Wolfe looked around in a panic. His headlights revealed a narrow old gravel road off to his right. He jerked hard on the wheel and stomped down on the accelerator. The sedan shot down the side road. Its wheels caught gravel, spitting it back out onto the main road.

But all the gravel hit was bare asphalt. The kid was already gone.

"This is crazy!" Sweat poured down Wolfe's brow. "It

can't be happening! Who *is* he? How—?" Then he remembered. *He was one of the four who helped carry away the Harrison kid.*

Clark stepped out into the middle of the gravel road, just a few dozen feet ahead.

"YOU CAN'T ESCAPE!"

"It's a trick! Has to be!" Wolfe gritted his teeth, his panic turning to fury. "You wanna play chicken, punk? Okay—!" He put his foot to the floor and sent the car rocketing straight for the boy.

"You idiot! NO—!" A split second from impact, Clark leaped straight up, ten feet into the air, jumping over the car as it passed under him.

Wolfe stared back in shock. He never saw that the road ended just ahead in a T-intersection. The car shot off the road. Its front wheels bounced off the edge of a ditch, and it went airborne for about twenty feet. The flying car was finally stopped by an old oak tree.

Wolfe had never buckled his seat belt.

With the car's air bags already deflated, Wolfe was flung through the windshield, its safety glass exploding outward in a shower of pebbles. He landed hard, headfirst, in the field beyond the tree. The satchel landed beside him, just a few feet away. Behind him, the car gave one last mechanical shudder and erupted into flames. Fire shot up the tree, turning it into a torch that could be seen for miles.

Clark reached the body in seconds. His X-ray vision confirmed what he already suspected. It was too late to save James Wolfe.

"Why . . . ?" He stood there, shaking his head. Once again, he heard the wail of a siren approaching from the distance.

Clark took a step back into the field and disappeared into the night.

CHAPTER 19

"This is K-T-O-W . . . Smallville! The Voice of News for Lowell County!"

"It's six-oh-seven. I'm Paul Treadwell, and these are the stories we're covering this Wednesday morning.

"Fourteen members of the Ascendance Foundation escaped serious injury yesterday evening, when a barn on the Foundation's Carter Road Compound caught fire. Among those who escaped the fire was Dr. Donald Jacobi, a founder of the organization. There were no known fatalities.

"Rescue workers on the scene reported that the fourteen survivors appeared dazed and confused following their ordeal. They were treated for smoke inhalation and transported to the Smallville Medical Center, where all were admitted suffering from carbon monoxide poisoning.

"Five members were listed in critical condition and later transferred to Metropolis General. The names of those rescued have not yet been released.

"None of the rescued were able to remember how they had escaped from the burning barn. According to local authorities, preliminary medical evidence showed that the Foundation members had all been drugged with a common sedative.

"Three companies of firefighters were called to the scene, where they battled overnight to contain the blaze. Fire Chief William Kone called the barn a total loss.

"Sources within the Lowell County Sheriff's Office called the fire suspicious. The cause of the fire remains under investigation.

"In a related story, State Police responded to a report of a car fire yesterday evening in the southwest corner of the county. There, they discovered the body of Foundation co-founder James Wolfe in a field just a few yards from the burning wreckage of a late-model sedan. The vehicle was believed to be registered in the name of another Foundation member. State Police Sergeant Jack Rodrigues reported that Wolfe had apparently been driving at a high rate of speed and missed a turn on the old Stringtown Pike.

"State Police believe there may be a connection between the two fires. An investigation is under way—"

Jonathan Kent reached across the kitchen counter and turned off the radio. He and Martha looked on as Clark sat at the table, mashing the cornflakes in his bowl with a spoon.

"If you keep that up, Son, you'll soon have nothing but mush."

"I'm not especially hungry anyway." Clark pushed the bowl away.

Martha put her hands on his shoulders. "Dear, we know you're upset . . ."

"I didn't want it to end that way, Mom. I wanted to stop him." Clark rested his elbows on the table and clasped his hands together. "I didn't want him dead."

Jonathan sat down across from Clark. "We know, Son. But you saved fourteen lives last night. Think about that."

"I have, but . . . if only I could have reacted a little faster . . ."

"Clark, that maniac hit you with his car! And then he tried to run you down again. He drugged those people and left them to die—they *would* have died, if you hadn't risked your life to save them."

"Clark, what have we always told you?" Martha sat down beside him. "You can't save everybody. Even with all of your powers, you can't do the impossible."

"I know, but . . ."

"Son, we all want things to come together perfectly in the end, but sometimes—despite our best efforts—they just don't." Jonathan looked Clark in the eye, the way he always did when he wanted to make a point. "Sometimes, other people write their own endings."

"I guess you're right, Dad. But I still don't like it."

"No one ever does."

"It's just . . . it was all so *random*. I wouldn't have gone out to the Compound in the first place, if I hadn't run into Lex. If he hadn't been there at the Talon . . . all those people would have died."

"Good things can happen without reason, Son, just like the bad."

"Yeah, I suppose . . ."

"Besides, how random was this, really?" Martha caught his eye. "You stop by the Talon all the time since Lana re-opened it. And Lex has a stake in the place, so he's often there as well." She glanced over at Jonathan. "To his credit, Lex has never been an absentee landlord."

"That's . . . right." Jonathan nodded. "Your talking to Lex wasn't totally random."

"And once you got to the Compound, things weren't random at all." Martha took Clark's hand. "You acted just as I would've expected you to. Even up against such terrible odds, saving all those people. We're so very, very proud of you."

"That we are, Son." Jonathan hesitated. This next bit was tough for him to say. "And if a talk with Lex was what led you to rescuing those people, then . . . I'm glad that you're friends. I hope he never gives you reason to regret that friendship."

"Dad . . ."

"I don't want to see you hurt, Clark. Lex is fighting two

decades of being a Luthor, and those are some pretty long odds. I just want you to be careful."

"I'll do my best."

"You do that, Son."

"Yes. That's all we ever ask, dear."

Clark smiled at his parents. "Ya know, I've been thinking a lot about the day you found me." A wistful look crossed his face. "I know it never could have happened . . . but I sometimes wish that you could have adopted Lex, too."

Martha looked at Jonathan, a tear in her eye.

Jonathan lowered his eyes and stared at his hands. "Sometimes, Clark, so do I."

◆◆◆

In a helicopter high over Metropolis, Lionel Luthor scanned his newspaper with an air of supreme satisfaction.

"Interesting reading in the late edition of the *Daily Planet*, Damian."

"Is there, sir?"

"Yes. The State Police have been able to connect James Wolfe to that fire the other day out in Lowell County. Evidently, it was started by a firebomb, and enough pieces of a timer survived for the fire investigators to link it to a receipt with his name on it." Lionel pointed out a particular paragraph. "And an unnamed federal source has confirmed that Wolfe had a passing acquaintance with such incendiary devices in his youth. He apparently had a very shady past."

"Imagine that." Damian glanced out the window, seemingly unconcerned.

"In fact, there have been a number of new revelations about this Ascendance Foundation. Between all the money and papers discovered on the late Mr. Wolfe, and the information that was retrieved from the Foundation's computers, the state Attorney General's Office has found reason to initiate criminal proceedings against the good Doctor Jacobi. He's going to be a busy boy once he gets out of Metropolis General. They're calling him a fraud."

"You can't trust anyone anymore." Damian brought his hands together and cracked his knuckles. "What are they saying about that kid he was supposed to have saved?"

"Young Stuart Harrison? His family physician is quoted here—quite extensively—about that 'cure.' He's calling it a case of spontaneous regression. Highly unusual, but not unheard-of. And the Harrison family appears to be accepting that now. Not surprising, in light of the fact that their son was one of the survivors of that fire." Lionel folded the paper and slapped it across his knee. "At any rate, it would appear that the land I sought will soon be back on the market. A job well-done, eh?"

Damian looked at his employer. "I don't know what you're talking about, Mr. L. I didn't do anything."

"Of course you didn't, Damian." Lionel smiled. "None of us did."

◆◆◆

"Earth to Clark. Come in, Clark."

"I can hear you, Pete." Clark leaned back against his locker.

"I might be more willing to believe that if you stop trying to stare a hole in that wall. Man, you have been out of it most of this week."

"I've had a lot on my mind."

"Well, don't bother to tell me about it. I've only known you most of your life." Pete followed Clark's gaze, as Lana and Whitney came around the corner. "Oh."

To Clark's eye, Lana looked a little unsettled, but

nowhere near as distressed as she'd been last week. Whitney, on the other hand, looked as happy as he'd ever seen him.

"Ross! Kent! How goes it?"

"It goes, Whitney." Pete tried to keep it light, but he could tell what Clark was thinking: *They've patched things up. Again.*

"Say, Whit . . ." Pete moved in to buttonhole the quarterback. "What do you think of the Monarchs' chances this year? Think they can win the pennant?"

"Good question. Talbot's arm was looking mighty fine in spring training. Their batting's pretty good. But a lot's going to depend on the fielding . . ."

While his pal steered Whitney off into a discussion of shortstops and ERAs, Clark took the opportunity to have a few words with Lana. He lowered his voice. "So . . . how are things on the home front?"

"Much improved. Nell's getting most of her money back and is busy pretending she never knew anyone named Donald Jacobi." Lana smiled shyly. "I'm finally starting to see the sense in Whitney's advice to just block it out. I want to thank you for helping me see the bigger picture, Clark."

"Oh . . . well . . ." He smiled weakly. "That's what I'm good for, I guess."

"Hey, guys!"

They all turned to see Stuart hailing them from down the corridor.

"Stu! You back so soon?" Whitney clapped him on the back. "I thought your doctor wanted you to take it easy."

"He does. And I am." Stuart grinned back. "But Doc Manning said I could stop by to pick up my books and a few assignments. Gotta keep those grades up, y'know."

"Aw, you can do it! You beat the Big C, you can beat anything!" Whitney could afford to be expansive. He was back together with Lana, and he no longer worried about Stuart as a rival. He poked his buddy in the ribs. "Hey, you still thinking of becoming a New Age preacher?"

"Please!" Stuart rolled his eyes and shook his head. "I'm not sure what I believe anymore. Sure has been a long, strange trip. But at least now I'm not dying any faster than the rest of you guys."

"Give it a rest, Whitney." Pete surprised himself, challenging the upperclassman. "Like you would have behaved any differently if you'd been the one to get the miracle cure."

"Yeah, Ford-Man." Stuart poked him back. "You would probably have taken over and started *running* the show. I know how you hate to let anyone else play quarterback."

Pete drew himself up. "Hut one, hut two! Hallelujah, brother!"

Stuart hooted, and even Whitney had to chuckle.

Clark glanced over at Lana. He noticed that she had become very quiet, very distant. "Lana? Are you all right?"

"Is something wrong, Babe?" Whitney immediately turned to her, instantly solicitous. "I know, we probably shouldn't have been joking about this stuff."

Lana looked up at him. "Oh—why not?"

"Huh?" That was clearly one response Whitney hadn't expected. "You're not bothered?"

"No, I was just . . . distracted. There's been all of this craziness in our lives lately, and most of it's been way beyond our control. We either have to laugh or cry, and there's been too much crying. At times like this, I think we all need a good laugh."

"That's a great way to look at it, Lana." Stuart turned to Whitney. "You are one lucky son of a gun, you know that?"

Yeah. Clark slouched back against the row of lockers. *Tell me about it.*

"Say, Clark—I owe you another thanks." Stuart reached out and shook Clark's hand. "You were there for me, when I really needed it."

"I was?" Clark swallowed uneasily.

"During the fire at the Compound . . . or maybe after it. I'm not sure, I was kind of out of it. I kept trying to make sense of things. And I imagined I heard your voice, asking me what was happening. I think that must have gotten me through it somehow."

"Ah." Inwardly, Clark breathed a sigh of relief. "Well . . . you're welcome."

"Stuart . . . ?" There was a hint of hesitation in Lana's voice, as if she was reluctant to bring something up. "Are there going to be any more problems . . . with your medical bills? I mean, with all the suits being brought against Jacobi . . ."

"No, nothing to worry about there. Those bills were all settled a week ago. Of course, the folks still have to find a new insurance policy, but they're not the only ones in that boat. And at least we're all in good health now." He tapped his head. "Knock on wood."

"Oh. Good. I'm glad."

"You sure?" Stuart looked at her. "You don't sound too glad."

"No, I am. Really. It's good that you're not in need of a benefit. It's just . . ." Lana turned red, embarrassed and flustered at the same time. "Oh, this is going to sound awful! There was so little we could do to help, and planning that concert was the one thing that *was* under our control—and even *that* got yanked away from us."

Whitney slapped his hands together. "So yank it *back*!"

"What?"

"The benefit concert was a good idea. Hold it anyway. There must be *someone* around here who could use the help." Whitney faltered for a moment, then forged ahead. "Stu, you mentioned the problems with finding good health insurance. Maybe the concert could raise money to start some kind of local fund. We could get it registered as a non-profit, the whole nine yards."

"Yes!" Lana threw her arms around Whitney. "What a great idea!"

Stu clapped him on the back. "Ford-Man, you're a genius!"

Pete nodded with grudging respect. "Way to go, Whitney."

"Yeah." Clark smiled halfheartedly.

Stuart shook his head. "Why didn't I think of that?"

"Hey, you would have"—Whitney patted his buddy on the head—"if you only had a brain!"

Stuart and Whitney traded a few mock punches, then the group started breaking up. Stuart went off to check in with his teachers. Lana walked off—arm in arm—with Whitney, making plans anew. And Clark slumped against the wall, looking even more out of it.

Pete leaned back alongside his friend. "Just offhand, I'd guess that you're bummed that you didn't make the great concert suggestion first."

"What a brilliant deduction, Holmes." Clark hoisted a book bag over his shoulder and started down the hall.

Pete hustled to keep up. "Even worse, you're thinking if you hadn't been bummed over Lana and Whitney to begin with, maybe you *would've* come up with the idea first."

"Huh. And some people say that *I'm* perceptive."

"Hey, being the youngest of a multi-kid family, I've seen it all before." Pete tried not to look too smug. "The breakups, the broken hearts, the rivalries, the feeling that no one in the history of the world could have been so stupid . . ."

"I hear *that*."

"Clark, I've seen the strategies that work, the ones that fail, and the ones that will turn around and bite you on the butt."

Clark stopped and turned to Pete. "So what do you prescribe, Doctor Ross?"

"Cut down on the *brooding*, man. Don't cut it out completely—the 'dark, brooding soul' could be a good look for you. A lot of the ladies go for that in a big way." Pete grinned. "Just cut it back to where it doesn't trip you up anymore. You're twice the thinker that Whitney is—at minimum. I know that, Chloe knows that, you know that. But if you stay wrapped up in your thoughts, who else is ever gonna know? Not Lana, that's for sure."

"Pete"—Clark looked his friend over—"that *is* brilliant."

"See? You're already thinking better!"

Clark and Pete entered the *Torch* office, only to find Chloe pounding the desk alongside her keyboard.

"Ohhh! I don't believe this!"

"What's wrong?" asked Pete. "Screen freeze up?"

"*Much* worse." Chloe looked up from the monitor. "I just got some new e-mail from the Ascendance Foundation."

"*What?*" Clark was astonished. "But how?"

"Evidently, our Doctor Jacobi still has a few believers. A couple of the unshakably faithful have taken over maintenance of the website, and they want everyone on the list to know that it's just been updated. This is crazy! They're saying that the charges against Jacobi are all part of a government conspiracy to discredit him."

Clark looked over her shoulder at the monitor. "Incredible. How did they manage to tie all of that to the Kennedy assassination?"

"Believe me, you *don't* want to know." Chloe threw up her hands. "*I* don't want to know!"

Pete gave Chloe's chair a half swivel, turning her away from the screen. "Hey, so there are some nut-jobs out there who still think that Jacobi's eventually gonna show 'em how to join the space people. So what? Some people think that Elvis is still alive."

"Yes, but the Elvis people don't have a vested interest in *me*. From now on, the Foundation website is going to attract nothing but the total lunatic fringe. And the links there still lead them *right* to my site. It's bad enough that all the major papers beat me to the punch with their Foundation exposés. But *this*—!" She smacked the side of the monitor. "This is like being chained at the ankle to the town idiot. It'll be *twice* as hard to get anyone to take me seriously."

Clark bent over the computer. "There's no way for you to break the link?"

Chloe shook her head. "Not without hacking into their website. And ethical questions aside, I'm not quite enough of a cyberwizard to hack in and erase a link without getting caught. All I can do is change the name of my site and hope they don't track me down."

"Where did I put that proclamation? Ah, yes!" Pete plucked a sheet of paper from the recycling bin and pretended to read from it. "On this momentous occasion, it gives me great pleasure to induct one Scoop Sullivan into the Federal Website Protection Program."

" 'Scoop'?" She snatched the paper away from him, wadded it into a ball, and tossed it at Pete, hitting him square in the chest.

"Uungh! She got me!" Pete clutched the paper ball and collapsed back into a chair—which promptly tipped over and dumped him onto the floor.

Clark took Chloe's hand and raised it over her head. "The winner, and still champion!"

She smiled with considerable satisfaction. "Hey, if I've

told him once, I've told him a thousand times—don't make light of the media."

"Okay, okay." Pete pushed himself up on one elbow. "Somebody want to give me a hand?"

Clark and Chloe immediately began applauding.

"Comedians!" Pete started laughing. "I'm surrounded by comedians!"

"Hey! Cut that out, you." Chloe drew her forefinger across her throat. "That's *my* line."

CHAPTER 20

That night, Jonathan and Martha found Clark sitting on the back steps, staring out at the stars.

"Is this a private party, Son, or can anyone join?"

"Be my guest. There's plenty of room." Clark slid to the middle of the step as his mother and father sat down on either side of him. "I was just thinking about the meteorites, and wondering what weirdness they'll cause next."

"Don't be morbid, dear." Martha reached over and brushed an unruly forelock out of his eyes. "Things turned out fairly well this time."

"They sure turned out well for Stuart. And who knows, maybe someday doctors *will* find controllable uses for the space rocks. It wouldn't hurt if a little more good came out of that meteor storm." Clark scooped up a handful of pebbles from the ground and started shaking them in his hand. "I just wish I knew why those space rocks make me so sick. And why the effect is so immediate. Most folks don't seem to have any reaction to them at all. And for the few who have suffered freaky reactions, the changes took anywhere from days to years to occur."

He tossed the pebbles back down. "And as far as I know, no one else has ever suffered crippling pain like I do. Okay, they're Earth people, and I'm not. But that's just a fact—it doesn't *explain* anything."

"Good point, Son. Your reaction to the meteorites is certainly the most extreme. It's almost like an allergic reaction." Jonathan leaned forward on his knees. "You know, most folks can eat peanuts by the pound without ever suffering anything more than a bellyache. But a few people will go into shock and collapse after eating a single peanut. Maybe those space rocks are your poison peanuts."

Martha pulled her sweater around her as a breeze picked up. "Whatever the reason for Clark's reaction, maybe we can someday find something that will block the effects."

"I already have." Clark gave a single dry laugh. "But it's not always practical to carry a sheet of lead around."

"No, not like that, dear. I was thinking more along the lines of immunizing or desensitizing you to the radiation. I've read of people—deathly allergic to bee stings—who were slowly desensitized to the venom." Martha made a mental note to do a search for that article. "And I remember a college classmate who used radioactive iodine in her research project. Before starting an experiment, she would saturate her system with nonradioactive iodine. That way, even if she did get exposed to the 'hot' stuff, her body wouldn't absorb any of it. Maybe we could find a treatment like that for you."

"Maybe." Clark sounded doubtful. "One thing's for sure, the meteorites aren't going to go away. There are too many of them scattered across the county."

"And there's no use in dwelling on that, Son. It'll just get your stomach in a bind." Jonathan threw an arm around Clark's shoulders. "Since we can't eliminate the problem, we'll just deal with it as it comes."

"Yeah." Clark smiled. "And maybe someday I'll find some scientist who can help me handle it."

"Yeah, a real scientist. Not another quack like Jacobi."

"Well, there is one other good thing that came out of this." Martha joined her arm to her husband's in hugging Clark. "A lot of those darned green rocks were gathered up from around the countryside. And according to the *Ledger*, some environmental cleanup company is carting them away for study. Far away, I hope!"

◆◆◆

Around midnight, Dr. Hamilton looked up from his computer terminal, roused from his studies by the rumble of an engine. Suspicious, he grabbed an old baseball bat from a corner of the barn and cautiously eased the door open. There, in the middle of his drive, lit by the light of the moon, sat a panel truck.

"Who are you? What do you want?" Hamilton took a step away from the barn, brandishing the bat like a samurai sword. "You're on private property. No trespassing is allowed."

"Dr. Hamilton?" A gruff, bearded figure, outfitted in coveralls and a hard hat, climbed out of the truck cab, clipboard in hand. "Got a shipment here for you."

"Shipment? I haven't ordered anything. Certainly nothing that would be delivered this time of night. You just keep your distance."

"Take it easy, Doctor." As the figure drew closer, his voice assumed a more familiar tone. "I think you'll change your mind when you see what I'm delivering."

"Luthor?" Hamilton lowered the bat, shielding his eyes from the glare of the truck's headlights. "Is that you?"

"Yes. *C'est moi!*" Grinning, Lex removed his hard hat and peeled away the false beard.

"Very funny." Hamilton stuffed the bat under one arm and took the clipboard. "I'm used to seeing you drive up in something a little sportier. What's the big idea of the masquerade?"

"Just doing my best to keep this delivery our little secret."

Hamilton turned the clipboard toward the truck's headlights, to read the shipping manifest. Across the top of the page was an unfamiliar logo. Associated Disposal and Transport Services?

"A little dummy corporation I set up for just this kind of situation, Doctor. Of course, I hired temp crews to handle the loading and initial hauling. I picked up the truck at a rental depot for the last leg of our cargo's journey."

Hamilton skimmed over the rest of the manifest. "This just says 'Research Materials.'" He stopped. "You don't mean . . ."

Lex threw open the back of the truck and pried the lid from one of the crates that filled the cargo bay. "I told you that I would handle the Foundation, Doctor. Their loss is your gain." He plopped the hard hat back on his head. "This should provide enough raw material for you to continue your work, don't you think?"

Hamilton didn't say a word, he just stared at the rocks packed into the big wooden crate. The center of each and every one of them sparkled with an eerie green glow.